WASHINGTON

THE MOUNTAINEERS BOOKS
is the nonprofit publishing arm of The Mountaineers, an organization founded in 1906 and dedicated to the exploration, preservation, and enjoyment of outdoor and wilderness areas.

1001 SW Klickitat Way, Suite 201, Seattle, WA 98134

First edition: first printing 2005, second printing 2013, third printing 2015, fourth printing 2018

Manufactured in the United States of America

Acquiring Editor: Laura Drury and Christine Hosler
Project Editor: Mary Metz
Copy Editor: Julie Van Pelt
Cover Design: Karen Schober
Book Design: Kristy Thompson
Layout Artist: Marge Mueller, Gray Mouse Graphics
Climbing topos: David Whitelaw, Adventure Images
Maps and photo overlays: Marge Mueller, Gray Mouse Graphics
All photographs by author unless otherwise noted.
Overlay photographs: Pages 28, 38 and 45: Jim Nelson; pages 71, 77, 87, 91 and 99: David Gunstone; page 108: Chris Greyell; page 124: Philip Leatherman; page 224: Jennifer Keller
Cover photograph: *Ron Cotman on* Loaves of Fun, *Pearly Gates*
Frontispiece: *Paul Warner on the spectacular second pitch of* Midway Direct *at Castle Rock*
Page 5: *Leland Windham on the upper section of* Carrot Top *at Banks Lake*
Page 6: *Climber working up under the big roof on* Wild Child *at Royal Columns*

Library of Congress Cataloging-in-Publication Data
Whitelaw, David, 1955–
Weekend rock : Washington selected trad and sport climbs from 5.0 to 5.10a / David Whitelaw.— 1st ed.
    p. cm.
Includes bibliographical references and index.
ISBN 0-89886-984-6
1. Rock climbing—Washington (State)—Guidebooks. 2. Washington (State)—Description and travel. I. Title.
GV199.42.W2W45 2006
796.52'23'09797—dc22
                2005020929
ISBN (paperback): 978-0-89886-984-2
ISBN (ebook): 978-1-59485-134-6

Contents

AREA
OF
MAP

1 Washington Pass
2 Mount Erie
3 Darrington
4 Static Point
5 Index
6 Half Moon Crags
7 Leavenworth
8 Exit 38
9 Tieton River
10 Frenchman Coulee
11 Banks Lake

WASHINGTON

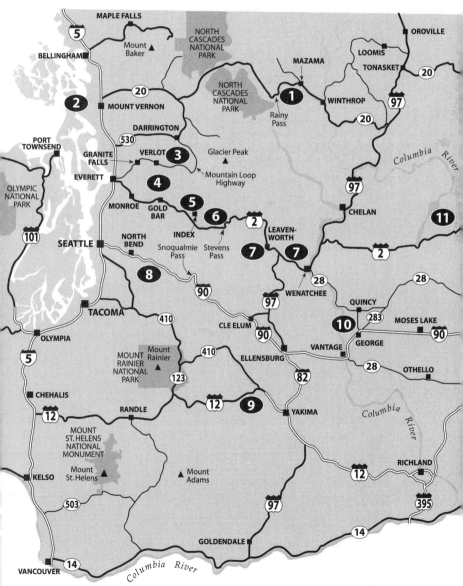

MAPLE FALLS

BELLINGHAM

Mount Baker

NORTH CASCADES NATIONAL PARK

OROVILLE

LOOMIS

MAZAMA

TONASKET

20

97

WINTHROP

NORTH CASCADES NATIONAL PARK

1

Rainy Pass

20

MOUNT VERNON

DARRINGTON

530

VERLOT

3

Glacier Peak

GRANITE FALLS

4

EVERETT

Mountain Loop Highway

Columbia River

97

MONROE

GOLD BAR

5

6

2

CHELAN

11

SEATTLE

NORTH BEND

INDEX

Snoqualmie Pass

Stevens Pass

LEAVEN-WORTH

7

7

2

PORT TOWNSEND

OLYMPIC NATIONAL PARK

101

8

90

28

WENATCHEE

QUINCY

28

MOSES LAKE

TACOMA

410

97

CLE ELUM

283

10

90

OLYMPIA

MOUNT RAINIER NATIONAL PARK

Mount Rainier

90

VANTAGE

GEORGE

ELLENSBURG

28

OTHELLO

5

123

410

82

CHEHALIS

12

RANDLE

12

9

YAKIMA

Columbia River

MOUNT ST. HELENS NATIONAL MONUMENT

Mount St. Helens

Mount Adams

12

RICHLAND

KELSO

503

97

395

14

VANCOUVER

14

GOLDENDALE

Columbia River

DESTINATION CHART

Destination	Drive time from Seattle	Drive time from Spokane	Approach times	Climbing season	Rock type	Climbing type
Washington Pass	3¼ hours	5 hours	1–2 hours	March/May–November	Granite	Traditional alpine rock climbing/mountaineering
Mt. Erie	1½ hours	5¾ hours	5–30 minutes	March–October	Diorite	Sport, moderate traditional routes, and a few mixed routes
Darrington	2 hours	5½ hours	30–90 minutes	late March–late October	Quartz diorite (granite)	Multipitch, traditionally bolted slab and knob routes
Static Point	1½ hours	5¾ hours	1–2 hours	year-round with some restrictions	Granodiorite	Traditional slab climbing
Index	1¼ hours	5 hours	30 minutes	March–November	Granodiorite	Traditional, although high-standard sport climbs are common as well
Half Moon Crags	1½ hours	4½ hours	20–60 minutes	Early June–October	Granodiorite	Traditional, sport, and mixed climbs
Leavenworth	2½ hours	3½ hours	2 hours	March–November	Granodiorite, Swauk sandstone	Traditional, sport, bouldering, bolted slab
Exit 38	45 minutes	3½ hours	10–40 minutes	April–early October	Metamorphosed basalt	Sport
Tieton River	2½ hours	3½ hours	10–30 minutes	April–October	Columnar andesite	Primarily traditional crack climbing, although bolted arêtes do exist
Frenchman Coulee	2½ hours	2 hours	30 minutes	March–November	Columbia River basalt	Sport, traditional
Banks Lake	4 hours	1¾ hours	15–30 minutes (by canoe)	April–late October	Granite	Traditional cracks, mixed routes, and sport climbs

Acknowledgments

An old saying has it that the one good thing about being wrong is the pleasure it brings to others. That being said it should be pointed out that the following list of people are among those who have chosen to forgo certain hours of joy in favor of giving me an opportunity to get it right. My appreciation runs deeper than they can know.

For their enthusiasm, contributions, suggestions, and patience I would especially like to thank Jan Keller, Chris Greyell, Mark Hanna, Laura Drury, Victor Kramar, Jim Donini, Ron Cotman, Dave Bale, Rich Carlstad, Dallas Kloke, Mitch Blanton, Christine Hosler, Don Brooks, Matt Perkins, Jim Nelson, Peter Gunstone, David Gunstone, Roger Bown, Jay Brazier, Jim Archambeault, Joe Ferrare, Doug Walker, Linda Sears, Sarah Trebwasser, John Fleming, Stephen Packard, Jonn Lundsford, John McGowan, Duane Constantino, Sarah Doherty, Victoria Wentz, David Burdick, Chris Carlsten, Noel Blake, Paul Warner, Dave Wolfe, Scott Buzan, Gary Paull, Darryl Cramar, Mike Schoenborn, Dan Dingle, Ben Stanton, Matt Morrison, Andy Fitz, Phillip Leatherman, Micah Lambeth, Leland Windham, Steve Arnold, Matt Walker, Julie Van Pelt, and Mary Metz.

Preface

The idea for this volume has been kicking around in my head for many years. Inspired in ages past by Steck and Roper's *Fifty Classic Climbs of North America*, I've long thought that a guidebook selected not only for quality but also for difficulty would find a welcome audience.

As the sport climbing phenomenon has gained momentum, and guidebook and magazine articles more and more often feature routes with dizzyingly stellar grades, it seems apparent that the cutting edge of the sport has advanced dramatically in all disciplines. At the same time, there are increasing groups of active and committed climbers whose weekend adventures and annual trips find expression in routes that are currently viewed as being of more modest difficulty.

That is what forms the basis for this compilation, a survey of great Washington routes that range from quality first-lead candidates to some of the state's more accessible 5.10s. An emphasis has been made throughout to feature the most classic examples of each grade. At the same time, it's a pleasure to introduce several never-before-published areas that have been my personal favorites for many years.

Finding selection criteria that made sense for six or seven different climbing areas scattered across half a state and involving half a dozen different kinds of rock and styles of climbing took some serious pondering and much discussion, deleting, and editing.

As the decades since Fred Beckey's first climbs on Castle Rock have unfolded, Washington has continued to reveal itself as a beautiful and expansive wonder of rock set against high mountains, forests, rivers, and deserts. Generation after generation has been inspired by the rich and diverse experience of Washington climbing. A look at the lists of first ascents for the passing decades gives testimony to the quality of this experience. Many of those listed in this book have made significant impacts in other areas of the world as well.

What follows is a compilation of some of the best climbing to be had in a state with embarrassing riches. Some are new and hardly known, and others have been well-traveled favorites since the days of steel biners and basketball shoes. Whatever the rating... they're all 5.*fun!* Enjoy.

Opposite: *Mr. Mount Erie himself, Dallas Kloke cruising up* Zig Zag *on Mount Erie*

Introduction

Welcome to Washington's *Weekend Rock*! Whether you're a weekend visitor or a seasoned resident, you're in for one of the widest selections of varied rock climbing in America and, most months, you'll find there's a dry piece of rock somewhere.

The core idea for this book is to assemble some of the finest examples of moderate climbs found in Washington. There's something for everyone in this grandly varied state, which offers sandstone pinnacles, alpine granite, and cliffs rising out of anything from sand and cactus to full-on jungles.

This great variety of rock also fosters a great variety of climbing styles, and both sport climbing areas and traditional areas are covered in this guide. The opportunity to sample so many different types of stone and styles of climbing can certainly contribute to a greater proficiency in the vertical realm.

It is now almost sixty-five years since the first Washington "crag" climb took place on Castle Rock, and the sport has blossomed all across Washington, the nation, and the world. Twenty-five years ago a book the size of this one covered all the known climbs in the state. Now the Leavenworth guide alone weighs in at over 1000 routes!

While the choices for good climbing have become virtually limitless, the increase in population and pressures on the natural environment are more acute than ever. Land-use managers are called on more and more to take notice and find ways to mitigate the impacts of all of us who seek out natural places.

In *Selected Climbs in the Cascades, Volume 2*, Jim Nelson and Peter Potterfield made the following comments about the wilderness ethic and modern times:

> To climbers, by nature iconoclastic and irreverent, rules and regulations have often seemed unnecessary or counterproductive. But in this particular time of the planet, regulations are unavoidable. Enjoy the mountains, but take care of them. Make it your responsibility. As a user, take seriously your stewardship of the Cascades so these wonderful mountains will remain a place of beauty, pleasure, and renewal.

These ideas have become even more important and it has become

Opposite: *Pax stylin' through the finishing sequence of* Toxic Shock

more of an imperative that each of us accepts personal responsibility for the stewardship of these lands. It is important for us as climbers to practice sound habits and join in discussions about the future of these lands if we expect them to remain open to the pursuit of our sport.

ACCESS ISSUES

Access issues have become much more a topic of concern in the last decade and a half. Increasing population pressures have taken their toll on the native lands and land-use managers have more and more often been forced to make difficult decisions regarding use and access to the great outdoors. Various user groups have banded together with some degree of success to try and insure the health of their own particular sport or point of view. The government charges numerous fees and tariffs to use different types of public lands and access has become a very, very politically charged arena.

The Access Fund (*www.accessfund.org*) probably represents one of the strongest and most thought-out climber advocacy groups. It has funded land acquisitions, trail and anchor rehab projects, and even litigation at countless sites throughout America. Anyone with a serious interest in climbing will want to at least familiarize themselves with this group, its record of accomplishments, and its guidelines for thoughtful, minimum-impact climbing. For the last decade Washington climbers have been truly fortunate to have local climber Andy Fitz as an Access Fund regional coordinator. Many are unaware of the thousands of hours he has spent working on behalf of Northwest climbers and we owe him a huge thanks for his years of effort. Please contribute to the Access Fund!

Increasingly, land-use managers are finding it necessary to define who gets to do what on public land and this is being accomplished by management plans that typically call for public and user-group input. The Washington Climber's Coalition (*www.washingtonclimbers.org*) is a local, grassroots group that formed with the help of the Access Fund so that climbers' interests could be represented where needed.

While specific permit requirements are detailed in each chapter of this guide, climbers should be aware that these days just about any trailhead with signage, kiosks, and restrooms can be expected to fall into some sort of fee category. Many of the areas in this guide will require a Northwest Forest Pass, although a good number of them are still free and a few others are in state parks where one is usually able to pay on-site via provided envelopes. Some areas, such as the Icicle Creek Canyon area, have a mixture of free and permit parking. Again, climbers will find specific information in each chapter.

WEATHER AND CLOTHING

Washington enjoys a truly horrible reputation for incessant rain and gloom. Perhaps it's best that the huddled masses never realize that it takes rain *and sun* to make all the green. That notwithstanding it probably *is* true that if you can learn to stay warm and dry in the outdoors of Washington State, then you will know your craft intimately enough to do well just about anywhere.

For Washington climbers the big distinction is whether the weather is better east of the Cascades or west. All Washington climbing areas are subject to rain, although western Washington receives as much as ten times more of it than does the eastern part. For generations of Northwest climbers from Vancouver to Portland the "rain shield" of the Cascades has provided fairly easy access to a drier climate when the western slopes are locked in mist.

Summertime climbing temperatures in our state can range from just above freezing in the mornings at Washington Pass to over 100 degrees in the midday heat at Frenchman Coulee. Eastern Washington may be somewhat less prone to sudden changes of weather, but anyone climbing on the west side needs to be prepared for a day that starts out sunny and bright and ends up cold and wet. Know what kinds of clothing work for you and bring it along.

GEAR CONSIDERATIONS

There are no specific peculiarities to climbing in Washington State with regard to climbing hardware and no tools of any sort that are used here and nowhere else. The Southwest Couloir on the South Early Winter Spire (Washington Pass area) is the only route in this compilation that is not a rock climb and requires the use of ice ax and crampons. Early-season approaches to any of the Washington Pass climbs can be facilitated by an ice ax and crampons, however.

Unless otherwise stated, ropes will be assumed to be 50 meters in length. A good many of the routes in this book are descended by multiple rappels and many climbers prefer to do these with double ropes of

This non-venomous gopher snake seemed to think it had found a kindred spirit.

various configurations. For the last forty years, climbing ropes have gradually gotten longer and longer. In the 1970s climbers began to move away from 150-foot (45m) ropes in favor of 165-foot (50m) versions and much discussion was sparked about the relative merits of this. Currently a similar but more varied transition is in process, as some climbers employ 60-meter ropes for various reasons and climbing styles. A large number of the routes at Exit 38 are set up to be climbed with single 60-meter ropes. This length rope is becoming quite common although a good many routes detailed in this guide involve rappels of more than 30 meters.

EMERGENCY MEASURES

Phone numbers and street addresses for emergency facilities are included in the appendix section of this guide. While a majority of the areas in this book are not open to cell-phone coverage, the fact remains that many in America owe their continued good health to a cell-phone initiated response. It is a good idea to know your own cell provider's coverage zones and how far you need to travel to reach coverage. It is not uncommon for climbers with a lifelong interest in the sport to receive some training in first aid.

Who to call and where to go in the event of an accident can vary with regard to the nature of the accident, where it took place, and even the time of day. Over the life of this book emergency phone numbers will certainly change, and rescue people themselves advise the following instead of searching for emergency phone numbers: In the event of an accident try to understand the injuries and stabilize the victim. Send someone for help or to a place where a telephone call can be placed, be it a cell call or a phone booth. Dial 911 and try and be as specific as possible about the nature of the accident and the location of the victim. Finding an accident scene from the air can be a difficult process even in good weather. GPS coordinates may help save time if they are available.

Once again, maintain composure. ***Call 911.*** Be specific about the injuries and location of the accident. Listen carefully and follow directions given by rescue personnel.

TEN ESSENTIALS: A SYSTEMS APPROACH

1. Navigation (map and compass)
2. Sun protection (sunglasses and sunscreen)
3. Insulation (extra clothing)
4. Illumination (headlamp or flashlight)
5. First-aid supplies
6. Fire (firestarter and matches/lighter)
7. Repair kit and tools (including knife)
8. Nutrition (extra food)
9. Hydration (extra water)
10. Emergency shelter

The Mountaineers

HOW TO USE THIS BOOK

A selected climbs book such as this one is really a compilation of miniguides to a number of autonomous and individual destinations. With such a diversity of choices it quickly becomes apparent that about the only thing the different venues have in common is that they are all in Washington State. The rock type, weather, gear, and access issues are all peculiar to each climbing area and topics such as these, conventionally discussed in guidebook introductions, have instead been deferred to the introductory paragraphs of each specific area.

The main introductory pages for this book contain a destination chart that can help climbers quickly determine the relative merits of each area. On another layer, the introduction to each area will feature a "beta box" that further illuminates area key points with a quick, at-a-glance format. Emergency services are listed in the appendix section of this book.

Finally, the appendix also contains various comparison charts that index the routes and sort them by difficulty, type, and quality.

RATINGS

Generally, a guidebook author tries to achieve some consistency with regard to ratings and popular consensus. For example, most of the 5.8s should generally be about the same difficulty—but only if they are *within the same area*. With a book of this scope, it needs to be pointed out that you can't always assume a 5.8 is a 5.8 is a 5.8.

In some cases a crag detailed in this guide will present six or seven routes that fit the selection criteria and one route that is (usually) more difficult. In those instances the more difficult route has been included purely to eliminate confusion when locating the other routes and not because it may be an especially excellent route. No route over 5.10b is included for any other reason than to make sure it doesn't get mistaken for a more moderate neighbor.

With over half a dozen different types of rock featured in this guide, it should be stressed that the techniques, ambiance, and equipment requirements vary slightly with each type of rock. A steep and crimpy sport climb should not be approached in the same way as a runout friction route. Climbers should expect to have different perceptions of difficulty as they sample different areas—that's where the adventure lies. We are fortunate in the Northwest to have such an incredible variety and scope of rock to climb on. Further, several distinct climatic zones mean that we can choose venues as divergent as desert sandstone and alpine ice.

I set out to faithfully maintain the published difficulty ratings of various climbs and to assign the quality ratings based more to my own tastes. Alas, I was mostly successful at not changing the difficulty ratings but a few have varied historically to begin with and a few others were just too far outside my own personal definitions. The quality ratings are much more a reflection of my own tastes. Ultimately though, the choices were my own throughout and your individual experience may well be different. Make sure to bring a few grains of salt.

Difficulty Ratings

This book uses the venerable Yosemite Decimal System (YDS), in wide use throughout North America. Anyone climbing in the United States or at least within the areas detailed in this book should understand this system and its implications before attempting to lead climbs. Most of the climbs found in this book will be at the 5.0 through 5.10a/b level.

Class difficulty is defined as follows:

Class 1: Flat walking with no obstacles.

Class 2: Trail walking with perhaps some uneven surfaces, roots, and boulders.

Class 3: Scrambling. Steep enough for use of hands. Beginners will not want ropes.

Class 4: Serious enough for fatal consequences. Most climbers use a rope and some protection techniques.

Class 5: Technical rock climbing. A rope, specialized equipment and procedures will always be used to protect against falls. Class 5 climbing is subdivided using decimals to indicate higher levels of difficulty.

To complicate the issue somewhat, the system employs a further level of definition that begins at the 5.10 level. Starting with 5.10a and proceeding through 5.10d, each decimal level from 5.10 on up is subdivided using letters. Thus 5.10a advances through 5.10d and then follows with 5.11a and so on.

5.0–5.6: Most novices have their early experiences at one of these levels. Easy for experienced leaders.

5.7–5.9: Most weekend climbers become comfortable in this range, although every route may not be suitable for every climber. Climbing at these levels requires competence and mastery of specific climbing techniques and uses of gear.

5.10a–5.10b: Many committed weekend climbers attain this level with some practice and persistence. Sport climbs at this standard are often considered to be moderate endeavors while traditional routes at this standard can be quite serious.

5.10c and above: For our purposes this is the realm of the "rock jock" or true expert. These routes often demand a level of training, ability and commitment that falls outside the scope of this book. Statistically few climbers are able to cleanly onsight beyond the mid-5.11 range.

Overall Grade Ratings

There are a great many short climbs in this book. For these climbs, grade ratings (overall difficulty and seriousness ratings) are really not applicable. The grade chart found below details the various criteria. However, it should be noted that grades I and II have not been labeled as such in this book. Climbers are better advised to count the pitches and look at the YDS ratings to estimate how much time is needed for the shorter multipitch climbs. Grade ratings have only been retained on climbs that may take a good part of the day and require strong overall skills.

Stephen Packard on the spectacularly exposed third pitch of Orbit *on Snow Creek Wall*

The class system tells how hard a given climb might be, and the grade gives a clue to overall commitment and time needed for a *competent* team to complete the route:

Grade I: One to three hours.

Grade II: Three to four hours.

Grade III: Four to six hours or a solid half day.

Grade IV: A completely full day by a competent team.

Grade V: One bivouac needed. A hot team can sometimes crank through in a day.

Grade VI: Two or more nights on the wall.

Seriousness Ratings

Seriousness ratings sometimes appear in this guide. This system, long in use throughout the country, more or less emulates the letters commonly associated with motion-picture ratings, albeit with a sometimes more immediate connotation. A 5.9 route with no seriousness notations can be expected to offer reasonable protection for crux passages but may still involve runouts in middle grade terrain. Typically, X-rated routes are not in the scope of this book although they may appear in various locator photos. It should be remembered that on routes with fixed protection, a missing or damaged piece may indeed turn the route into something much more serious than anticipated. *Always* be on your guard for dangerous situations and back up fixed gear when possible.

PG: Generally a fairly secure route, but not entirely so. May have a short runout, or tricky protection.

R: Potential for serious falls; runout, poor protection or both; injuries are likely to be serious.

X: Death fall potential; difficult or crux sections with death fall hazards; injuries likely to be fatal.

Quality Ratings

This volume uses a three-star rating system for route quality. As this book is a select compilation it should be assumed that almost every route will have something going for it with regard to quality, history, position, and so on. Even so, quality ratings are intended to be a gauge against other climbs *within the same area*. A one-pitch, three-star route at Banks Lake may be as good as it gets at Banks but shouldn't necessarily be compared to climbs in other areas.

No stars: In this book they are okay routes, but maybe not the first choice.

★: Totally worthwhile climbs. May contain some lower quality portions.

★★: These are excellent climbs, some of the best of their genre at each area.

★★★: Truly transcendent routes. Absolutely the best of the Northwest at each area.

Artificial Climbing

On the whole, most climbers do far more free climbing on Saturday afternoons than they do fiddling with aiders or gingerly putting weight on a nest of stacked-up pitons. Still, many climbers aspire to, or enjoy, the occasional wall route, and some still train for proficiency in this genre. Wall-type climbing and mixed free and aid routes are certainly not for inexperienced climbers. The combinations of skills and techniques are usually the product of some years of climbing in many environments. With that said, the aid routes included in this guide are short and fairly straightforward examples of their genre. If you've led enough traditional 5.9 to be fairly confident, led a few straightforward aid pitches without

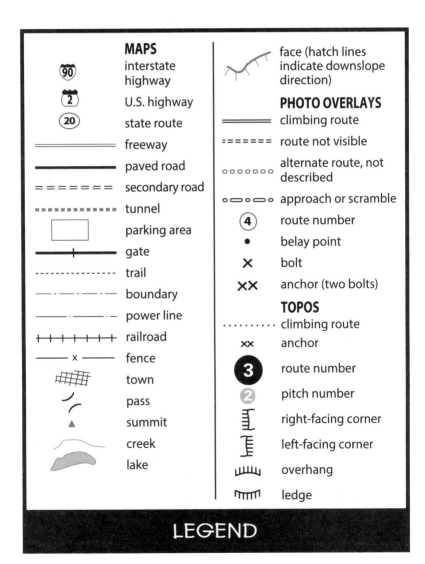

incident, and perhaps read a few books on the subject, then the aid routes included here should prove to be pretty fun.

Aid climbing is currently divided into five rating classes, A1 through A5, depending on the difficulty of finding and arranging a string of placements that will all sustain at least body weight. With A1 it will not be very strenuous or difficult to make the placements and most of them will be pretty much "bombproof." With A5 each placement is so tenuous that the failure of one piece would certainly rip enough other pieces to send the leader on a 100-foot fall.

Aid climbing ratings are sometimes given using a scale designed to represent "clean" or hammerless climbing. If the aid climbing can be done without resort to hammering pitons or even tapping on nuts it will be designated with an upper case "C" preceding the numerical difficulty. For example, C1 indicates solid aiding on *relatively* easy to reach pieces of gear. C2 will involve *mostly* solid pieces of gear with some awkward reaches or high-steps required to make the placements. A2 represents more or less the same feeling of reliability, but requires a hammer and pitons. C3 and beyond represent some pretty serious climbing and are beyond the scope of this book.

Washington Pass

Climbing in the Washington Pass area is an experience unlike that offered by most of the other areas detailed in this book. With summits just shy of 8000 feet, these climbs are distinctly mountains. It is the fortuitous proximity of the road that has allowed these climbs to be tackled as sunny alpine rock jaunts instead of remaining the remote granite summits they were at the time of their early ascents.

Anywhere else and these spectacular spines of rock would only be detailed in an alpine guide. Now, some 31/4 hours from Seattle, they present a jaw-dropping sight as US 20 swings past the Washington Pass Overlook and practically underneath the huge eastern ramparts of Liberty Bell, Concord and Lexington towers, and the Early Winter Spires.

This is one of the few regions in the state where true granite dominates, and the high quartz content and large crystal structure of the stone here provide a relatively rough and textured climbing surface compared to, for instance, the quartz diorite of the Darrington area.

Presented below is a selection of climbs at increasing increments of difficulty. The South Arête on the south spire is mostly a scrambling route with only a couple of short fifth-class sections. Liberty Bell's *Beckey Route* is a quality 5.2–5.6 adventure and the Southwest Rib of the south spire contains

Chris Greyell on the third pitch of the Beckey Route. *All the other summits in the Liberty Bell group are visible from this point of view.*

several excellent passages in the 5.6–5.8 range. One of the most difficult and awesome rock climbs in this guide is the Direct East Buttress on the south spire. The route is climbed completely free at 5.11a, but a good many experienced climbers enjoy the route as a 5.9/A0 adventure by standing in a few slings and grabbing a couple of bolts.

The approaches here are generally short and speedy by any peak-climbing standards, and the most distant of these routes can be reached in less than 2 hours of hiking. With a reasonable respect for the law and a light pack, you can be roping up with the mountain goats at the base of the south spire about 5 hours after leaving home in Seattle.

Mosquitoes at the Blue Lake trailhead are legendary and can approach Alaskan standards for infestation. For a few weeks each year in midseason they are a real consideration. Generally a speedy departure will leave them in your wake and the breezes above tree line often foil them entirely. Be packed and ready to walk fast!

WASHINGTON PASS BETA

Drive time from Seattle ▲ 3 1/4 hours
Drive time from Spokane ▲ 5 hours
Approach times ▲ 1–2 hours

Getting there: From I-5, 35 miles north of Seattle, take the Arlington/Sylvana exit 208. Turn east onto SR 530 and continue 35 miles east to Darrington. Turn left onto the SR 17-A and continue to its junction with US 20 (North Cascades Highway) at the town of Concrete. From there the road leads to Marblemount (last gas) and on past several dams, Rainy Pass, and finally Washington Pass. The Blue Lake Trail starts 1 mile before the Washington Pass crest. The big hairpin turn below the Early Winter Spires is 0.5 mile beyond the crest.

Season: The North Cascades Highway opens for the season anywhere from March to May and usually stays open until snow closes it sometime in November. Expect snow to linger on the lower, forested portions of the Blue Lake Trail into May and sometimes June. July and August are likely to provide the highest frequency of climbable days, with temperatures commonly into the 60s and 70s.

Regulations: To date, permits are not required for climbing at Washington Pass although the controversial Northwest Forest Pass is mandated at the Blue Lake trailhead. Routes approached from parking spots along the highway are not covered under this requirement. For information and up-to-date regulations, call the Okanogan National Forest, Methow Valley Ranger District in Winthrop (509-996-4003).

Camping: Camping is prohibited at Washington Pass itself, although bivouacking below some climbs has traditionally been permitted. There are several campgrounds located along the North Cascades Highway; the nearest is to the east, about halfway to Mazama.

Concessions: The nearest reliable concessions are either in Marblemount to the west or Winthrop to the east. Sometimes a country store is open in Newhalem.

Climbing type: Traditional alpine rock climbing/mountaineering
Rock type: Granite

Gear: Medium traditional rack with gear to 4 inches. Extra dark-colored slings/rappel gear, 2 ropes, approach shoes, mountain clothing.

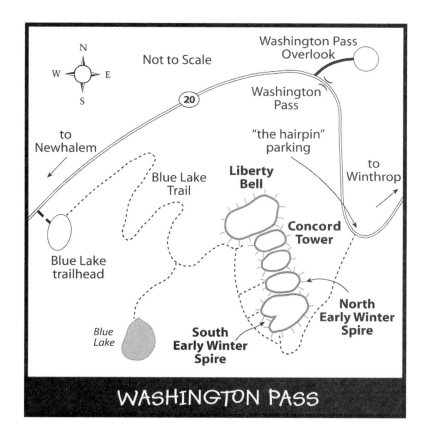

South Early
Winter Spire

North Early
Winter Spire

Liberty
Bell

Lexington
Tower

Concord
Tower

Minuteman
Tower

LIBERTY BELL GROUP
(from the east)

Liberty Bell (7720 feet)

You can only imagine the roadless vista from the summit of Liberty Bell
at the time of its first ascent in 1946. While it's now quite common to
make one-day jaunts up this mountain from the Seattle area, consider
the arduous 16-mile approach Fred Beckey made in order to bag the first
ascent of this striking feature, perhaps the most sublime in the state.
Viewed from the Washington Pass Overlook, the peak best resembles its
namesake shape, and the awesome east face plunges almost 1200 feet
from the summit to the talus- and spruce-covered slopes immediately
adjacent to US 20.

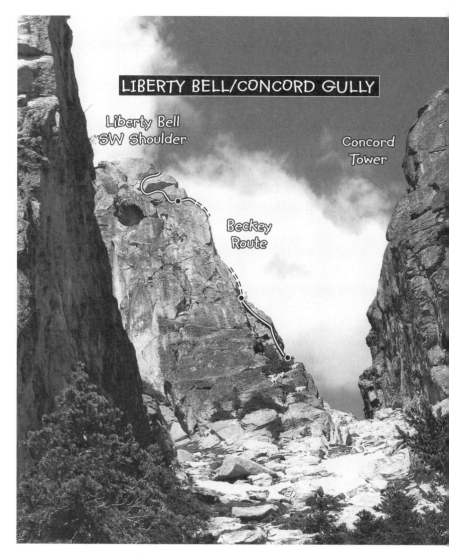

All of the Washington Pass routes described in this book (except the Direct East Buttress on the south spire) involve use of the Blue Lake Trail, which begins 1 mile west of Washington Pass at the obvious 5200-foot trailhead. Northwest Forest Pass required.

Approach: Follow the Blue Lake Trail about a mile and a half until a sharp right turn in the trail at an open boulder-strewn meadow signals the turnoff to the left and the steeper slog on up to the peaks. Follow a well-worn path up through slabs and bits of forest until able to trudge up into the sometimes loose and sandy gully that descends from between Liberty Bell and Concord Tower. If you find yourself in a large boulder field below and to the left of the gully you'll probably find the well-worn trail farther to the right, in trees and meadow.

1. OVEREXPOSURE 5.8 R ★

FA: Ron Burgner, Don McPherson 1966

Overexposure begins about 15 feet left of the actual notch-edge or the highest point you can scramble to before dropping off to the east. This route represents the shortest distance from the notch to the summit but has some less-than-perfect qualities. Among them are that it is also the line of the standard Liberty Bell rappel descent. It does have some short bits of enjoyable climbing, though, and may be a satisfactory alternative if the *Beckey Route* is crowded. **Pitch One:** Find a somewhat decomposing crack/seam that trends up and right. Careful gear placements in the short initial crack are vital and it is advisable to place several. Make a couple of moves to arrange your pro and then style up and right through a short crux. Things quickly improve, however, and the difficulty eases to 5.5 or so. Finish the pitch by climbing cracks and blocks up to a good ledge with a stout tree and many rappel slings. **Pitch Two:** Climb the obvious lieback crack up from the right side of the ledge a short distance before another ledge interrupts the corner. Twenty feet of decent corner remain, or you can scramble out right and on up to the rappel terrace. The summit is a short scramble away and the white bouldering friction slab of the *Beckey Route* remains to be climbed. A single 50-meter pitch allows you to reach scrambling terrain by omitting the last short bit of the corner. Gear to 3 1/2 inches. Rappel the route.

2. RAPPEL GRAPPLE 5.8 ★★

This route features some quality crack climbing on excellent, clean alpine granite. There are two commonly used starts, although the route has been previously described as using the *Beckey Route* for access. One disadvantage of using that start is that the *Beckey Route* is often occupied. The right-hand start allows a totally separate line. **Access Pitch:** Use the same first-pitch options as the *Beckey Route*, only continue another 30 feet right on the ledge at the top and belay at trees near the base of the left-facing dihedral. *Variation: 5.8* Start about 15 feet left of the *Overexposure* route, just right of some blocky reddish overhangs and climb a short pitch up and left until you gain the ledge system. Move left 15 feet or so and belay beneath the open book. **Pitch One:** Climb the delightful open book and belay at

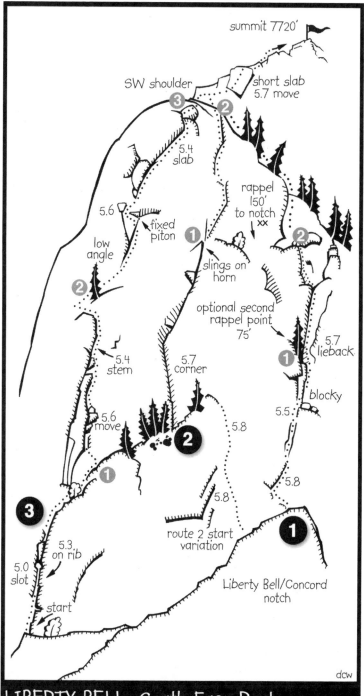

LIBERTY BELL   South Face Routes

slings below a steep orange wall. **Pitch Two:** Climb up and right passing some steep cracks and corners. Ledgy blocks and flakes at about the same height as the fixed pin on the *Beckey Route* lead to a dogleg crack and the top of the difficulties. Proceed or descend as per the *Beckey Route*. Gear to 3 1/2 inches with multiples in the 1/2- to 2-inch range.

3. BECKEY ROUTE 5.6 ★★★
FA: Fred Beckey, Jerry O'Neil, Charles Welsh 1946

This is the original route on the mountain and is still the most traveled, although the spectacular routes on the east face have also received considerable renown. The three short pitches and some scrambling of the *Beckey Route* were once described by Beckey as "400 feet of distinctly sporting climbing." Although the gully you slog up to reach the route is fairly nasty, the route itself is on great rock and is distinctly alpine in character. Hike up the gully until about 40 feet shy of the notch and find a ledge that leads out to the left past a struggling tree. **Pitch One:** Organize a belay at the left end of the ledge (please spare the little tree and use gear) and either climb the chimney or the rib to its right (maximum 5.2/5.3) until you can move right to a tree belay below a chimney with chockstones. **Pitch Two:** Climb the chimney and over the chockstones (awkward 5.6) and then stem up the beautiful rock above until you can exit left and belay beneath a low-angle slab. **Pitch Three:** Scramble up the slab to the right of center using cracks to where it steepens and a fixed angle piton under a small overlap is found. From the piton make a few moves left (5.6) to turn the overlap and climb pleasant flakes and cracks up to the right under a steep headwall to exit the pitch. Belay from robust trees at an obvious shoulder. Many people cache their gear here and continue on to the summit unroped. Although the remaining distance to the top is barely third class, a 12-foot slab with an unprotected 5.7 bouldering move will be encountered a short distance beyond. Leaders with novice partners may wish to arrange a belay for this short move and a half. Take a small rack to 3 1/2 inches and a number of slings for protection and slinging trees. **Descent:** Downclimb about 200 feet back to the shoulder where the gear was stashed, perhaps giving each other a spot or handline at the slab bit on the way. From the shoulder scramble down to the east about 100 feet through trees and past boulders and good emergency bivouac sites until an exposed ledge beneath a steep wall leads back west to reach a pair of 3/8-inch rappel bolts. Although a single 150-foot rappel can be made all the way to the notch with 2 ropes, retrieval is much easier if two shorter rappels are made with a single rope. A solid tree anchor with copious slings will be found for this about halfway to the notch.

Concord Tower (7560 feet)

Concord Tower is the summit immediately south of Liberty Bell or on the right as you ascend the couloir toward the start of the *Beckey Route*. Several fairly short but interesting routes exist on its north face and it's common to combine an ascent of Liberty Bell with one of these enjoyable lines. Most of the routes on Concord descend by rappeling down the north face. From the summit, two 50-meter ropes just reach the tree bench low on the North Face route. From there another 40-foot rappel from the trees regains the notch.

1. PATRIOT CRACK 5.8 ★

The *Patriot* is the right-hand of the two obvious crack lines located on the steep wall left of the regular North Face route. Protection is generally good but requires some insight to place effectively. **Pitch One:** Climb the standard first pitch of the North Face route to the bench with trees about 40 feet above the notch. Scramble left across the bench until underneath the cracks and belay. **Pitch Two:** Climb up a move or two between the cracks and then step right to reach the main crack. Work up the offset corner (5.6) until a short bulge forces a crux move (5.8) and then a few more feet lead to the belay. **Pitch Three:** Step up onto the stacked blocks on the right side of the ledge and move up under an overlap just like the standard route. Instead of following the crack out left on the North Face route, continue straight up, behind and beside the flake feature and aim for the 5.7 hand crack in the summit ridge. This last pitch has been described in the red Beckey guide as a variation option for the north face. Gear to 3 1/2 inches. **Descent:** Rappel a full 165 feet (50m) from the summit to the left end of the tree bench near where the crack starts and then make another short rappel into the notch.

2. NORTH FACE 5.7+ ★

FA: Fred Beckey, John Parrott 1956

This route makes a great follow-up to the *Beckey Route* or something interesting to play with while waiting. The short, flared crack on the last 10 feet of the route is distinctly more difficult, and a blue and yellow TCU may be the only options for reasonably protecting it. The following

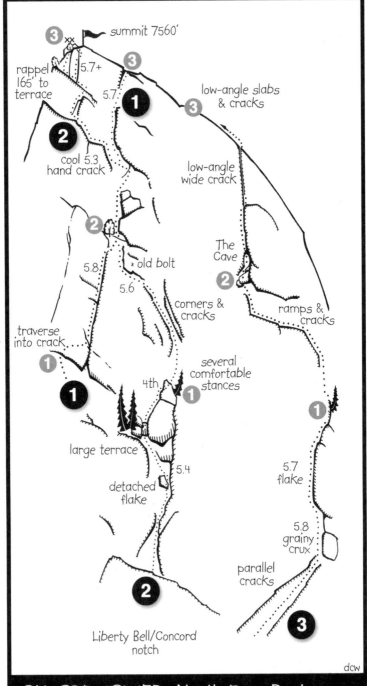

summit 7560'

③

③

5.7+

③

1

5.7

low-angle slabs & cracks

③

rappel 165' to terrace

2

cool 5.3 hand crack

low-angle wide crack

②

old bolt

The Cave

②

5.8

5.6

corners & cracks

ramps & cracks

traverse into crack

1

4th.

①

several comfortable stances

①

1

large terrace

detached flake

5.4

5.7 flake

①

5.8 grainy crux

parallel cracks

2

3

Liberty Bell/Concord notch

dcw

CONCORD TOWER North Face Routes

pitches can be combined in any number of ways. They are short but wander a bit and short pitches mean you don't need to have as much gear with you. **Pitch One:** Start about 30 feet below the actual notch and climb a crack and flake system some 40 feet to a large terrace with windblown trees and slings. Continue up to the right about 20 feet to a smaller ledge with a small tree and belay. **Pitch Two:** Climb cracks about 40 feet and then work up and left across slabs and ramps (5.6), passing a fixed pin and an ancient bolt. A juggy flake leads to a small alcove with a bush. **Pitch Three:** Continue up and left, using a fun 5.3 hand crack and then up a 5.0 friction slab to turn the corner and find the ledge just under the summit block. Extend pitch 3 to include the short but flaring and awkward (5.7+) crack just a few short feet to the summit on the east side. *Variation: 5.8*

EARLY WINTER SPIRES
(from Concord Tower)

The steep, 15-foot summit crack just right of the previous one and still on the north face looks much more intimidating but really isn't much harder and takes gear better. Gear to 3 1/2 inches. **Descent:** Rappel a full 165 feet (50m) from the summit to the left end of the tree bench near where *Patriot Crack* starts, and then make another short rappel from the trees into the notch.

3. CAVE ROUTE 5.8 ★
FA: Ron Burgner, Don McPherson 1968

The *Cave* starts a little farther down from the notch than the North Face route. Find a spot about 75 feet below the notch where you can gain a pair of nearly parallel cracks. **Pitch One:** Climb out right using the two obvious crack/ramps. Pass a dead stick that was the tree mentioned in the Beckey guide. From the end of the ramp make a few cruxy moves on grainy rock to gain the hand crack on the left side of a large flake. Belay from a tree a short distance up and right. **Pitch Two:** The second pitch remains on the north face and from the belay tree works out left and up on ledges and ramps beneath a diagonal roof line. A short crack provides a cruxy section, as you are able to move up and into the big cave above. **Pitch Three:** Creep through the cave and climb out its west entrance at a place where obvious knobs lead out onto the low-angled west face. A long but easy crack (5.2) leads to even easier slabs. Another 60 feet or so of fourth then third class scrambling lead to the top. Gear to 3 1/2 inches. Rappel via the standard North Face descent.

North Early Winter Spire (7760 feet)

The north spire is the right-hand of the two Early Winter Spires when viewed from the big hairpin highway turn beneath the massif. The north spire is usually accessed from the Blue Lake Trail, for its most popular routes are on the side facing away from the highway. From the meadows beneath Lexington and Concord towers, the worn lichen footpath of the West Face route can be seen firing straight up the impressive black wall.

Descent: Descend the peak by scrambling southwest from the summit a few feet and finding the rappel station just over the edge, above the chasm between the two spires. After a steep rappel, scrambling down the gully to the southwest reaches a large chockstone. One last rappel from the chockstone's right side is required before the meadows are reached.

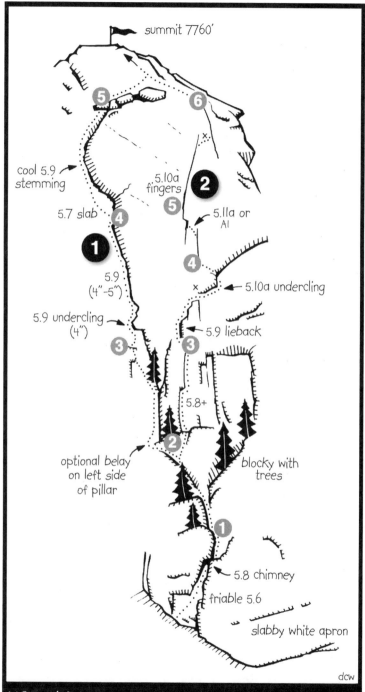

summit 7760'

5

6

cool 5.9
stemming

5.10a
fingers

2

5

5.7 slab

4

5.11a or
AI

1

4

x

5.10a undercling

5.9
(4"–5")

x

5.9 undercling
(4")

5.9 lieback

3

3

5.8+

2

optional belay
on left side
of pillar

blocky with
trees

1

5.8 chimney

friable 5.6

slabby white apron

dcw

NORTH EARLY WINTER NW Corner & West Face

1. NORTHWEST CORNER III, 5.9 ★★

FA: Paul Boving, Steve Pollack 1976

This fine route shares its initial pitches with the West Face and then wanders out left and around a corner before it gets down to business. **Pitches One and Two:** Climb blocky cracks to a ledge with trees as per the West Face route. On the second pitch continue around the buttress/pillar to the left and belay at a comfortable station. **Pitch Three:** Work up the dihedral above the belay until you reach a crack/flake (5.8) system. Set your belay at a comfortable stance a bit below and left of an obvious undercling. **Pitch Four:** Difficult and awkward moves lead right off the belay and a strenuous 5.9 undercling is encountered before the big crack in the main dihedral is reached. Climb the wide crack in the corner (4 to 5 inches, 5.9) for some distance and belay as the corner starts to arch out left over your head. **Pitch Five:** Face-climb out left to escape the roof (runout, 5.7), and head back up into the dihedral to a point where a few steep 5.9 stems fight their way out the wall on the right. Easier scrambling leads a short way to the top. Gear to 6 inches.

2. WEST FACE III, 5.10 A1 (or 5.11a) ★★

FA: Fred Beckey, Dave Beckstead 1965
FFA: Steve Risse, Dave Tower

This climb features outstanding and exposed crack climbing. For climbers skilled at leading 5.10a in a mountain setting the experience is awesome. Grabbing or aiding on just a couple of gear placements gets you past the crux moves in short order, although the climb still presents some 5.9 and 5.10a passages. The route was originally done with a substantial amount of direct aid and was rated 5.7/A1. If you aid only the short crux section, then you'll encounter a bit of 5.10a thin crack climbing on pitches five and six. **Pitches One and Two:** Climb blocky cracks past some marginal 5.6 and a chimney (up to 5.8) to the obvious ledge system with trees. **Pitch Three:** Move up cracks on the left side of the alcove (5.8+) and onto the face above. Climb above a tree and then make a short traverse right until a belay can be set. **Pitch Four:** Power through some difficult lieback moves (5.9) above the belay and higher find a 3/8-inch bolt protecting a short 5.10a undercling. Continue to an airy belay spot below the thin crack. **Pitch Five:** Climb the crux, a thin crack above the belay, using several TCUs or similar gear for protection or aid. In a dozen feet or so the difficulties relax to 5.10a and a face-climbing move left leads to the final crack and the belay near an old snag. **Pitch Six:** This is the pitch that's so visible from the trail, a white stripe of worn lichen that marks the final hand crack. The crack starts out thin (5.10a) but quickly widens to accept hands and becomes 5.9 and then 5.8 as the angle kicks back. High on the pitch a bolt marks a few moves to the right and a final crack is reached. Scramble a short way to the summit from the top of this pitch. Gear to 3 1/2 inches with multiples in all medium and smaller sizes.

South Early Winter Spire (7807 feet)

This is the highest feature in the Liberty Bell Group, and for a time during earlier years it was sometimes confused with Liberty Bell itself. This is a spectacular mountain! Viewed from the east, the peak looms more than 2500 above the road as an awesome fang of rock. That such a thing has several classic and moderate routes and that it also exists adjacent to a major highway is nothing short of lavish good fortune for us climbers.

There is something for everyone on this amazing formation. From

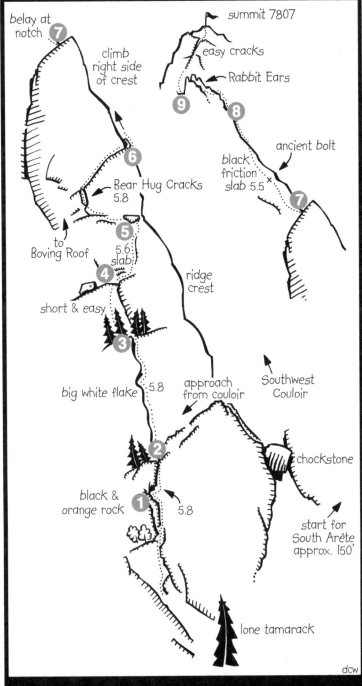

belay at notch ⑦

climb right side of crest

summit 7807

easy cracks

Rabbit Ears

⑨ ⑧

ancient bolt

black friction slab 5.5

⑥

Bear Hug Cracks 5.8

⑦

⑤

to Boving Roof

5.6 slab

ridge crest

④

short & easy

③

Southwest Couloir

big white flake 5.8

approach from couloir

②

chockstone

black & orange rock

① 5.8

start for South Arête approx. 150'

lone tamarack

dcw

SOUTH EARLY WINTER West Face/Southwest Rib

the relaxed scrambling on the South Arête to the stunning exposure of the Direct East Buttress—and indeed all the way around the peak—there are quality routes with picture-postcard positions.

The south spire can be approached from a couple of different directions depending on the route in question and personal inclination. Generally speaking, most people approach all Washington Pass routes in this book from the Blue Lake Trail. The exception to this is the Direct East Buttress, which is approached from the hairpin turn in the highway below the spires.

The large bowl to the south of the south spire often presents excellent early-season ski conditions. A popular agenda for many climbers has been to hike up the bowl from the hairpin in the morning, flash one of the sunny south-side routes, and then enjoy a stunning ski run back to the car under the magnificent south face of the spire. A day at Washington Pass doesn't get much finer!

1. WEST FACE/SOUTHWEST RIB III, 5.8 ★★★

FA West Face: Fred Beckey, Jim Madsen 1967
FA Southwest Rib: Donald Anderson, Larry Scott 1964

This climb is an outstanding alpine rock climb on excellent stone. The long, narrow rib is almost the twin of the easier South Arête but features more interesting fifth-class climbing on every pitch. The popular link-up described below is a combination of the lower pitches of the West Face and the upper portion of the original Southwest Rib.

Follow the Blue Lake Trail about 1.5 miles until a sharp right turn in the trail at an open boulder-strewn meadow signals the turnoff to the left and the steeper slog on up to the peaks. Follow a well-worn path up through slabs and bits of forest until able to trudge up into the sometimes loose and sandy gully that descends from between Liberty Bell and Concord Tower. If you find yourself in a large boulder field below and to the left of the gully you'll probably find the well-worn trail farther to the right, in trees and meadow.

From the Blue Lake Trail branch off to the left as for Liberty Bell and proceed toward the southern toe of the south spire. About 100 feet downhill and to the left of the Southwest Couloir, find a substantial lone tamarack tree that marks the gearing-up point of the route. A low-angle ledge or ramp leads out to the left, and in about 40 feet you reach another smaller, spindly tree at the belay point below a broken and blocky right-facing corner/crack system. **Pitch One:** A short pitch (some 5.6) leads up the blocky corner about 50 feet or until a large comfortable

Jim Nelson on the famous "Bear Hug Cracks", SW rib of the South Spire

ledge presents itself beneath a short hand crack. **Pitch Two:** A short bit of 5.8 jamming in the hand crack leads up to easier terrain. A fourth-class section continues to a comfortable belay beneath an obvious, white-edged flake. **Pitch Three:** Step out to the left and gain the spectacular scalloped flake (5.8), which is easier than it looks from below; 3- 4-inch gear will be welcome, however you can belay at a large ledge at the top of the flake. **Pitch Four:** Move left behind a tree and climb a 30 foot, low-angle crack leading up to ledges and terraces beneath the Boving Roof. Note: Pitches three and four may be linked. **Pitch Five:** Traverse out right from the belay and creep around the buttress crest on an obvious ramp. From a ledge about 30 feet around the corner, ease up onto the slabby face and trend up and right (somewhat runout 5.6 friction) as holds and short cracks allow. An exciting step to the right, near the end of the pitch gains easier features. **Pitch Six:** From the left side of the ledge two parallel wide cracks (the Bear Hug Cracks, 5.8) give access to an easy ramp that leads up and right and to another comfortable belay. **Pitch Seven:** Walk around a leaning block on the right side of the crest and scramble up easy ground to another terrace on the ridge. **Pitch Eight:** From a notch on the west side of the ridge, gain a blackish friction face (5.5) with an ancient bolt and move up and right to regain the ridge. Belay on easy terrain on the ridge. **Pitch Nine:** Continue a short distance until pitch ends at a large block with slings. From there a short (15-foot) rappel from the Rabbit Ears drops down into the sandy gully, from which the last short bit is gained. You can also ease right and off the rib just before the slings and scramble down into the gully. **Pitch Ten:** Climb the short, 30-foot wall (5.3) out of the gully to the summit.

Variation: Southwest Rib original start 5.9

After surmounting the chockstone at the bottom of the Southwest Couloir, trend up and left a minimal distance on ramps and terraces until a steep arching finger crack is found on a wall facing into the couloir. Climb the crack (5.9) and move right and up more ramps until a moderate (5.6–5.7) corner system leads up onto the ridge crest at the end of pitch four described above. A small to medium rack should suffice, as the difficult sections are usually short. A #4 Camalot works well on the white flake but is almost too small for the Bear Hug Cracks. **Descent:** The descent for all the routes on the spire is usually done by downclimbing the South Arête and perhaps making a short rappel at the chimney section and again a bit lower at a tree, from which a single-rope rappel reaches the ground.

2. SOUTHWEST COULOIR ★

FA: Kenneth Adam, Raffi Bedayn, W. Kenneth Davis 1937

This route is notable primarily because of the personnel on the first-ascent party. The erstwhile Raffi Bedayn had a significant hand in the development of technical rock climbing in America and is perhaps best remembered for his part in the first ascent of New Mexico's Ship Rock. This group also made the first ascent of nearby Cutthroat Peak during their 1937 visit to the area. These days the route's primary interest is an early-season snow climb, which can be pleasant in proper conditions. **Route:** From the start of the South Arête, scramble down and left around the corner and underneath a large chockstone that blocks access to the couloir. Surmount the chockstone and the next several hundred feet are low angle (25- to 30-degree) snow or gravel. At about midheight the couloir forks. Take the right fork and here find that the angle increases to 40 degrees or so and can sometimes contain ice. Continue to where the couloir terminates just a few feet short of the summit. Most people will use the South Arête as the descent route, however anchors can be arranged on the right wall of the couloir if a descent proves necessary.

3. SOUTH ARÊTE 5.6 ★★

FA: Fred Beckey, Helmy Beckey 1942

This is primarily a scrambling route so it isn't shown on an overlay. The route is approximately 600 feet long and once the initial half-pitch is overcome, the climb presents only occasional short moves and problems, primarily at a short chimney about a third of the way up. Some people belay only a couple of sections, and other parties prefer to pitch out the entire climb. In any case it's possible to break the pitches up in just about any conceivable pattern and anchors are plentiful. If you make an attempt to stay as far out right as possible the difficulty and exposure can be enhanced to a degree. **Pitch One:** Start at the obvious, well-stomped-out sandy platforms at the highest possible location. Move up on blocks and work up through an awkward (5.6 or 5.7), left-facing flaring slot. Make a few tenuous moves left to exit the slot and climb a steeper but well-broken (5.3) buttress to reach a tree heavily decorated with rappel slings. **Pitch Two:** Move up and right some, then start up the gully/chimney that leads the entire way along the crest. Belay a bit below a chockstone that blocks the chimney. **Pitch Three:** Climb some exciting moves up and around the chockstone on the left (5.4) and belay from an obvious tree just above. **Subsequent Pitches:** From above the chockstone, scramble/climb several more rope lengths until a narrow spine of rock is encountered that must be traversed. Many parties rope up again here and belay across the hand-traverse/friction slab. A bolt hidden on the far side about halfway across may ease the pressure a bit for some. From just past the hand traverse it's only a short scramble up and to the left, across the top of the Southwest Couloir and onto the spectacular summit. Gear to 3 inches. Descend by reversing the route, either by scrambling or rappeling or a mixture of both.

4. DIRECT EAST BUTTRESS IV, 5.9 A1 ★★★

FA: Fred Beckey, Doug Leen 1968

This fabulous line would be a great classic anywhere. It takes a jaw-dropping line, has no real nasty pitches, and is of a reasonable enough standard that many can enjoy its awesome position. Nonetheless the route should not be underestimated; it is a good bit more difficult and

EARLY WINTER SPIRES
(from highway hairpin turn)

South
Early Winter
Spire

North
Early Winter
Spire

South
Arête

Direct East
Buttress

approach
from
hairpin

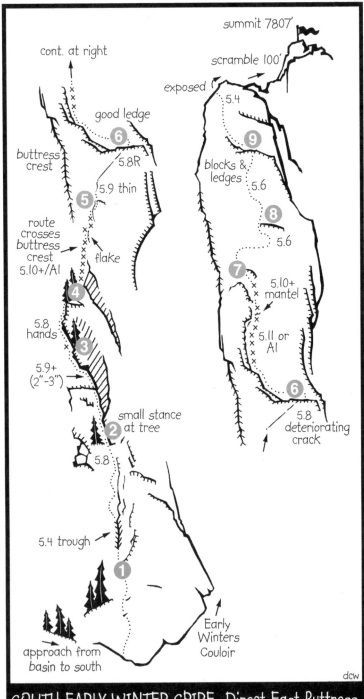

summit 7807'

scramble 100'

cont. at right

exposed
5.4

good ledge
6
5.8R

buttress
crest

blocks &
ledges
9
5.6

5.9 thin
5

8
5.6

route
crosses
buttress
crest
5.10+/A1

flake

7
5.10+
mantel

4

5.11 or
A1

5.8
hands
3

5.9+
(2"-3")

6

small stance
at tree
2

5.8
deteriorating
crack

5.8

5.4 trough

1

approach from
basin to south

Early
Winters
Couloir

dcw

SOUTH EARLY WINTER SPIRE Direct East Buttress

committing than almost any other route in this guide and climbers will want to be both swift and confidant on traditional 5.8–5.9 terrain before they tackle this one!

From the hairpin turn on the highway, hike up into the basin beneath the southeast face and work right until out beneath the buttress. Some third- or fourth-class scrambling may be encountered as you near the face. **Pitches One and Two:** Nondescript pitches of 5.6–5.8 climb up to a tree belay beneath steepening cracks. **Pitch Three:** Make a few moves to the left and reach a long hand crack in a left-facing corner. A short move left around an overlap two thirds of the way up the pitch provides added and cruxy (5.9+) excitement for a couple of moves. Continue to a decent stance and belay. **Pitch Four:** Another hand crack continues on in the same direction but just a little easier (5.7–5.8) until it's possible to climb out of the corner to the right and move past a couple of trees to a comfy belay ledge beneath a steep and imposing-looking rampart. **Pitch Five:** A bolt ladder shoots up the wall above (A1 or 5.10+), and from its end free climbing leads out around the corner to a short crack (5.9) and an especially airy semihanging belay. **Pitch Six:** Moderate (5.6) terrain leads out right across an obvious edge/crack. Protect when you can because the edge kinda peters out and so does the crack. Some solid 5.8 happens here about 15 feet sideways from your gear. Persevere and a great stance is soon reached. **Pitch Seven:** Easy ramps and ledges lead 40 feet up and left across the face to a funky, blocky feature. A couple of difficult moves reach a bolt ladder (A1 or 5.11), which takes you up past the difficult terrain. **Pitch Eight:** Wander back and forth on ramps and ledges (5.6) and belay. **Pitch Nine:** Climb more blocks and ledges (mid-fifth class) for a full pitch. **Pitch Ten:** Aim for the upper left-hand corner of the face. A tricky move down off a block takes you to the walking terrain of the South Arête. Medium-large rack to 3 1/2 inches; doubles in hand sizes. Descend the South Arête.

Mount Erie

Mount Erie is the only climbing area in this guide that is actually inside a city limits. Although there are (as yet) no burger stands on the ledges, the excellent views contribute to a rather large tourist quotient. Mount Erie is owned by the city of Anacortes and technically is a part of the Anacortes Community Land System. This destination features some 30 miles of hiking trails as well as popular teenage party sites and exceptional views of the Olympics and Puget Sound.

The rock is somewhat odd and has been described in a number of ways, although it apparently is a kind of diorite, or a granitic stone without the quartz. This highly textured and featured stone is excellent to climb on but presents few continuous cracks and few cliffs of any significant size.

While top-roping with climbing classes on the Summit and Powerline walls may be a first rock experience for generations of Northwest natives, the area is something less than user-friendly for beginning leaders. Many of the trad routes here feature fairly good climbing with difficult or poor protection and despite moderate grades these routes don't make safe experiences for novice leaders. The newer sport climbs tend to feature sandbag ratings (harder than expected) and rather unpredictable rigging, so it's advisable for leaders to scope out logistics prior to launching out on the sharp end! Indeed many come to Mount Erie with

Mitch Blanton stepping up off the ever-thrilling Springboard

49

no thoughts beyond a day spent top-roping and admiring the stunning views from these friendly red crags.

The summit of Mount Erie itself is about 1300 feet above sea level but there are no really large expanses of rock. Myriad short cliffs and crags are hidden in the steep madrona, fir, and hemlock forests of Erie's

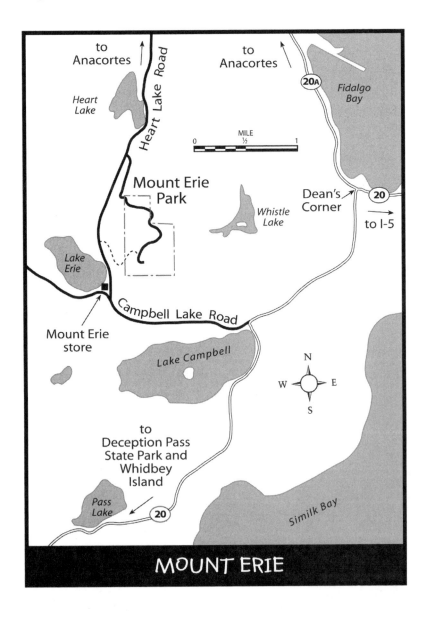

MOUNT ERIE

flanks and readers are referred to Dallas Kloke's *Climbing Mount Erie* for in-depth explanations of the complicated trail system and locations to the many newly developed sport crags.

Many Anacortes and Everett area climbers regularly visit Mount Erie and the mountaintop parking sites can sometimes become congested and full. Of particular note to climbers is the more than thirty-year presence of local climber Dallas Kloke. Although widely traveled throughout North America, Kloke calls Mount Erie home and he has been the leading force in the area since its pioneer days in the 1970s. For decades a virtual backwater of the Washington climbing experience, Mount Erie now seems perched on the edge of a renaissance as the growing number of modern climbs become more widely known.

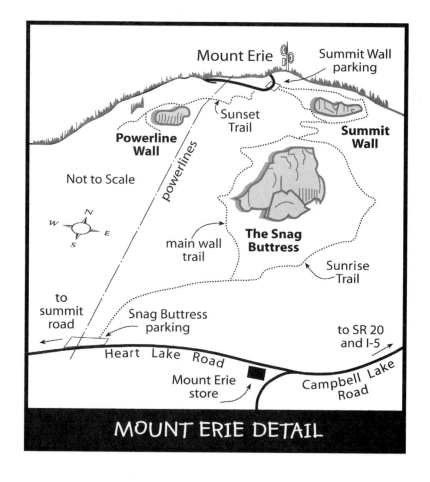

MOUNT ERIE DETAIL

MOUNT ERIE BETA

Drive time from Seattle ▲ 1 1/2 hours
Drive time from Spokane ▲ 5 3/4 hours
Approach times ▲ 5–30 minutes

Getting there: Exit I-5 at Burlington and take SR 20 west for about 15 minutes. Make a left at an obvious stoplight and (still on SR 20) head out toward Deception Pass. In a few miles reach a fork and trend right on Campbell Lake Road. Mount Erie will be visible on the right. In a few more miles the vintage Mount Erie Grocery marks the right-hand turn onto Heart Lake Road, and in one more mile the state road to the top will branch off to the right. Several miles up the winding road leads to the summit parking areas.

Season: Located in the rain shadow of the Olympics, Mount Erie offers the potential for dry climbing any time of year. Devoted climbers can find something to climb on most months of the year, but changeable maritime weather is the rule here. March to October commonly allows good chances of sunny, dry weather.

Regulations: The city of Anacortes has apparently sought to avoid liability issues by not getting involved in the climbing scene. Please exercise good judgment when climbing at this popular area.

Camping: There is no camping at Mount Erie, per se, although several campgrounds are located nearby.

Concessions: The Mount Erie store, located at the junction of Heart Lake Road and Campbell Lake Road, offers sandwiches, beer, sodas, and energy bars as well as the Kloke's local guidebook.

Climbing type: Sport, moderate traditional routes, and a few mixed routes

Rock type: Diorite

Gear: Small rack of gear to 3 inches and quickdraws. Most routes can be descended with a single 50-meter rope.

Summit Wall

This is the highest (not tallest!) of the popular crags on Mount Erie and is home to several moderate trad leads, although many climbers come here specifically to top-rope. There are several bolted anchors and convenient trees located at the top of the feature from which top-roping is facilitated.

MOUNT ERIE

summit towers

The Snag Buttress

Powerline Wall

Like many of the Mount Erie crags the Summit Wall is rather nondescript and not easily viewed in its entirety. The left side of the crag is comprised of easy, left-trending ramps and slabs. Roughly in the center of the crag is the obvious and surprisingly nose-like protruding feature of *The Nose*, with the short crack on its left being *The Open Book*. The large tree 30 feet farther right marks the start of *King of Diamonds*.

To reach the summit area, drive up the Mount Erie road until just shy of the summit towers. As you drive underneath the powerlines near the top, the Summit Wall parking area (not the main summit area parking and viewpoint) is visible directly ahead and on the right as the road swings sharply left. There is only room for two to three cars here, but the main city park parking area is only another several hundred feet along the road.

Approach: From the parking area, two trails head south to the buttress. The left trail leads to the top of the crag and the lower or right trail leads out through the madrona trees and across an exposed step-around bouldering move to reach the bottom of the crag. At least one (nonclimber) fatality has occurred at the step-around move. Please exercise extreme caution or set up a belay at this point.

1. THE OPEN BOOK 5.6 PG ★

Wander up easier and lower-angled ground beneath the feature and climb the short and sweet crack in the left-facing corner. Minimal protection on the lower portion beneath the corner. Bolted anchors on top. A popular top rope takes the overhanging "nose" immediately to the right.

2. THE NOSE 5.8 TR

FA: Dallas Kloke, S. Masonholder 1970

Climb *The Joker* until at about the same height as the open book, then traverse left to reach the feature. Look for key holds on the left edge of the slab.

3. THE JOKER (AKA JOKER'S WILD) 5.6

This is the obvious crack/groove 30 feet right of *The Open Book*. Work up and slightly right to reach bolted chain anchors at the top. Gear to 3 inches.

4. JACK OF DIAMONDS 5.8 PG ★★

Just right of *Joker's Wild* is a smoothish wall that stands out just a bit from the rock to its left. The *Jack* is the left-hand of the two obvious crack

SUMMIT WALL

routes on this part of the wall. It's a fun little route, but the overhanging moves at the start require precise placements of small brass nuts to keep it safe. Gear to 3 inches, with emphasis on smaller stoppers and offset nuts. Rappel from bolts.

5. QUEEN OF DIAMONDS 5.8+ TR
FA: Dave Seman and party 1970

This climb was originally led with 2 bolts. The bolts have long since been chopped, however, and now the route is commonly played as a top rope.

6. KING OF DIAMONDS 5.8+ PG ★★

This is the right-hand and perhaps not quite as nice of the two leads on this part of the rock. Start immediately beside the large tree and climb the overhanging groove until buckets can be reached on the left. A wired stopper or blue TCU can be arranged to protect the initial overhanging moves. Climb toward the higher tree and make a tricky move out left to reach scrambling terrain below the bolts. Gear to 3 inches. Rappel from the *Jack of Diamonds* bolted anchor.

7. BLACK JACK 5.4

This short route starts a few feet to the right of the big tree. It features good stone with some pretty easy moves. Belay from the higher tree or continue beyond a short distance to the anchor above the playing-card routes.

Powerline Wall

This rock is home to some of Mount Erie's more popular adventures and is probably among the most visited crag in the group. The left or west side of the feature contains some excellent sport climbs, and the right part of the wall hosts several classic trad routes as well as a couple of less demanding sport climbs.

Most climbs at the Powerline Wall finish at bolted anchors, although these anchors are sadly lacking in rappel hardware. Many people find that a belay set in the trees above *Intimidator* allows them to belay their friends out onto the exposed top anchors to set or retrieve quickdraws and carabiners. Please do not leave webbing tied around these anchors.

Park at either the Summit Wall or summit area parking lots and walk back down the road a short distance until you find the Sunset Trail on the left. Continue down the trail until you are above the crag. A scrambly path to the bottom of the crag is on the left (see the Mount Erie overview map).

Approach: Most of the routes right of *Terminator* are accessed by scrambling up the blocky corner (5.0 move) and then walking along the main ledge system. Another, higher ledge system can be accessed via *The Right Stuff* and provides a link-up to *Tyndall's Terror* and *Scarface*. Continuing right, along the main ledge past *The Right Stuff* and past an obvious tan-colored dirty section, leads to a single-bolt anchor on the ledges beneath *No Holds Barred* and *The Finishing Touch*.

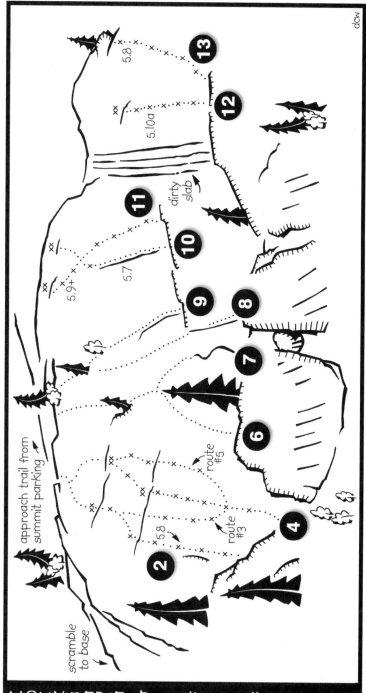

MOUNT ERIE Powerline Wall Area

1. LASTING IMPRESSION 5.7–5.10 TR

The left shoulder of the rock, left of the bolted routes, can also be accessed by top rope from trees.

2. FALSE IMPRESSION 5.8 ★★

Pass 4 bolts leading almost straight up and then angle somewhat right past 2 more until you can reach the anchor bolts of *Lethal Weapon*. 6 clips.

3. LETHAL WEAPON 5.10d

Climb the opening moves of *Intimidator*, until it's possible to step left and pick up this line of bullets. 6 clips.

4. INTIMIDATOR 5.10a ★★

This was the original bolted line on the cliff... since upgraded from 1/4-inch to modern 3/8-inch. Climb straight up the fingery and sustained bolt line past one set of anchors to the top. 8 clips.

5. TERMINATOR 5.10b ★★

This one is more or less the twin of *Intimidator*, except a touch harder. 6 clips.

6. TREE SHADOW 5.8 R

Tree shadows tend to be where moss grows. Included for orientation purposes.

7. PSYCHO 5.7

A short diversion up casual cracks left of *The Right Stuff*. Gear to 2 inches. Walk down to the left.

8. THE RIGHT STUFF 5.4

This easy crack system leads up some distance to a tree and then to the top. Mostly the bottom half of the route is used to access *Tyndall's* and *Scarface*.

9. LEANING CRACK 5.5

Another short and obscure "one-move wonder." Step out left from the stance at the bottom of *Tyndall's* and move up through a few feet of decent rock. Gear to 3 inches.

Mitch Blanton working hard not to give a False Impression

10. TYNDALL'S TERROR 5.7 ★★

Named for Reed Tyndall, one of Mount Erie's earliest climbers and developers, *Tyndall's* takes a sweet little crack up through some steep terrain. **Pitch One:** Climb about halfway up *The Right Stuff* and step right to reach a decent belay stance below the crack. **Pitch Two:** Step up and right just a touch to find the bottom of the crack and move up that until 2 bolts allow a blank section to be passed. The proper finish is up and right from there, but currently climbers often stay near enough to clip the bolts on *Scarface*.

11. SCARFACE 5.9+ ★

This is the bolted route that starts just right of *Tyndall's*. Perhaps a bit of a squeeze job, but interesting climbing nonetheless. The last bolt is now generally also used to finish *Tyndall's*. 6 clips.

12. NO HOLDS BARRED 5.10a ★

From near the right terminus of the main ledge system, find a single-bolt anchor on the ledges beneath this short route. The lower angle makes it a bit easier than some of the longer 5.10s on the left. Finish at another pair of bolts with no rappel hardware and make a short scramble pitch to gain the trees above. 5 clips.

13. FINISHING TOUCH 5.8 ★★

Use the same bottom anchor as the previous climb, only angle up and right past 5 bolts. The short crux is probably at the last bolt, and then a somewhat runout but barely fifth-class bit leads up onto some blocks where a stout madrona tree can be used as the top anchor. 5 clips.

The Snag Buttress

This feature is one of the largest crags at Mount Erie and is host to quite a number of routes in all difficulty and quality ranges. The buttress is named for the obvious silver snag located on the ledge in the middle of the feature and is an intensely developed crag with many difficult sport climbs located on the steep wall beneath the snag.

Approach: Climbers traditionally have hiked up to the base of the Snag Buttress by starting at the gated, chain-link trailhead located on the right just a few hundred yards beyond the Mount Erie store. Some will prefer to hike down from the top, however, and leave packs above the routes.

1. NEW CREATION 5.9

Currently the left-hand line on the cliff and a touch licheny. Sadly, no anchors exist at the top of this line and you must pick a spot and then traverse to the top bolts on *Potholes* to finish. 6 clips.

2. POTHOLES 5.10a ★

Big bathtub holes lead up to a short, fingery crux move in the middle of this 100-foot line. 10 clips.

3. COWBOYS DON'T CRY 5.10a ★

A somewhat shorter and maybe a little bit harder version of *Potholes*. Move out right on the flake/block to reach the first bullet. 7 clips.

The Headwall

The Snag

SNAG BUTTRESS

4. ZIG ZAG 5.7 ★★

This is probably the premier moderate trad route for Mount Erie and its three short pitches have been popular since the 1970s. **Pitch One:** Climb the obvious right-facing corner (5.6) near the left side of the formation. From the top of the corner make a few moves up and left and then across to the right to access a pair of belay bolts. **Pitch Two:** Move up from the anchors and find a set of ledges, cracks, and features that lead up and right (5.6) across the low-angled slab. Continue all the way across the slab and belay from trees on top of the Snag Buttress. **Pitch Three:** Scramble up and left across easy ground until under a short right-leaning flake/overhang. Pull up and around the 'hang (5.7) and then

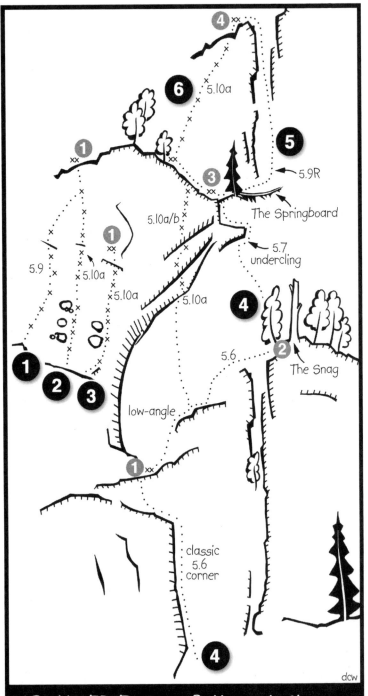

4 — 5.10a

6

1

3 — 5.10a/b

5 — 5.9R

The Springboard

5.7 undercling

1 — 5.9 — 5.10a — 5.10a

1 2 3

4

2 — 5.6

The Snag

low-angle

1

classic 5.6 corner

4

dcw

MOUNT ERIE Snag Buttress Left

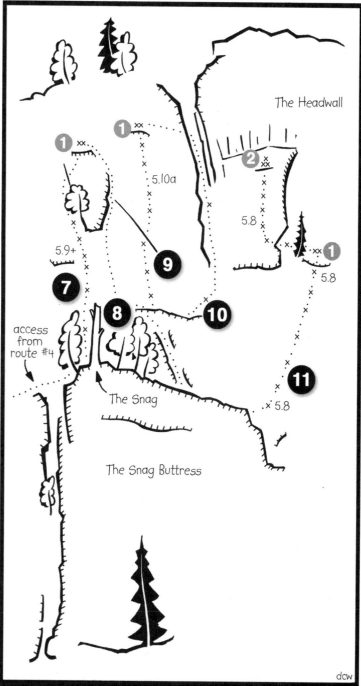

The Headwall

5.10a

5.9+

5.8

5.8

5.8

access
from
route #4

The Snag

The Snag Buttress

1

1

2

1

7

8

9

10

11

dcw

MOUNT ERIE   Snag Buttress Right

cruise up easier terrain to the bolts on the *Springboard* ledge. From here
an easy traverse up and left on ramps leads off, or you can finish with
either *Springboard* or the last pitch of *Eagles Wings*. Moderately small rack
with at least one piece of gear to 3½ inches.

5. SPRINGBOARD 5.9 R ★★

This route makes a great direct finish for the *Zig Zag* route, but is
substantially more difficult and with some questionable protection.
From *Zig Zag*'s pitch-three bolts, tiptoe out right on the well-traveled
springboard and make a difficult move (5.9 crux) with scant protection
to reach the angling crack on the right. Once in the crack (fixed pins
obvious) the difficulty eases a bit, but protection requires no small
expertise to arrange solidly and the crack continues at a sustained 5.7–5.8
level. Belay from bolts at the top. Gear to 3 inches, with small stoppers
and TCUs helpful.

6. ON EAGLES WINGS 5.10a ★★

This description is only for the last pitch of a route which starts at
the bolted anchors at the top of the first pitch of *Zig Zag* and works up
through the tiered roof system above the slabs. The last pitch starts some
20 feet left of the *Springboard* belay and is one of the more moderate
5.10s to be found at Mount Erie. **Route:** Climb *Zig Zag* until you reach
the bolted anchor at the start of *Springboard*. Climb out left along the
ledge and belay at a pair of bolts. Then climb the clean wall above that
is the last pitch of *Eagle's Wings*. Six clips lead up and right to the shared
anchor on top of *Springboard*.

7. REDEMPTION 5.9+ ★

Climb the first two pitches of *Zig Zag*. From a viewpoint with the old
dead snag right behind you, look up and find a line of bolts that leads
around the right side of a roof feature and then up the wall beyond. Pass
a tree on the upper part of the pitch and wander back right to the shared
anchor with *American Warrior*. 6 clips.

8. AMERICAN WARRIOR 5.8 PG

Start with a left-trending gully/ramp and locate a line of holds,
cracks, and textures to the right of *Redemption*. Work right, around the
blob at the top where *Redemption* goes around to the left. Belay at the
same anchors. Gear to 3 inches.

9. FREEDOM FIGHTER 5.10a ★★

This is the sport climb immediately left of the *Ray Auld* route. 7 clips, with an optional red Camalot useful as well.

10. RAY AULD MEMORIAL ROUTE 5.8 PG

This is the obvious groove/crack/chimney that defines the left margin of the headwall. Use the left-trending ramp mentioned on *American Warrior* and move right past the bolts at the start of *Freedom Fighter*. A single-anchor bolt exists beneath the route. Exit to the left before the actual top to use a pair of anchor bolts at the top of *Freedom Fighter*. Gear to 31/2 inches.

11. TOUCHING THE SKY 5.8 ★★

FA: Dallas Kloke and party

This is a spectacular new sport climb that takes an exciting position on the left side of the Snag Buttress headwall. It can be done in one long pitch with a 60-meter rope, but is more commonly done in two. **Pitch One:** From the right side of the big ledge on top of Snag Buttress make an awkward move out and right to pick up the bolt line. Pass a diagonal crack and move up steep ground past a small overhang to find the belay bolts to the right of a small tree. 7 clips. **Pitch Two:** Step left above the overlap and follow bolts up the exposed wall above. 6 clips. Rappel 150 feet back to the start and either rappel off from the left side of the buttress near the snag or finish with another route.

Darrington

Welcome to Darrington! The mountains, rivers, and creeks around Darrington contain some of the most wild and beautiful scenery of any of the popular rock climbing centers in Washington. Granite is the word here. Spectacular domes of exfoliating stone rising from old-growth forests of cedar and hemlock provide stunning views from belay stances. Several regionally immense glaciated peaks flank the granite-filled valleys of Clear, Copper, and Squire Creeks, and Whitehorse Mountain seems to loom over the small Darrington town site.

Without question, the mountain country around Darrington is full of surprise and awe. The region is one of the most accessible wild areas in the state for rock climbing, and the weather and general conditions are somewhat friendlier than local traditions would suggest. D-Town is the archetypal western Washington climbing area: dirt roads, approach hikes, glaciated peaks, old forests and clear-cuts, all nestled against the western slope of the Cascades.

Among the distinguishing characteristics of the Darrington area is that several densely forested valleys have large intrusions of granitic domes. Some of the more outstanding of these are Exfoliation Dome, Three O'Clock Rock, the Green Giant Buttress, and Squire Creek Wall. Of the rocks included in this guide, Three O'Clock Rock and the Green Giant Buttress are located

Matt Walker cruising up the fourth pitch of Silent Running

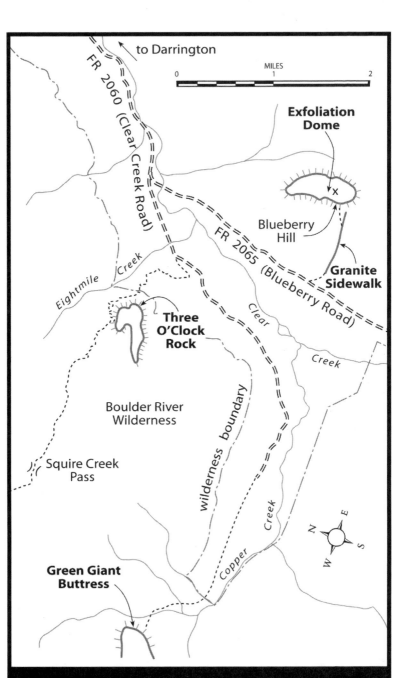

to Darrington

MILES
0   1   2

FR 2060 (Clear Creek Road)

Exfoliation Dome

X

Blueberry Hill

FR 2065 (Blueberry Road)

Granite Sidewalk

Eightmile   Creek

Clear

Creek

Three O'Clock Rock

Boulder River Wilderness

wilderness boundary

Squire Creek Pass

Copper   Creek

N
E
S
W

Green Giant Buttress

DARRINGTON

within the Boulder River Wilderness. Exfoliation Dome is not in the wilderness.

The best climbs are pretty clean and dry out relatively quickly, although morning mist can sometimes make the early pitches slippery. The season usually does provide lots of sun-baked days on the granite expanses.

Darrington climbs are moderately angled slab and knob climbs. While never particularly steep they do tend to feature thought provoking moves on smooth granite at a somewhat greater distance from protection than many might be used to. Mostly, the cruxes of the featured routes are well protected but significantly easier sections may still be runout. From the standpoint of climbers from the "old days" the modern D-Town routes are much safer than before; from a sport climbing point of view they are still pretty sporty and runout, if not steep. Climbers desiring more comprehensive information about this climbing area are directed to this author's recent interactive CD-ROM, *Rattle and Slime*, available at local stores or from the author at *www.DarringtonRock.com*.

DARRINGTON AREA BETA

Drive time from Seattle ▲ 2 hours
Drive time from Spokane ▲ 5 1/2 hours
Approach times ▲ 30–90 minutes

Getting there: From I-5, 35 miles north of Seattle, take the Arlington/Sylvana exit 208 and continue on SR 530 another 35 miles east to the town of Darrington. Make a right at the Shell station located at the junction of SR 530 and the Mountain Loop Highway and proceed south 2.8 miles to Forest Road 2060 (Clear Creek Road), which is on the right just opposite Clear Creek Campground. At about 8.4 miles from the Shell station the road forks and in another half mile the right fork reaches the Three O'Clock Rock parking area. The left fork (Forest Road 2065, Blueberry Road) crosses a cement bridge and reaches the base of the Exfoliation Dome approach (Granite Sidewalk) in a bit over a half mile.

Season: Condition of the Clear Creek Road is the primary criterion for access to Darrington. Typically the road sustains damage each winter and requires some work to become passable in the spring. This can happen anytime from late March to sometime in April. The season usually lasts through the end of October. In spring, south-facing aspects of the crags may be dry long before the roads and approaches are feasible.

Regulations: With the exception of Exfoliation Dome most of the climbing in Darrington takes place in the Boulder River Wilderness and climbers are advised to familiarize themselves with the specific regulations attached to such. As this book goes to press plans are in place to upgrade the road and parking area and institute Northwest Forest Pass requirements.

Camping: Clear Creek Campground, located at the junction of the Mountain Loop Highway and the Clear Creek Road, is convenient both to the climbing and for jaunts into town. Traditionally climbers have used several sites on the Blueberry Road and at the end of the Clear Creek Road as unofficial bivy sites.

Concessions: Darrington offers limited concessions but the Shell station/minimart located at the junction of the Mountain Loop Highway and SR 530 is a popular spot for outdoor enthusiasts.

Climbing type: Multipitch, traditionally bolted slab and knob routes

Rock type: Quartz diorite (granite)

Gear: Medium traditional rack with gear to 3½ inches. Extra dark-colored slings/rappel gear, approach shoes, multiple ropes, mountain clothing.

Three O'Clock Rock

Three O'Clock Rock, long the locus of Darrington climbing, appears as a pair of twin buttresses on the valley side opposite the west face of Exfoliation Dome. Approaching 700 feet in height, these features offer exciting slab and knob climbing at a moderate steepness. Three O'Clock Rock boasts the highest quality approach trail of any in the Darrington Group and has lately benefited from several years of volunteer trail-maintenance projects. Much of the climbing here is relatively straightforward on very sound rock with most routes being a mixture of gear and bolts. The climbs range from one to eight pitches and all are exited via rappel. With a few exceptions most rappel routes require two 50-meter ropes. A single 60-meter rope works for only some of the one-pitch routes.

Approach: The Eightmile Creek Trail currently leads straight to the slabs at the bottom of the North Buttress before continuing past the rock and on up through the forest to Squire Creek Pass. From the pass the trail

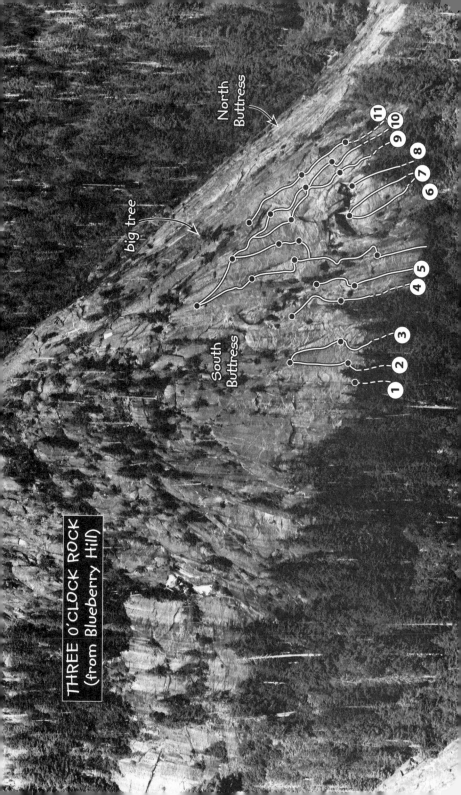

THREE O'CLOCK ROCK
(from Blueberry Hill)

North Buttress

big tree

South Buttress

11 10
9
8
7
6

4 5

2 3
1

Mark Hanna starting up the big runout on the second pitch of The Rash

leads down the other side into the Squire Creek drainage and, eventually, to the remains of the old logging road.

The South Buttress of Three O'Clock Rock is reached via a path that leaves the main trail about 100 yards shy of the North Buttress and heads up and left through vine maples and granite blocks. This steeper spur trail reaches the bottom of the South Buttress a bit right of the obvious large crack of the Big Tree routes.

THE SOUTH BUTTRESS

The South Buttress is home to fully three-fourths of the routes on Three O'Clock Rock, thus presenting a much broader range of climbing opportunities than its northerly twin. The rock gets steeper farther around to the left, and as this happens the knobs tend to get bigger. Several of the early routes on the South Buttress were pushed through for five and six pitches, but newer routes, which constitute most of the better climbing here, tend to be in the two- to four-pitch range, allowing for a number of different routes to be climbed in a day.

1. MISTRESS JANE'S CHAINS 5.9

FA: Buckaroo Bonsai, the Knob Queen

This is a 60-foot bolted slab route 150 feet left of *The Rash*. Balancey 5.9 near second bolt. 1/4-inch bolts. Rappel from obvious chains.

2. LUKE 9:25 5.10a/b ★★

FA: Tom Heins, Mike Altig 1988

Hike down and left a bit from the ramp that starts *When Butterflies Kiss Bumblebees*, then scramble up another narrow ramp. There you will find a bolt line on a knob-littered slab. **Pitch One:** Clip 6 bolts and climb some fun 5.8 to reach the glue-in ring anchors. **Pitch Two:** Climb straight up (5.10a/b) from the belay past 7 bolts and gear to a small stance that is the top of *The Rash*. 1/4-inch bolts except for the modern anchors; #0 and #1 TCU recommended. Rap from new chains.

3. THE RASH 5.8 R ★★★

FA: Don Brooks, Chris Syrjala 1980

This is an amazing track of huge, fun knobs that shouldn't be missed! When the trail peaks about 150 feet left of the *Tidbits* dike, find two parallel left-facing, dirty corners. Just a bit left of these is a clean flake system. **Pitch One:** Climb the flakes and angle right across some 5.7 to cross a small overlap and reach new chain anchors above. **Pitch Two:** Climb out and leftward to reach the incredible "rash" coming down from above. It's easy class 5, but totally unprotected for about 70 feet. Just when you're starting to wonder, a bolt appears at the top of the feature. Pass the bolt and move up and left to get some gear underneath a flake. Move up and left, past another bolt (cruxy 5.8) to the chain anchor finish. **Note:** Originally the route traversed 15 feet left from the first bolt at the top of the rash to another bolt that is now part of *Luke*; this keeps the final portion of the second pitch at 5.7. TCUs and stoppers. Rappel either route.

4. DIRT CIRCUS 5.9+ ★★

FA: David Whitelaw, Allison Woods, August 2002

Not dirty at all, and some excellent climbing too. The first pitch is only minimally 5.9 at the second bolt and gets progressively easier as you go up. **Pitch One:** Start about 20 feet left of *Magic Bus* and move up and over the same initial overlap using some small pro about 8 feet off the ground. Follow bolts up and slightly left (5.9) to reach the lower

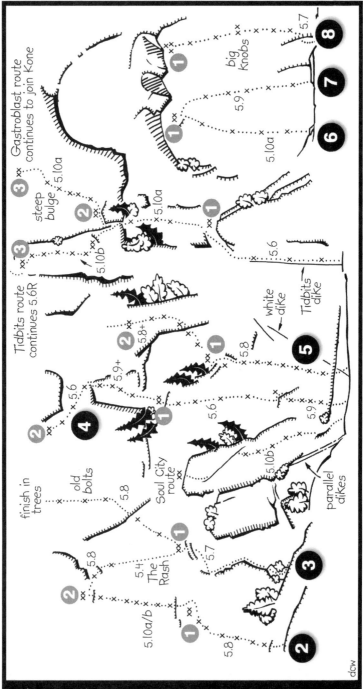

THREE O'CLOCK ROCK The Rash Area

right corner of the knobby face above. Climb more or less directly up the middle of the wall (5.6) and belay at chains just below the hanging cedars. **Pitch Two:** Climb straight up the featured wall above the belay past 4 bolts (5.9+) and step right at the top of the step to gain the upper slab. Move up and left past three more bolts (5.6) to reach the anchors. One yellow TCU for the first pitch, second pitch is 1/4-inch bolts. Rappel the route.

5. MAGIC BUS 5.8+ ★

FA: Steve Risse, Mark McKillop, Peter Wojcik 1979

This multipitch route rarely gets much action beyond the delightful first pitch. The second pitch is every bit as good, if only a little bit harder. Walk about 30 feet left of the *Tidbits* dike and look for a solution pocket above a small overlap about 8 feet off the ground. **Pitch One:** A line of 8 fairly decent 1/4-inch bolts takes off above this feature (max 5.8, mostly 5.6/5.7) and belays on a sloping ledge. **Pitch Two:** Move out right across the slab (5.8) and pass a bolt on the way to the corner. Find a bolt here and step around right onto the narrow slab above. Excellent climbing leads another 35 feet or so past 2 more bolts (5.8+) to the anchors. **Beyond:** Several more unknown pitches have been done up this way. 1/4-inch bolts. Rap the route.

6. 20TH CENTURY CLOCK 5.10a A2

This is the left-hand and perhaps least aesthetic of the three routes under the arches. It's just barely 5.10 at one spot and climbs to a shared anchor with *Charlie Chan's*. It's unclear where the aid portion of the route ends up. 1/4-inch bolts.

7. CHARLIE CHAN'S NUMBER ONE SUSPECT 5.9 ★

This is the middle climb of the three routes under the arches. It's somewhat easier and has a nicer position on the slab than its neighbor on the left. Shares anchors with *20th Century Clock*. 1/4-inch bolts.

8. UNDER THE BOREDWALK 5.7 ★

FA: Tom Heins and party 1988

This is the right-hand of the three routes under the arches and is barely 5.7 near the start. Start at the bottom of an 18-inch thick, left-facing, corner/arch. Place something in the 1- to 1.5-inch range, and step right onto the slab to reach knobs and the first bolt. Follow the bolts straight up past huge buckets and knobs (5.4) to reach the chain

Victoria Wentz on the first pitch of Dirt Circus

anchors. Please rappel the route using two ropes so as not to continue to litter the slab with bright rappel slings tied on intermediate bolts.

9. TILL BROAD DAYLIGHT 5.9 ★★

This excellent route starts 50 feet left of *The Kone* and can be reached either from the *Kone* ledge or by scrambling up and right from the area beneath the arches. **Pitch One:** Climb a low-angle slab up and slightly left past a couple of bolts and bulges to reach the steepening overlap wall. Exciting moves and devious step-arounds distinguish this pitch as one of the finest 5.8s in Darrington. Finish at a semihanging bolted belay stance. **Pitch Two:** Move out and right from the belay, step around another overlap, and reach a corner that can be climbed for some distance to the shared belay with *The Kone*. **Pitch Three:** Climb out left from the stance and cross the overlap at its lowest point. Move generally up and left (5.7) to clip two bolts and then a longish traverse left to the anchors. **Pitch Four:** Climb straight up the bolt line (5.9) above to join *The Kone* at the left edge of the overlap. **Pitch Five:** Climb the last pitch of *The Kone* route. 1/4-inch bolts; take 4–5 TCUs to 2 inches. Rappel *Tidbits*.

10. THE KONE 5.9 ★★★

FA: Duane Constantino, David Whitelaw 1978

From the top of the access trail, hike left about 100 feet until a short (25-foot) scramble leads up through blocks and bushes to the ledge at the bottom of *The Kone*, *Cornucopia*, and *Daylight* routes. There are 3 bolts on a short slab just right of this access scramble. **Pitch One:** Climb up the center (5.9) of the narrow slab that is about 25 feet left of the *Cornucopia* flake. Move left around the overlap at the top and belay at the chain anchors. **Pitch Two:** Move up and left across moderate terrain (5.3) to the shared anchors with the *Daylight* route. **Pitch Three:** Climb straight up from the belay past some gear placements (5.9) to reach a bolt. Traverse

THREE O'CLOCK ROCK

North Buttress

South Buttress

21

20

19

18

17

16

15

14

13

12

11

10

9

8

3

2

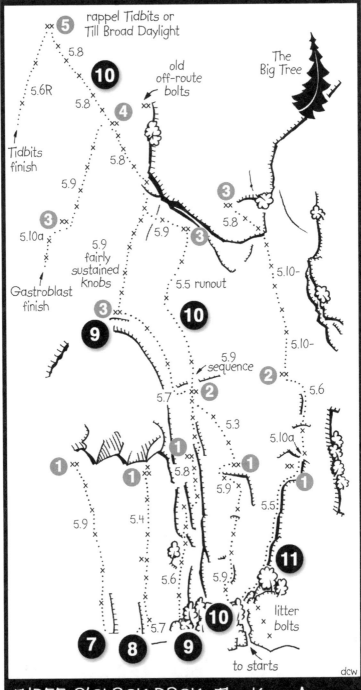

THREE O'CLOCK ROCK The Kone Area

to your left on a minimal ramp to find another bolt and then up to the hanging stance above. **Pitch Four:** Move out left from the belay past a bolt and a small crack (5.9) to another bolt, then climb up and left around the overlap above. Once the overlaps are cleared, look for bolts leading out and left to the chain anchors. **Pitch Five:** Climb up and slightly left (5.8) past 5 bolts to the chain anchors shared with *Tidbits*. Rappel *Tidbits* or (less desirable) down *Daylight* till above the roofs and then down to the top of *Boredwalk*. Take a small rack to 2 1/2 inches.

11. CORNUCOPIA 5.10a PG ★★

FA: Don Brooks, Chris Syrjala 1980

This fine route takes the obvious left-facing flake that shoots upward about 20 feet right of *The Kone*. **Pitch One:** Lieback up the flake (5.5) and find a chain anchor a bit higher. **Pitch Two:** Step up from the right edge of the ledge and finesse past a bolt and a 5.10a move to find another bolt. Get a yellow or orange TCU in the crack and aim for the short corner above. More gear is possible before launching up and left to the chains. **Pitch Three:** Interesting moves lead directly above the belay; continue up and somewhat left using knobs, dikes, and friction. Seven clips lead to the 2-bolt anchor. From here it is possible (but not recommended) to climb out to the right, and then up a short corner to reach the *Big Tree*. Modern bolts and gear to 3 inches.

12. BIG TREE ONE 5.8 ★

FA: Manuel Gonzalez, Don Williamson 1970

BT One is one of the more obvious routes on Three O'Clock Rock. From the point where the access trail to the South Buttress emerges from the forest at the base of the rock, look up and see an obvious 4-inch crack doglegging its way to the Cedar Ledges above. **Pitch One:** Climb the wide crack, crux near the bottom (5.6) and belay at one of numerous spots on the ledges. **Pitch Two:** Follow an indistinct rib right of the bushy corner past a bolt to the right edge of the roof above. Lieback up the right side of the roof and find a horizontal 5-inch crack heading back left. Scramble left 20 feet and step down a few moves to the bolted anchor. **Pitch Three:** Work up and left from the anchors and climb around and over flakes and the odd bush until a left-facing corner system is followed to a bolted anchor. Don't get lured out left, onto the bolts of *Cornucopia* unless you're looking for a more difficult finish. **Pitch Four:** Continue up the corner past another bush, and move right over the corner to follow a line of bolts heading up the exposed slab to a chain anchor. **Pitch Five:** Climb left

Dan Dingle on the first pitch of Till Broad Daylight

some 40 feet (5.0, no pro) and climb flakes to reach the Big Tree. Rappel *Big Tree 2000* or straight down from the chain anchors.

13. BIG TREE 2000 5.10a PG ★★
FA: Matt Perkins, David Whitelaw 2000

BT 2000 adds yet another choice to the Big Tree group and technically is a variant of *BT One*. **Pitch One:** Climb the wide crack described in the previous route and belay from trees on the ledge system. **Pitch Two:** Start up the second pitch of *BT One* and continue as far as the 5-inch horizontal crack, at which point several bolts (5.10a) will be visible leading up and right to a chain anchor. **Pitch Three:** The next exciting pitch climbs directly up the apron and includes some traditional style runouts (i.e., longer) on challenging (5.10a) but quality terrain. Finish the pitch at the chain anchor common to all the Big Tree routes. **Pitch Four:** This is a short, unprotected 5.2 pitch that leads horizontally to

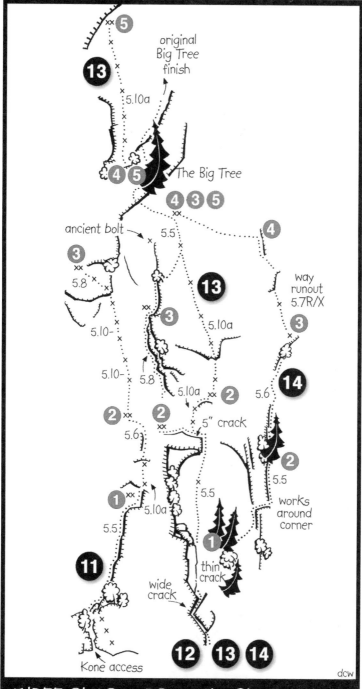

THREE O'CLOCK ROCK The Big Tree Area

just underneath the Big Tree and up to the ledges beneath the last pitch. **Pitch Five:** Climb straight up the clean slab above (5.9/5.10a) to a chain anchor beneath a big overlap/corner. Small rack to 4 inches or so for the bottom pitches. Rappel the route.

14. BIG TREE TWO 5.7 R
FA: Jim Friar, Don Williamson 1970

This was apparently the first climb at Three O'Clock Rock and follows a fairly circuitous and runout path to the Big Tree. The climb is okay for three pitches but missing bolts and 50-foot runouts make the fourth and fifth pitches unappealing. It's best to rappel down *Stance or Dance* from the top of the third pitch. **Pitch One:** Same as for *BT One*. **Pitch Two:** From the tree belay, move out to the right and make a couple of sketchy

5.6 moves to reach a left-facing corner system. Climb the wide crack a short distance to where the rib can be crossed over to the right. Work up the right-facing corner to the tree and belay. **Pitch Three:** Continue up the corner or just right of it (5.6) until a bolted anchor at a small bush is reached. **Pitch Four:** A 40- to 50-foot runout up and left to a distant and ancient bolt then continues up to a flake/stance where a belay can be set. **Pitch Five:** A long and mostly unprotected (5.4/5.5) traverse leads left to the shared chain anchors. Small rack to 4 inches. Rappel.

Chris Greyell on the first pitch of Stance or Dance

15. STANCE OR DANCE 5.10a ★

This is the leftmost of the three routes at the toe of the South Buttress. Multiple short pitches lead up through the trees and offer the possibility of linking up with *Big Tree Two*. All three of the routes in this area are pretty decent climbs, and the cracks on this route and its neighbor are a rare treat at Darrington: deep, parallel-sided, real cracks. Enjoy! **Pitch One:** Find a short, 6-foot crack and climb past it and 4 bolts (5.10a) to reach a 20-foot hand crack. Above the crack, 2 more bolts protect easier moves to the anchor. **Pitch Two:** Move left a bit to find an ancient fixed pin and a forested passage through the trees. Climb out and left onto more moderate slabs above. **Pitch Three:** Another short pitch past several bolts leads up to the anchors at the third pitch of *Big Tree Two*. Gear to 2 1/2 inches plus modern bolts. Rappel the route.

16. NORTHWEST PASSAGE 5.9+ ★

A one-pitch variation of *Stance or Dance*. Climb the technical finger crack 25 feet right of *S or D* and then the line of bolts above. Make a few moves leftward from the last bolt to reach the *S or D* anchors. 1/4-inch bolts. Rappel.

17. PUCKER UP 5.10b ★

This is the right-hand and perhaps most obvious of the three routes here. Find an 8-foot flake, from its top reach the first of 8 bolts. Crux is probably between the third and fourth bolts. There is no second pitch on this route! Rappel from 1/4-inch bolts.

THE NORTH BUTTRESS

This is the right-hand and tallest of the multiple formations comprising Three O'Clock Rock. The Eightmile Creek Trail runs into the rock precisely at the rope-up point for *Silent Running*. The North Buttress presents longer unforested sections of rock than the South Buttress and tends to be a bit lower angled and smoother than its southerly twin.

One great tour of the North Buttress is to start with *Silent Running* and follow it to a point on the second pitch where a traverse left leads to *Penny Lane*. Climb *Penny Lane* to the top of its third pitch and rappel to the bottom of the fourth pitch of *Total Soul*. Finishing with *Total Soul* yields ten pitches of climbing and finishes on the summit of Three O'Clock Rock.

18. TOTAL SOUL III, 5.10a/b or 5.11a ★★★
FA: Matt Perkins, David Whitelaw 1998
FA Rubber Soul route: Don Brooks, Don Harder, Donn Heller 1973
Considered by many to be the premier route on Three O'Clock Rock,

Total Soul blends two original pitches with six modern ones to create this challenging and interesting excursion. Start several hundred feet left and uphill from *Silent Running* at the bottom of the Great Divide. *Total Soul* starts on the right near a slanting crack. **Pitch One:** Step out right onto a short slab at the extreme bottom corner of the north buttress. Move up into a short crack and pass 2 bolts to find the chain anchors beneath a slabby shield. **Pitch Two:** Move up from the belay and get some TCUs into the arching overlaps. Finesse up onto the smooth slab (5.9+) past another bolt and friction on up the rest of the pitch. **Pitch Three:** Step left out of the corner and up some 5.7 slabs. Pass a horizontal crack and pleasant 5.6 climbing, which leads to a belay at the crescent-shaped ledge. **Pitch Four:** Climb the white dike (original *Rubber Soul* route) shooting up from the belay past gear and bolts. A final few 5.9+ moves reach a semihanging, 3-bolt belay. **Pitch Five: Anti-Fly Option 5.10a** Lieback up to the second bolt and traverse left 20 feet to find a bolted flake and seam system above the overlap. Make an exposed few moves right from the top of the flake to join the final moves of the *Superfly*. **Pitch Five: Superfly Option 5.11a** Climb up from the anchors past several bolts and a short finger crack to gain the upper slab. Smooth slabs lead past several bolts before the route swings left (5.11a) and up to a comfortable belay at the Ant Farm Ledge. **Pitch Six:** Scramble up the right side of the thin flake above the anchors and launch out across a smooth slab (5.9) to

find some large solution pockets and a path through the overlaps above. Negotiate the overlaps and edges (5.10a/b) to emerge onto a lessening slab and the belay. **Pitch Seven:** Move out left about 25 feet from the belay and find a clever way (5.8) through the overhang and up alongside the right-facing corner above. Climb the corner a short distance and move up and left past a bolt. A committing sequence leads up to an important 11/2-inch gear placement in a left-facing corner before moving off left again to reach cracks that lead to the anchor ledge. **Pitch Eight:** Move up and left from the anchors and pick up a line of bolts (5.10b) leading up the final short pitch. **Descent:** From the summit of Three O'Clock Rock move about 75 feet right to find a large tree from which you can rappel 60 feet to bolted anchors on the brink of the cliff. A double-rope rappel from here reaches the top of the sixth pitch of *Total Soul*. Rap *Total Soul* from there.

19. PENNY LANE 5.10c ★★

FA: Chris Greyell, David Whitelaw, Stephen Packard

Penny Lane is an independent line for four pitches and then joins *Total Soul*. The route starts at a blocky ledge about 35 feet left of the start of *Revolver* and is best accessed by climbing over from there rather than scrambling directly to its start. The first two pitches make an excellent 5.8 route and the third pitch is one of the best pure slab pitches (5.10a)

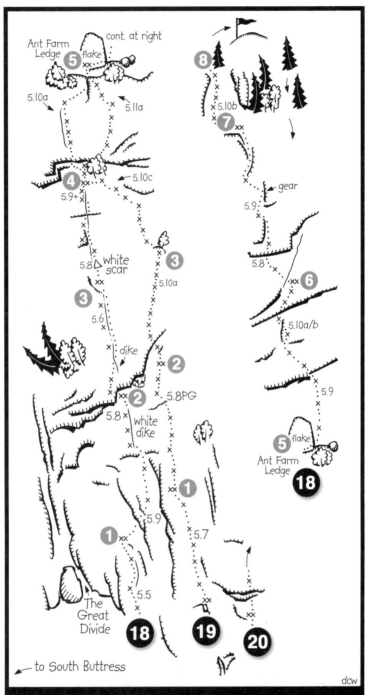

Ant Farm Ledge
⑤ flake   cont. at right
5.10a
5.11a
④ 5.10c
5.9+
5.8 △ white scar
③
③ 5.6
5.10a
dike
② 5.8PG
② white dike
5.8
① ①
5.9
5.7
5.5
The Great Divide
18
19
20

⑧
5.10b
⑦
gear
5.9
5.8
⑥
5.10a/b
5.9
⑤ flake
Ant Farm Ledge
18

to South Buttress

dcw

THREE O'CLOCK ROCK Total Soul Area

Four O Clock Buttress

THREE O CLOCK ROCK
(from north)

North Buttress

South Buttress

20

19 20

18

17

15 16

10 11

12 13

14

21

at Three O'Clock. **Pitch One:** Climb up and somewhat left past 5 bolts and generally 5.7ish terrain. **Pitch Two:** Move out left from the anchors and climb directly up to an overlap where several good pieces can be placed. Cross the 'lap and move left and up (5.8 PG) to the chain stance. **Pitch Three:** Climb up from the anchor and cross the overlap to find the line of bolts (5.10a) leading to the bush station a full pitch above. **Pitch Four:** Climb up to the left of the bush and follow bolts up and right and back left again to a crux friction sequence (5.10c) that reaches the bolts on *Total Soul*. Gear to 2 1/2 inches. Rappel either route.

20. REVOLVER 5.10a ★★

Until recently this was a rusting relic climb that seemed forgotten. The first half of the first pitch was the original start for *Silent Running*. Several options exist for reaching the anchors at the start: the most straightforward is to make a 40-foot, fourth-class traverse left from the second bolt on the second pitch of *Silent Running* (see topo). **Pitch One:** From the bolted belay stance move directly up to the overlap, place some 3/4- to 1 1/2-inch gear in the horizontal crack and step over (5.8+) onto the slab above. Pleasant 5.6–5.8 passes 6 bolts and leads directly to the anchors. **Pitch Two:** Climb straight up past a bolt and left across some broken rocks to reach a smooth slab (5.8) and 4 bolts leading to a sling belay. **Pitch Three:** Move out left from the anchors and step over some small overlaps before heading up the slab. A small headwall (5.9) leads to the belay. **Pitch Four:** Climb straight up past some runout 5.7 and find a right-arching crack in the slab above. Turn the overlap on the right before moving left again (5.9) to the anchors. **Pitch Five:** Climb straight up the flake, passing bolts when it ends. Continue up the smooth slab (5.10a) to a unique slot in the flake above. Reach over the flake and step up and right to turn another roof on its right. Finally, ease up a short crack above the overhang and hand-traverse right a few feet to the anchors. Take 6 to 7 pieces to 2 1/2 inches. Mostly modern, but a few 1/4-inch bolts remain. Rappel.

21. SILENT RUNNING 5.9+ PG ★★★

FA: Don Brooks, Brent Hoffman 1973
FA complete version 5.10a/b: David Whitelaw, Matt Perkins, Chris Greyell

The Eightmile Creek Trail reaches the North Buttress precisely at the start of this classic route. **Pitch One:** Climb the 40-foot flake and crack

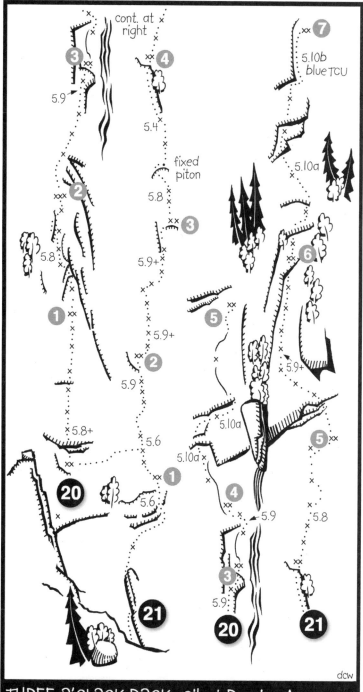

THREE O'CLOCK ROCK Silent Running Area

system and angle right to clip a lone bolt. Continue up and slightly right under the overlaps to find some opportunities for gear before stepping over the 'laps and climbing to the chains. **Pitch Two:** Climb straight up from the anchors past 6 bolts to a chain anchor in a crescent flake/ledge. A 5.9 move near the last 2 bolts sets the stage for the coming pitch. **Pitch Three:** Step out to the right and find a line of bolts (5.9+) leading up the amazing slab above. Move right a bit just past midpitch and find 3 more bolts leading to some easier flakes and the chains. This pitch was the heart of the original *Silent Running* route. **Pitch Four:** Move straight up from the anchor, passing 2 bolts before trending left for a few moves to find a crack and hidden fixed pin in the top of a flake. Above the pin, 2 bolts protect the remaining, easy fifth-class terrain. **Pitch Five:** Angle up and right past 5 bolts and some quality 5.8 to find the chains beneath the right edge of the huge overlap. **Pitch Six:** Step up past the overlap and move up and left to pick up a line of bolts (5.9+) leading up the narrow swath above. **Pitch Seven: Bonus Pitch 5.10a/b** Climb straight up into the bottleneck above the anchors and make several difficult moves through the chunky overlaps. Move right around some flakes, underclings, and bolts (5.10a/b) to finally lieback up a shallow right-facing corner to the top. This pitch requires a reasonable rack to 3 or 4 inches but save a couple of smaller TCUs for the final corner. Several pieces from 1/2 to 2 inches can be used on the first pitch. Rappel the route with 2 ropes.

Exfoliation Dome

Exfoliation Dome is the first granite feature visible as you are traveling up the Clear Creek Road. This amazing rock spur is located a bit over a mile northwest of Helena Peak and is arguably the most striking feature of the Darrington Group. The steep eastern flank, known as Witch Doctor Wall, is a bit over 1000 feet tall with an angle of about 75 degrees. The west face, Blueberry Hill, is somewhat lower angled and slabby with a greater number of established lines.

Exfoliation Dome is much more than a crag; the huge expanse of rock, difficult approach and general remoteness make an ascent of the dome a full-day affair on an exposed mountain with no straightforward descent.

Approach: Access to the Dome is via Forest Road 2065 (Blueberry Hill Road). Drive or walk up the road to the second of two long, narrow

Blueberry Hill Overview

Exfoliation Dome

North Ridge

descent

The West Slabs

1

Granite Sidewalk

granite "sidewalks" and scramble/hike for about an hour to reach the base of the West Buttress area. The Granite Sidewalk's lower terminus is the second location where a boulder-strewn creekbed crosses the road.

West Slabs Descent: There is no simple way off Exfoliation Dome! Numerous descent routes are viable but all have some less than straight-forward aspects. Currently, a reworked rappel route down the West Slabs seems to be the least problematic and has the benefit of returning you to the same place you started.

From the south end of the summit area find a rappel anchor situated for the rap down to the ridge above the West Slabs. Three or four lower-angled rappels from bolts lead down to the cleaner portion of the rock; you should aim for the chain anchors at the top of *Westward Ho!* for the most trouble-free descent. When you reach the top of the first pitch of *The Ho*, rappel left (facing down) to an anchor on a ledge where the original West Slabs route began. From there, one last rappel reaches walking terrain.

Descending the Granite Sidewalk in the rain is something you really don't want to do. A number of ways to facilitate this have been theorized by climbers watching big clouds rolling in while on the wall. The only first hand account the author has heard of involved reaching the big trees on the left-hand (climber's right, while looking up) side and descending through the big forest, thereby avoiding the slabs altogether.

BLUEBERRY HILL

The obvious focal point from Three O'Clock Rock, Blueberry Hill has historically received less attention despite the striking views. Perhaps rumors of horrific descents and the "gnarly" Granite Sidewalk have kept the traffic light. It should be kept in mind, however, that a summit visit and the ensuing descent are likely to take the larger portion of the day.

Approach: Move into the second granite wash that reaches the road and hike across shattered blocks and avalanche debris to reach the start of the slabs and the Granite Sidewalk. "Hiking" up this requires some moderately astute decision making as well as several short tree climbs at well-worn and obvious points. From beneath the Grotto a tree climb on the left leads up into the trees, and the trail works through the bushes alongside the drop until another tree climb regains the slabs above and left of the Grotto. Once past this somewhat dangerous point, acres of low-angled slabs lead upward many hundreds of feet past overlaps, water

Micah Lambeth on the sixth pitch of The Blueberry Route, *Exfoliation Dome*

slides, and small pools with frogs. Eventually it all works up to a point below the West Buttress where sandy platforms suggest roping up.

1. THE BLUEBERRY ROUTE III, 5.8+ ★★★
FA: Clark Gerhardt, Bill Sumner, September 1972

This has been the standard route on the peak for many years and features a relatively moderate and enjoyable subalpine rock climbing experience on medium-angled flakes and cracks. Recently a large rockfall that included a portion of the third pitch has altered the route and 2 protection bolts protect the new version. While the route is not particularly difficult, completing it to the summit and descending

EXFOLIATION DOME
(West Buttress)

rappel route

Blueberry Terrace

The West Slabs

Westward Ho!

The Blueberry Route

Dark Rhythm
(lower pitches not visible)

Blueberry Hill and then the Sidewalk makes for a big day. **Pitch One:** Climb a wide crack in the slabs, passing some bushes on the left and continue for another 25 feet or until you can step left at the base of a left-facing corner with a tree in the bottom of it. **Pitch Two:** Lieback up the corner to the base of the roof/overlap and undercling left 10 feet to round the roof. Continue another 40 feet to a belay at a ledge with several trees. **Pitch Three:** Climb up and left from the tree past flakes and cracks until you reach the main right-facing corner. Move up the corner past 2 bolts (5.8+) and continue until a gear belay can be set just past the obvious large splinter flake in the corner. **Pitch Four:** Continue up the corner until it's possible to climb up left, over the edge (5.8) and back onto the crest. A ramp and detached flake lead up to a comfortable ledge with a tree. **Pitch Five:** Make a short pitch up flakes just above the tree and move right onto a ledge just below a right-leaning finger crack. Belay from the crack. **Pitch Six:** Climb the widening finger crack for a few moves until a jog to the left reaches a wider but low-angle crack. Continue to a belay on a pedestal with a tree a full rope length above. **Pitch Seven:** Climb up and slightly right with little protection as the angle of the slabs eases and you find an obvious large tree with many slings. From there it's just a short scramble on up to Blueberry Terrace. **Pitch Eight (original):** Walk left on the terrace about 100 feet to find a 50-foot-high right-facing corner. Climb this (5.8) until it degenerates into brushy scrambling to the summit. *Recommended variation:* Walk past the previous corner to the extreme left end of Blueberry Terrace and make a belay at one of the final solid trees there. Then lead out left and up flakes and short slabs (5.7) about 75 feet or until a solid gear belay can be found. **Pitch Nine:** Wander a bit and find several options, all with somewhat runout 5.7/5.8 bits in the first half of the pitch, and then easier climbing and gear belays. **Pitch Ten:** Continue on up generally easy ground until the angle finally relaxes and you can walk to the summit ridge. Scramble up and right through blocks and trees to reach the top.

THE WEST SLABS

The Blueberry Route climbs the right-hand edge of a huge right-facing corner that divides the main portion of Blueberry Hill from the West Slabs. Sadly, the West Slabs are only sweet and clean in the lower portion, and following any of the routes through the upper reaches involves unaesthetic, low-fifth-class scrambling through bushes, intermittent

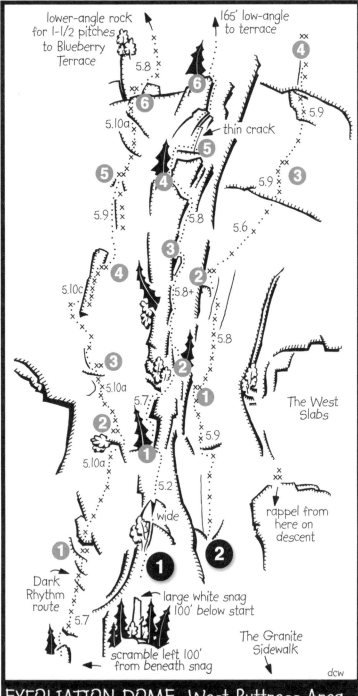

lower-angle rock
for 1-1/2 pitches
to Blueberry
Terrace

165' low-angle
to terrace

5.8

④

④

⑥

⑥

5.10a

thin crack

⑤

5.9

⑤

④

⑤

3

5.9

5.8

5.6

④

5.10c

③

②

5.8+

5.8

③

5.10a

②

②

5.7

①

The West
Slabs

5.9

①

5.10a

5.2

wide

rappel from
here on
descent

①

②

❶

❷

Dark
Rhythm
route

large white snag
100' below start

The Granite
Sidewalk

5.7

scramble left 100'
from beneath snag

dcw

EXFOLIATION DOME West Buttress Area

ledges, and so on for up to four pitches to reach the ridge crest just south
of the summit.

Approach: From the rope-up spot for *The Blueberry Route* you can
scramble up and slightly right another 50 feet or so to reach the bottom
of the big slot that divides the West Slabs from the West Buttress. This is
the best place to gear up for most any of the routes on the Slabs.

2. WESTWARD HO! 5.9 ★★★

FA: David Whitelaw, Mark Hanna, Chris Greyell, June 2001

This clean, four-pitch route provides a different perspective on the
West Buttress. Scramble up through a wide slot in the broken and reddish
colored rock between the buttress and the West Slabs to find a reasonable
set of stances and the rope-up spot, which is actually in the cleft. **Pitch
One:** Follow a small seam/edge about 25 feet (5.6) to reach the first
bolts. At the fourth bolt the angle steepens a bit below a small overlap,
and a tricky (5.9) move steps left under the 'lap and then continues up
the obvious line above. **Pitch Two:** From the chains move out right on
textured rock past 4 to 5 bolts (5.6) to reach the left-hand of two small
cracks coming down from the next belay spot. The angle steepens a bit
and some 5.8 moves with gear protection lead up and left to the chains.
Pitch Three: Climb up and right past 3 rather widely spaced bolts (5.6) to
a steeper area with 3 more bolts (5.9) and an exposed belay above. **Pitch
Four:** Climb up from the anchors past a bolt some 30 feet out (5.5) and
then float directly through the overlaps (5.9) past bolts and several wider
gear placements to reach the anchors. It's possible to reach the summit
ridge by continuing up four more pitches of less aesthetic brushy corners,
ramps, and headwalls, all with gear. Take 3 to 4 smaller TCUs, a #21/2,
#3, and #31/2 Friend, and 2 to 3 stoppers. Rappel.

Green Giant Buttress

The Green Giant Buttress is nearly 1000 feet tall and is famous for
being the location of *Dreamer*, a ten-pitch classic detailed in Nelson and
Potterfield's *Selected Climbs in the Cascades, Volume I*. The varied trail to
this rock passes old mining ruins, beautiful waterfalls, and striking scenery
before scrambling up ever steepening slabs to the base.

Access the buttress by driving several miles past the Three O'Clock
Rock parking area (or however far your rig can handle), and park in

one of several suitable turn-around areas. Be careful not to block the road... there may be more ambitious four-wheelers farther in!

Approach: The initial part of the hike follows the remains of this road another half mile or so into the forest past old logging operations and mining relics. Cross a braided creek drainage before encountering a boulder field with sections of old water pipe from the mining days. From here you can look directly up Copper Creek to the falls and the Green Giant Buttress dominates the view. From the water slides, tunnel through underbrush to the right for about 50 feet until you reach a rock and gravel wash coming down

John Fleming on the first pitch of Westward Ho!, Exfoliation Dome

from the wall. Once past a dangerous bit of vertical rubble and moraine, scramble up slabs to your chosen route.

Descent: Like Exfoliation Dome, the Green Giant Buttress is much more a mountain than a crag. Its remote position and technical descent conspire to create a degree of seriousness even if no one particular passage is inherently suicidal. The best way off the Giant is certainly to rappel *Dreamer*. This is not without its own issues, however, and climbers need to pay special attention to not getting ropes stuck at various points. The author has on at least one occasion been "saved" by other climbers being able to free a stuck rap line. The most notorious stuck-rope points are the textured wall that is the eighth pitch of *Dreamer* and the big yawning flake on the last pitch of *Giants Tears*, which seems to catch the falling ropes.

While it has been reported that you can walk down the back side of the buttress, this is really not the case as two or three rappels are normal and brushy slabs above exposure are common. However, if you

GREEN GIANT
BUTTRESS

Urban
Bypass

② 1

Urban
Bypass

Urban
Bypass

② 1

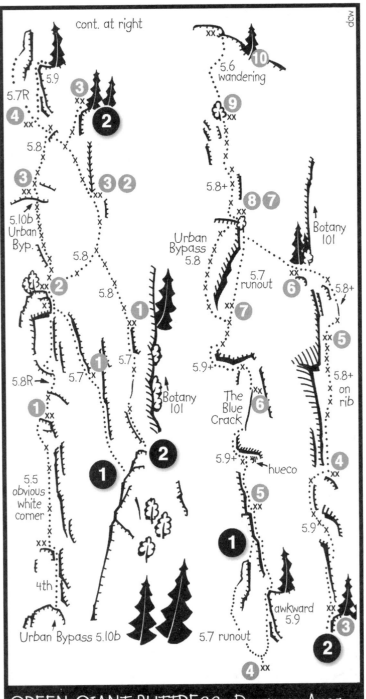

cont. at right

5.6 wandering

5.9

5.7R

5.8

5.10b
Urban
Byp.

5.8

5.8

5.8+

Urban
Bypass
5.8

5.7
runout

5.8+

5.8+
on rib

Botany
101

5.9+

The
Blue
Crack

5.9+

hueco

5.8R

5.7

5.7

Botany
101

5.5
obvious
white
corner

5.9

4th

awkward
5.9

5.7 runout

Urban Bypass 5.10b

GREEN GIANT BUTTRESS Dreamer Area

have a particular taste for S&M, then rap from trees on the summit into the big gully behind the buttress and scramble down the drainage until you can thrash around the brush to locate a couple of rappels over big, drooling chockstones. From the base, troublesome but not dangerous bushwhacking leads back under the wall to the start of the routes.

Neither of these descents could be recommended in the dark without a light, but if a light is available then rappeling *Dreamer* is still perhaps the preferred choice. The buttress is a big feature, with a rappel descent and some miles of approach, so it's best not to get caught in the dark!

1. DREAMER IV, 5.9+ R ★★★
FA: Chris Greyell, Duane Constantino 1979

Dreamer is certainly the main attraction on the Green Giant! This route took Chris and Duane three attempts before they got it to go. Since then it has altered and shifted a bit to reach its current form. **Pitch One:** Climb out left to find a short 5.7 flake/overlap and work up some awkward moves. **Pitch Two:** Move left again and follow a left-facing, thin overlap that diagonals up and left to near the ledge with bushes and bolts. **Pitch Three:** Friction out right from the anchors and find a bolt some distance out. Move up past a number of bolts to intercept the anchor near the bottom of small seam. **Pitch Four:** Climb up and left past several widely spaced bolts to find the anchors below and left of a short blocky left-facing corner. *The Giants Tears* and *Urban Bypass* join *Dreamer* at this point. **Pitch Five:** Climb out around to the left (5.7+ runout) or move up the blocky corner (5.8+) and then move left a bit to find the anchors about 30 feet below the roof/flake. **Pitch Six:** Climb up and slightly right to find a big hueco under the roof and then undercling (5.9+) back left to turn the corner and climb the offset flake (5.8+) known as The Blue Crack. Find the anchors above and right of the crack. **Pitch Seven:** Move up about 30 feet above the belay to an obvious bolt and start another undercling out left. Turn the corner and climb the face above (5.9+) to bolt anchors. **Pitch Eight:** Climb straight up from the anchors to where the angle steepens onto a textured and huecoed wall. Climb the wall (5.6) about 80 feet with only one runner and make a thrashy set of moves left (5.7 R) into some hanging bushes and onto the ledge. *Variation: 5.8* Just after starting the pitch move left and cross a large right-facing corner to gain a bolted knob wall that leads directly to the anchors at the bottom of pitch nine. **Pitch Nine:** Step a few feet left on a ledge and climb up (5.8+) and generally left on a steep wall past

Eric Mohler leading the Dreamer's *celebrated "Blue Crack" on the Green Giant Buttress. (Matt Perkins)*

6 bolts to find the last set of anchors. **Pitch Ten:** Wander up and left to find some overlaps and opportunities for protection, then swing back right a bit near the top and head for the trees on the summit ridge. Gear to 4 inches. Rappel the route with two ropes.

2. SAFE SEX IV, 5.9 PG ★★

FA: Matt Perkins and friends 1986

The climb starts at the base of the *Botany 101* dihedral. It shares portions of the *Dreamer* and *Botany* routes and has been responsible for some confusion as climbers follow the most visible bolts. The first four pitches of the climb lie on the slabs just left of the *Botany* dihedral and (mostly) right of *Dreamer*. Perhaps just a touch easier than *Dreamer*, this is a fine route that makes excellent use of the initial apron on the Green Giant. **Pitch One:** From the base of the *Botany 101* dihedral, climb up and left on a ramp past a fixed pin (visible from the ground) and some runout, but high-quality bolted friction climbing. Step left (5.7), negotiate an undercling, and climb a crack leading to the belay on a comfortable hidden ledge. **Pitch Two:** Move up and left past a bolt and over a bulge (5.8). Four more bolts follow fairly directly in line, with a thin crack and some stemming at the end of the pitch. This pitch is a full (50m) rope length, leading to a belay on a small ledge. **Pitch Three:** Climb left and up a rib next to the shallow dihedral above the belay. From the third bolt, head up and right past a fourth bolt (5.8) to a belay on a small ledge below a small tree. **Pitch Four:** Climb up crack/corner system above the belay and step over a small roof. From here, a bolted face leads up and left, but a step right leads to a rib (5.8) in the *Botany 101* dihedral (hangers are missing but nuts are on the 2 bolts here). *Variation:* After the small roof, climb the bolted face (5.9) to loose flakes (5.8) and a final move back right (at a bolt) to the belay. Belay on a large ledge in the main corner. **Pitch Five:** Climb up the corner, diverging briefly onto the right wall above the belay (5.7), and as you near the great roof, diverge again onto the right wall past 2 bolts (5.8+) then up and left to the belay on a small ledge next to a bush. **Pitch Six:** Climb up and right past a bolt (5.8+), then up and left past a bolt (5.4) to a belay on a large ledge just left of the *Botany 101* dihedral. **Pitch Seven:** Climb up and left on easy but poorly protected rock (5.4) and step left past a bolt (5.8) to reach the pitch eight *Dreamer* belay on a comfortable ledge next to a bush. **Pitches Eight and Nine:** Follow *Dreamer*. Gear to 3 1/2 inches. Rappel *Dreamer*.

Static Point

Static Point is a slabby, glacier-polished buttress coming off the southeast shoulder of Static Peak. The climbing is similar to that on Yosemite's Glacier Point Apron. For those of us in Washington, it is quite simply the finest slab climbing in the state. Static's southern exposure and lack of dirty cracks has made for a remarkable climbing surface and indeed one of the routes, *On Line*, has been celebrated in magazines, calendars, and route-of the-month selections almost to the exclusion of the area's other excellent routes.

Many Static Point routes are quite similar, featuring four to six pitches of mostly bolt-protected friction climbing. Unlike many domes, Static Point gets steeper as you get higher, and the difficulty tends to ramp up accordingly. While the cruxes of these moderately angled routes are mostly in the 5.10 range, there are also many 5.7, 5.8, and 5.9 pitches mixed in along the routes.

Climber on the fourth pitch of one of Static Point's classic slab routes, Lost Charms

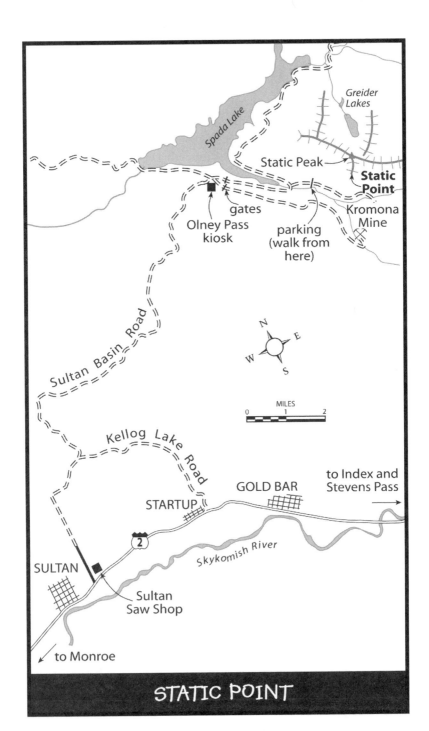

Greider
Lakes

Spada Lake

Static Peak

**Static
Point**

gates

Kromona
Mine

Olney Pass
kiosk

parking
(walk from
here)

Sultan Basin Road

N
W — E
S

MILES
0   1   2

Kellog Lake Road

GOLD BAR

to Index and
Stevens Pass

STARTUP

2

Skykomish River

SULTAN

Sultan
Saw Shop

to Monroe

STATIC POINT

STATIC POINT BETA

Drive time from Seattle ▲ 1 1/2 hours

Drive time from Spokane ▲ 5 3/4 hours

Approach times ▲ 1–2 hours depending on conditions at the gate

Getting there: From the east end of the town of Sultan on US 2, find a large wooden sign on the north side of the highway that says Sultan Basin Recreation Area. Turn north onto this road (Sultan Basin Road) and follow it about 15 miles to a three-way fork and a users' sign-in kiosk at Olney Pass. From here, follow the gated middle fork of the road (South Lake Shore Road). After the gate the road trends downhill and swings around sharply to the left on its way to Spada Lake. About a mile and a half from the gate, the Static Point road will be found on the right. Another mile or so along this track leads to a place where boulders block the road and the hiking begins.

Season: People have climbed at Static Point all months of the year, but the seasonally gated South Lake Shore Road may restrict access at times.

Regulations: Static Point exists in the Sultan Basin watershed, which in turn feeds Spada Lake (a reservoir) and provides drinking water for the city of Everett. Recreational activities such as hiking, boating, and rock climbing are permitted, although the Everett Public Works Department (425-257-8800) may close the gate due to poor road conditions at any time.

Camping: Primarily a day-use area, but a campground does exist at Olney Park, located about halfway along the Sultan Basin Road. People also throw their bags out at the trailhead when necessary.

Concessions: The town of Sultan, on US 2, is the last opportunity to make purchases.

Climbing type: Traditional slab climbing. The majority of the routes have been upgraded to modern gear.

Rock type: Granodiorite

Gear: Small rack to 3 inches, quickdraws, extra dark-colored slings/rappel gear, double ropes, approach shoes, mountain clothing.

Access for Static has changed continuously over its history and mountain bikes may be helpful for times when the gate remains locked during peak climbing season. Technically, outdoor recreation is permitted in the Sultan Basin although security concerns for the Everett watershed

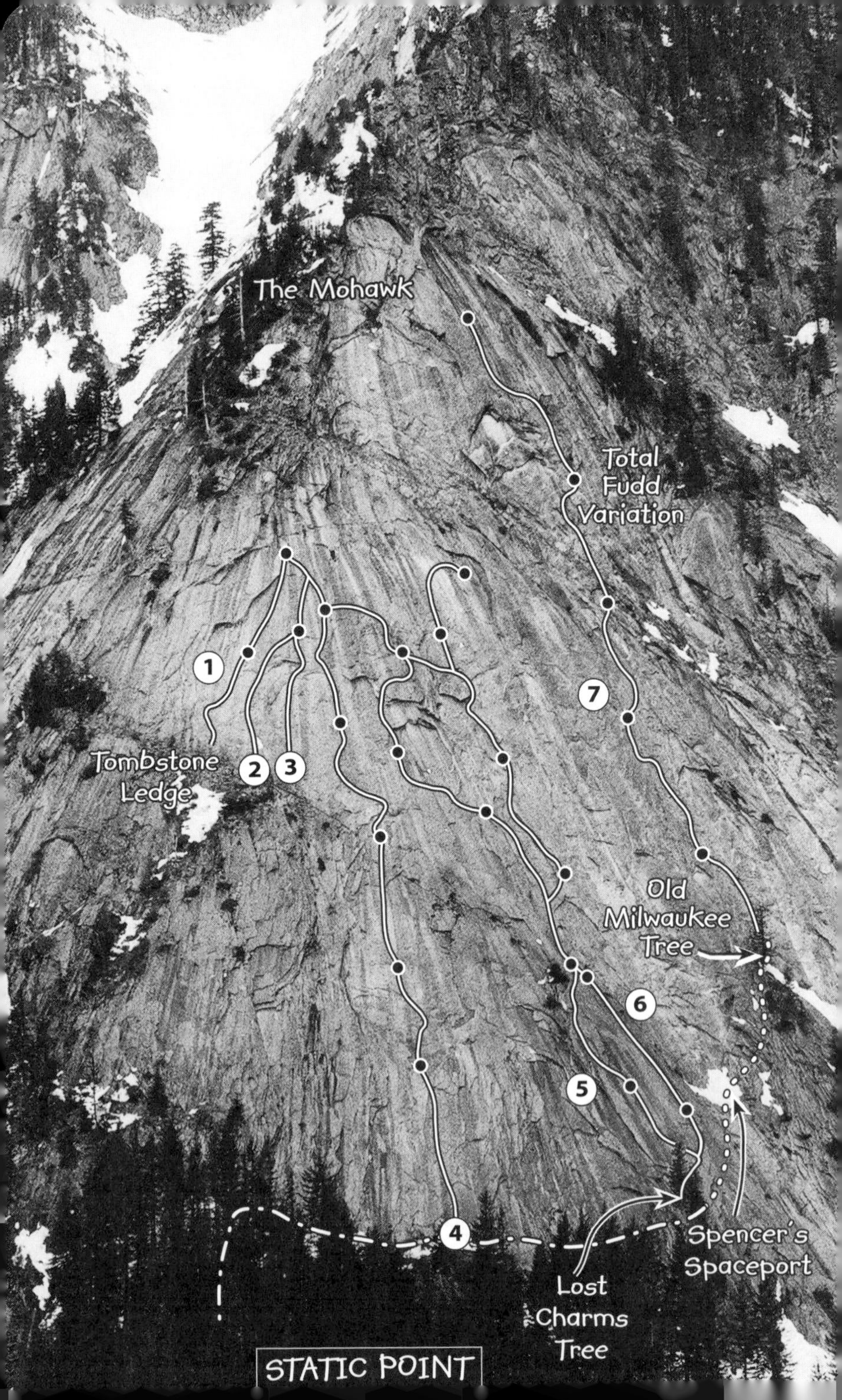

The Mohawk

Total
Fudd
Variation

①

Tombstone
Ledge

② ③

⑦

Old
Milwaukee
Tree

⑥

⑤

④

Spencer's
Spaceport

Lost
Charms
Tree

STATIC POINT

subsequent to 9/11 seem to have had an effect on exactly when these gates are open or closed.

Approach: From the parking area, hike the decommissioned roadbed a good mile up the valley, crossing numerous creeks and drainages. At one point a brief glimpse of the shoulder of Static Peak will be visible uphill to the left and shortly beyond that a large culvert pipe will be found lying on the roadbed with (usually) a cairn nearby. Immediately opposite the pipe, the trail ascends the dirt bank and in just a few feet passes a large tree stump before moving up into the old-growth forest.

Follow the clear trail uphill for about 45 minutes through the sublime old forest until a short steep section scrambles the last few hundred feet up to the crag. Fifty feet or so beyond where the trail leaves the woods is a flat spot that marks the start of *On Line* and the last place to gear up without scrambling.

Several hundred feet above where you exit the forest and to the left of the fourth pitch of *On Line* is a spacious ledge system known as Tombstone Ledge. Several excellent one-pitch routes start from here and although it's possible to scramble to this destination it's much more common to rappel here after climbing *On Line*. It's possible to climb *On Line* as far as the bottom of the crux pitch and from there rappel to the ledge. From trees at the right side of the ledge, rappel to anchors on *On Line* and continue down.

There is no real base at Static Point and moving around the feature to the right involves slabby scrambling to various destinations. Keep a biner handy, and a bolt makes a safer handhold on the scramble right from the *On Line* area. Several hundred feet right of *On Line* you come to the Lost Charms Tree and ledges from which the *Pillar* area routes begin.

Most people rope up to continue around to the right beyond the Lost Charms Tree. A long, barely fifth-class pitch up and right eventually leads to bolts at the left end of *Spencer's Spaceport*. The popular and challenging route *Shock Treatment* begins here, but the start of *Fuddhat* is located another 100 feet up and right at the Old Milwaukee Tree.

1. THE CASHMAN 5.10b R ★

FA: David Whitelaw, Bob DeChenne 1983

From Tombstone Ledge, start near the left side of the slab and smear up a short, left-facing, 2-inch corner before an unprotected move left reaches a "thank-god" hueco. Trend right on a ramp and move up past several more bolts and the crux to a bolted anchor. Rappel.

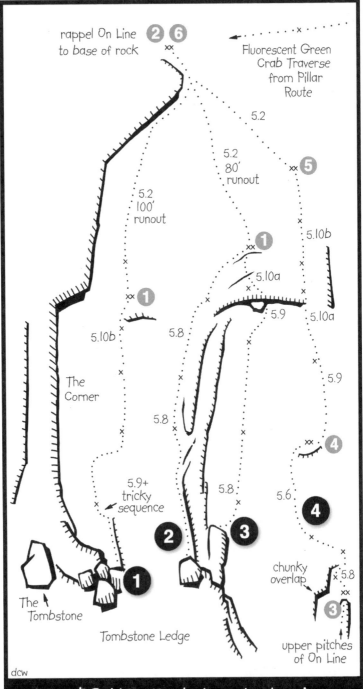

rappel On Line to base of rock ②⑥

Fluorescent Green Crab Traverse from Pillar Route

5.2

5.2 80' runout

⑤

5.10b

5.2 100' runout

① xx

5.10a

5.9

5.10a

①

5.10b

5.8

5.9

The Corner

5.8

5.8

④

5.9+ tricky sequence

5.8

5.6

④

② ③

chunky overlap

5.8

The Tombstone

③

Tombstone Ledge

① upper pitches of On Line

dcw

STATIC POINT Tombstone Ledge Area

2. BLACK FLY 5.8 PG ★

FA: Chris Greyell, David Whitelaw 1983

From Tombstone Ledge, just right of center, another left-facing, 2-inch corner stands about 10 feet tall. Climb up and a little left from here, past numerous small stoppers, to pick up the first bolt. Exciting climbing continues up and right, past several bolts to the anchor. A totally unprotected, 5.2 second pitch completes the route. Gear to 11/2 inches. Rappel.

3. AMERICAN PIE 5.10a R ★★

FA: David Whitelaw, Duane Constantino 1983

From the right margin of Tombstone Ledge, step up onto a grainy block and launch out up the slab from there. Moving left from the last bolt is more runout, but a bit easier than finishing directly. Bolts, and bring a #21/2 Friend.

4. ON LINE 5.10a/b PG ★★★

FA: Don Brooks, David Whitelaw 1984

The celebrated classic at Static Point, *On Line*'s six pitches scarcely deviate from straight up by more than 3 or 4 feet. This is the first route you walk by at the base of the rock and the first bolt will be visible some 40 feet up, above a small overlap. **Pitch One:** Climb 40 feet of unprotected 5.5 to the first bolt, where a couple of 5.6 sequences will be found. The rest of the pitch is easier and uses a couple of smaller TCUs in the arching crack above. **Pitch Two:** Climb up and right (5.7) past 2 bolts before a move left reaches the Potato Chip Flake and above that the anchors. **Pitch Three:** The scary looking Mirror Slab was worse in the days before sticky rubber! Clip the bolt above the anchors and make a 25-foot, 5.8ish runout up the smooth but low-angle slab. **Pitch Four:** A move left from the anchors works up a crack and passes chunky overlaps (5.8) before the line wanders to the bolts in the slab above. **Pitch Five:** Increasingly difficult climbing heads up from the anchor until the crux passage between the third and fourth bolt is reached. Easier climbing concludes the pitch. **Pitch Six:** A final, unprotected 5.2 pitch completes the climb. Bolts, but include 2 to 3 pieces to 11/2 inches. Rappel the route.

5. THE PILLAR 5.10b ★★

FA: Duane Constantino, Chris Greyell, David Whitelaw 1984

From the Lost Charms Tree several hundred feet right of *On Line*,

Tombstone Ledge

The Curious Cube

STATIC POINT
(from the base)

start of On Line

two direct pitches lead up to the ledges of the pillar formation. **Pitch One:** Climb out and right just a few feet as per *Lost Charms* and then move back left on a flake until you can friction (5.9) directly up the slab past a bolt to the belay. **Pitch Two:** This short pitch moves left and then climbs to a belay beneath the pillar. **Pitch Three:** Climb the pillar face until it makes more sense to lieback up the right margin. Belay from gear. **Pitch Four:** Work out and left from the pillar (5.8) past several obvious flakes until a bolt signals the moves up to the small gear stance. **Pitch Five:** Climb directly up from the anchor, past a small overlap until a bolt can be reached out to the left. Moving up to the overlap is the crux, and then good gear and easier moves pass the 'lap. **Pitch Six:** Two bolts climb a narrow little dike (short 5.10b sequence) up from the left end of the ledge system, and the Fluorescent Green Crab Traverse heads off left

Duane Constantino making the first ascent of the Fluorescent Green Crab *pitch*

and passes a distant bolt before reaching the top of *On Line*. Gear to 3½ inches. Rappel *On Line*.

6. LOST CHARMS 5.7 A0 (or 5.9) ★★★
FA: Chris Greyell, Bob DeChenne, Peter Skardvedt 1983

    Lost Charms is the classic moderate route for Static Point. A later direct finish has added a higher rating, but the original just barely scrapes 5.9 for one move, which can be easily aided by grabbing the bolt. There are only a few bolts on *Lost Charms*, but the route follows traditionally protected cracks and flakes for much its length. The best descent involves climbing the first pitch of the variation (5.8) and then rappelling to *Shock Treatment*

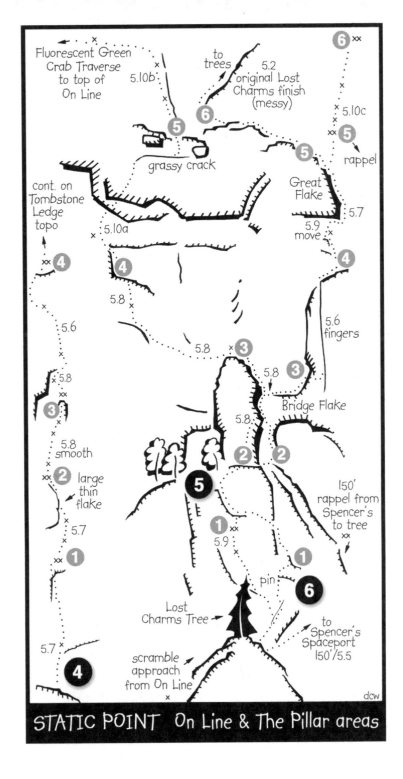

Fluorescent Green
Crab Traverse
to top of
On Line

to trees

5.2
original Lost
Charms finish
(messy)

5.10b

⑥ ✕✕

5.10c

✕ ✕✕ ⑤ rappel

⑤ ⑥

grassy crack

⑤ Great Flake

cont. on
Tombstone
Ledge
topo

5.7

5.9 move

5.10a

④ ④ ④

5.8

5.6

5.6 fingers

5.8

5.8 ③ ③

5.8 Bridge Flake

5.8 smooth

③

5.8

5.8

② large thin flake

② ②

⑤

5.7

150' rappel from Spencer's to tree

① ✕✕

① ①

5.9

✕✕

pin

⑥

Lost Charms Tree →

to Spencer's Spaceport 150'/5.5

5.7 ✕

④

scramble approach from On Line

dcw

STATIC POINT   On Line & The Pillar areas

Matt Perkins moving up through the crux section on the third pitch of
Fuddhat

and down. **Pitch One:** From the Lost Charms Tree, climb features up
and right past a fixed pin (5.7) until you reach a stance near the right
margin of the slab. **Pitch Two:** Continue up from the stance past shallow
corners until you reach the *Pillar* ledge. **Pitch Three:** Move up and right
across the unique Bridge Flake and belay from cracks on the other side.
Pitch Four: Climb the sweet, 5.6 finger crack above the belay until edges
lead right to reach the stance below a large roof. **Pitch Five (original):**
From the anchor, climb to a bolt-protected 5.9 move and then step out

115

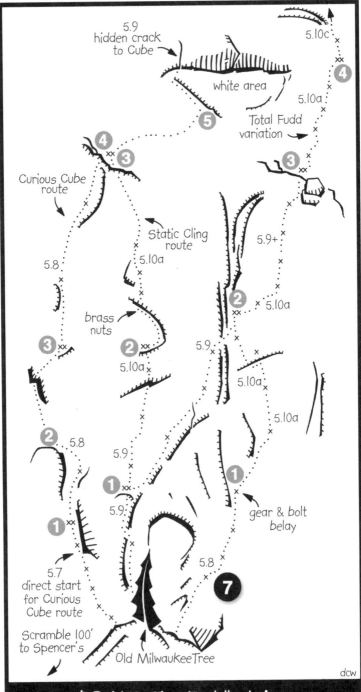

5.9
hidden crack
to Cube

5.10c

④

white area

5.10a

⑤

Total Fudd
variation

④
xx
③

Curious Cube
route

③
xx

5.9+

Static Cling
route

5.10a

②
xx

5.9

②
xx

5.10a

brass
nuts

5.10a

5.10a

②
xx

5.8

5.9

5.10a

③
xx

①
xx

5.9

①

5.9

gear & bolt
belay

②
5.8

①
xx

5.7
direct start
for Curious
Cube route

5.8

7

Scramble 100'
to Spencer's

Old Milwaukee Tree

dcw

STATIC POINT The Fuddhat Area

right, around the Great Flake, until it is possible to aim up and left to the communal anchor with *The Pillar*. **Pitch Six (original):** A dirty pitch trends up and slightly right on easy ground to reach the trees. Move left and rappel from trees to the top of *On Line* and continue down.

Variation: I Found It! 5.10c ★★

FA: Chris Greyell, David Whitelaw 1986

Pitch Five: Follow *Lost Charms* up around the Great Flake and then continue straight to a bolt anchor (5.8) instead of exiting left. **Pitch Six:** Extremely slippery moves work up past the bolts (5.10c) until the angle eases and you can traverse right to the anchors on *Shock Treatment*. Gear to 3 inches.

7. FUDDHAT 5.10a PG ★★★

FA: David Whitelaw, Chris Greyell, Dave Jay 1984

Fuddhat is located way around to the right on Static Point and is a sustained and outstanding route all on modern bolts. If you like slab climbing you won't want to miss this one! **Pitch One:** Start just right of the Old Milwaukee Tree and move up the slab. Careful route finding keeps it at 5.8 and passes 3 bolts enroute to the partly gear anchor in a corner. **Pitch Two:** Head out right past a similar corner to get lined up beneath the awesome slab above. Pass 3 bolts (crux 5.10a) before a sequence left picks up edges and another bolt on the way to the chains. **Pitch Three:** Move out horizontally right (crux 5.10a) to reach a stance in an obvious dish. Continue directly up the slab past 4 more bolts (5.9+) until blocks lead to the anchors at the Broken Band. Gear to 3 inches. Rappel the route.

Variation: Total Fudd (aka Kill the Wabbit) 5.10c ★★★

FA: Dave Tower, Chris Greyell 1985

From the top of *Fuddhat*, move up and right across the wall (5.10a) to visible set of anchors. Another pitch moves up past the overlaps (5.10b) before a crux (5.10c) sequence moves left to gain features that finish the pitch. Gear to 11/2 inches. Rappel.

Index

The Index Town Walls represent some of the steepest granite climbing featured in this guide. Located only 1 1/4 hours from Seattle on US 2, the area's easy access and huge supply of high-standard routes has made it a climbing pressure cooker for nearly forty years. In the early years and with the exception of what used to be called the "free area," Index featured aid climbing as its primary draw. Ultimately skills, attitudes, and mechanics evolved to the degree that free climbing became possible almost everywhere on these crags.

Index has been altered quite a bit by the hand of man: turn-of-the-twentieth-century quarry operations hauled away more than half of the lower wall. The quarried granite was installed across the state as curbs, foundations, and even in the steps of our state capitol. One of the moderate climbs on the lower wall still features a belay at the celebrated Railroad Bolts: giant, 1-inch diameter, iron eyebolts. They remain as reminders of the days when the stone-cutting operations steamed full tilt and the tracks, only yards away, were busy with daily trains laden with quarried stone.

A good deal of the Index climbing experience is outside the realm of this book. Exciting, difficult, and high-standard climbs have always been a hallmark of the area and all the climbs are considered stiff for their standard. Still, a useful, technical, and rewarding set of traditional skills can be acquired here at 5.10 and under, and many skilled and even legendary climbers of decades past learned their craft on the now-moderate free climbs detailed here.

Few amenities are available in the quaint town

Jay Brazier gets ready for the crux on Princely Ambitions.

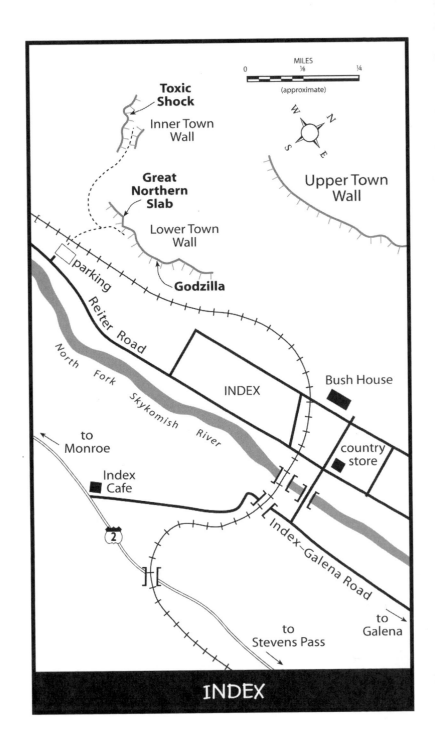

Toxic Shock

Inner Town Wall

Great Northern Slab

Lower Town Wall

Godzilla

Upper Town Wall

MILES

0   ⅛   ¼

(approximate)

W N S E

parking

Reiter Road

North Fork Skykomish River

INDEX

Bush House

country store

to Monroe

Index Cafe

2

Index–Galena Road

to Galena

to Stevens Pass

INDEX

site. But of course there is the rushing river, the front-row views of Mount Index and the stunning, striped granite walls that seem to hang above the small town site.

INDEX AREA BETA

Drive time from Seattle ▲ 1 1/4 hours
Drive time from Spokane ▲ 5 hours
Approach times ▲ Roadside to 30 minutes

Getting there: From the junction of SR 520 and I-405, drive north about 15 minutes on I-405 and follow signs to Monroe and Wenatchee via US 2. Drive US 2 through a number of small towns, and at the Index Café turn left and take the short bit of road that leads to the river and into town. The town is on the north side of the Skykomish River, opposite the spectacular fang of Mount Index.

Season: Hardcores can be found here almost any month of the year, whenever sun and a few dry days occur. Typically the season extends from March through November.

Regulations: There are historically few hassles here. The parking area for the Lower Town Wall is privately owned, however, so exercise discretion.

Camping: Several camp spots exist by the river, immediately across the street from the climbing. When open, the Bush House in Index offers great food and historic accommodations.

Concessions: Index offers scant concessions save a small country store and a rough bar. Sadly, the historic Bush House hasn't been open in a while.

Climbing type: Traditional, although high-standard sport climbs are common as well

Rock type: Granodiorite

Gear: Medium traditional rack with gear to 3 1/2 inches. Extra dark-colored slings/rappel gear, approach shoes, multiple ropes, mountain clothing.

The Lower Town Wall

The Lower Town Wall is by far the most frequently visited area at Index. With an approach time measured in seconds, the rock is about as close to the car as it can get. It's nearly forgotten that the lower wall was once substantially more vegetated than it appears now. In those early botanical years the only options for free climbing were found on the extreme

left margin of the lower wall, now referred to as the Great Northern Slab. In days past it was simply the "free area" and the rest of the wall was host to a wide array of nail-ups and thriller aid routes.

The Lower Town Wall now ranks as one of Washington's finest crags, with an unrivalled concentration of steep crack and face climbs. The steep rock and often thin cracks make for high standards, and most of the now free routes on the main wall go at stellar grades in the 5.11 and 5.12 range. There's certainly no lack of hard climbs to lust after here!

The wall is located just a few hundred yards southwest of town, beside the railroad tracks and across the street from the Skykomish River.

Pax on the athletic start to Godzilla

From town, make a left at the T intersection in front of the Bush House and follow that road past residences and down along the river a short distance to the spacious parking area located in the trees on the right.

Approach: From the parking area an obvious trail crosses the railroad tracks and leads through the woods for about 100 feet until you reach a stone amphitheater at the base of the Great Northern Slab. Several routes start at ground level and a number of others start on the first tier, which can be reached by scrambling up a short access chimney on the right.

The Great Northern Slab area is separated from the main lower wall by the huge left-facing dihedral of *Roger's Corner*, a somewhat less than aesthetic but nonetheless well-traveled 5.9 route in its own right.

Routes described from *Breakfast of Champions* to *Godzilla* are located on the main portion of the Lower Town Wall. An obvious trail leads out right from the base of the Great Northern Slab area and continues around the bottom of the wall as far as the boulder field.

1. VELVASHEEN 5.6 ★
FA: Mark Weigelt, Cheryl Greenman 1969
From the Railroad Bolts move up and left around the corner into the bottom of the infamous Leo Chimney and belay. Climb good cracks on the right side of the chimney until they lead out into a left-curving arch, giving access to the upper Great Northern Slab. Finally, cross a diagonal system of weakness and climb a short blocky 5.6 corner to reach the upper slab and belay tree. Gear to 3 1/2 inches. Rappel *The Great Northern Slab*.

2. ARCHIES 5.6
Archies is the scalloped exfoliation flake visible up and left of the fir tree in the middle of the Great Northern Slab. To reach it climb a bit of the way up *Velvasheen* and then exit up and right onto the Great Northern Slab proper. *Archies* has its own finish, but it's usually cleaner to finish up and to the left as per *Libra Crack*. Gear to 3 inches. Rappel the *GNS*.

3. THE GREAT NORTHERN SLAB 5.6 ★★★
FA: Paul Guimarin, Phil Leatherman 1965
This is the "standard" route on the slab, a three-pitch climb of good quality that makes use of the unique railroad bolts at the end of the first pitch. There are two ways to start this climb, either at the extreme left via a dirty (but easy) ramp/corner or via the access chimney detailed in the Lower Town Wall introduction. Either way, the good part of this climb and several others begins on the wide terrace 30 feet or so above the ground. **Pitch One:** From the left side of the terrace climb clean, arching cracks (5.2) up an indistinct corner to the obvious Railroad Bolts. **Pitch Two:** Climb the crack just left of the bolts and make some awkward moves up through a bulge (cruxy 5.6) and onto the slab above. Follow the obvious right-trending pair of thin cracks to the shared chain anchor at the top of *Libra Crack*. **Pitch Three:** From the chains continue directly up the corner and then up and left onto the upper slab. Pass a tree, then angle right on flakes and edges and make the final moves up to a belay at a large tree with many slings. Gear to 3 1/2 inches. Rappel the route.

4. LIBRA CRACK (AKA PISCES) 5.10a ★★★
FA: Mark Weigelt, Mike Berman 1969
Libra is the obvious splitter hand crack running up the Great Northern Slab. Various publications have billed it as, *The Great Northern Slab Direct*,

GREAT NORTHERN SLAB

flake gone

step-across

flaring chimney

access chimney

dihedral

terrace

5.10a

Railroad Bolts

Libra, and *Pisces.* The original version climbed the 5.10 corner problem at the bottom crag, the splitter crack to the bolts, and then angled out to take the left-hand finish. **Popular Version:** Use the same moves off the terrace as *The Great Northern Slab* route and work up easy ground to reach the steep part of the crack. A strenuous (5.10a) few moves through the short headwall lead up to a good stance below the easier hand crack. Continue up the crack (5.6) to the bolted, chain anchors. ***Variation: 5.6*** Climb to the railroad bolts and follow the *GNS* route up through the bulge. Traverse right, past the thin cracks of the *GNS* and reach a good stance at the base of the 5.6 hand crack that is upper *Libra.* Either set up a gear belay at the base of the crack or continue up it. Double-rope techniques can help minimize rope drag. Gear to 3 1/2 inches. Continue with the *GNS* or rappel.

5. TAURUS 5.9 ★★

FA pitch one: Ron Burgner, Thom Nephew 1970
FA pitch two: Dave Anderson, Rich Carlstad, Carla Firey, Donn Heller 1972

Taurus is sort of a catchall name for a number of pitches originally described as being variations of *The Lizard.* Only a short bit of the Blockbuster is 5.9 and can be avoided. **Pitch One:** From the terrace system use the sickle crack and continue with some athletic 5.9 moves up through the Blockbuster Overhang, or skirt around it (5.6) on its right. From the top of the block scramble left around a corner into a trough and move up and right to a belay. **Pitch Two:** Continue up and right across easier ground and then step out over some striking exposure to reach the right of two parallel cracks. Climb the exposed crack (5.7) to a belay near a small fir. **Pitch Three:** Continue up the slab using the last pitch of the GNS. ***Variation One: 5.4*** From the terrace climb up as per *Libra* but trend more right and work into the trough to the left of the Blockbuster. Continue as above. ***Variation Two: Swordplay 5.7*** This is the left of the two parallel cracks on the second pitch. Gear to 4 inches. Rappel the GNS.

6. THE LIZARD (AKA ARIES) 5.8 ★★

FA: Ron Burgner, Thom Nephew 1970

This one starts from ground level and takes a series of short features all the way up to the shared anchor at the top of *The Great Northern Slab.* Pitches can be linked in numerous ways depending on your tolerance for rope drag. The chimney pitch, traditionally rated 5.8, is thought by some to be as much as 5.9+. **Access Pitch:** From the ground locate the short hand crack leading up to a large flake and fist crack. Climb the short but strenuous (5.8) crack to the terrace above. **Pitch One:** From the right edge of the terrace climb a shallow left-facing corner with a thin crack and belay at its top. **Pitch Two:** Thrash up through the famous chimney above (said to be easier if you don't get in too deep) and belay at its top. **Pitch Three:** Climb up to the roof and continue out left, with a spectacular undercling. Exposed crack climbing (5.8) leads up to the bolted anchor on the *GNS*. Gear to 3½ inches. Rappel.

Railroad Bolts

GREAT NORTHERN SLAB (left)

7. BREAKFAST OF CHAMPIONS 5.10a ★★★
FFA: Julie Brugger, Carla Firey

Another classic Index hand crack. This one is steep, strenuous, and pumpy the whole way. Traditionally approached by climbing several pitches up *Roger's Corner*, it can also be reached by climbing one of the moderate Great Northern Slab routes and rappeling to the tree at the start of the crack. **Route:** Climb the left-hand of the two obvious cracks high on the right wall of *Roger's Corner*. This part of the climb, originally accomplished with some stemming off the convenient tree, was first climbed straight-on by Julie Brugger and Carla Firey—quite an achievement considering the gear of the day. Many find the crack a bit of a sandbag at 5.10a. The crack starts out thin and gets wider. Gear to 3 inches. Rappel from bolts.

8. PRINCELY AMBITIONS 5.9 ★★
FA: Clint Cummins, Jeremy Metz 1977

From the trail around the base, find a small track that leads 30 feet over to the rock just after reaching the main wall. Obvious flakes and cracks point out the start of this athletic and cruxy route. **Route:** Climb easy stacked blocks up and left, passing a bolt in a shallow corner. Climb obvious flakes up and right and then make a rightward move from a distinct hollow flake. A few technical moves lead to the crux hand traverse back left, and then blocky and somewhat easier moves lead up to the belay. The second pitch climbs the bulging, right-facing corner above and is not so commonly traveled. Gear to 3 1/2 inches. Rappel.

9. CITY PARK C1 ★★★
FA: Roger Johnson, Richard Mathies 1966
FFA (5.13c): Todd Skinner 1986

City Park is the obvious straight-in thin crack located 150 feet or so further right along the main wall from *Princely Ambitions*. Look for a short bolt-ladder leading to the crack. Although it has been free climbed, the first pitch of *City Park* has long been an outstanding place to experience steep, bomber aid climbing in a manageable environment. While it's probably not likely that anyone will be working the route free, it should be noted that the initial bolt ladder for the route is often free-climbed (5.10a) as a better protected start for *Godzilla*. **Route:** Aid directly up the bolts and reach the crack. Two or three places do exist for gear up to 2 1/2 inches, but mostly the crack takes many small wired stoppers. It's over 100 feet to the ledge, so bring enough gear to not compromise yourself

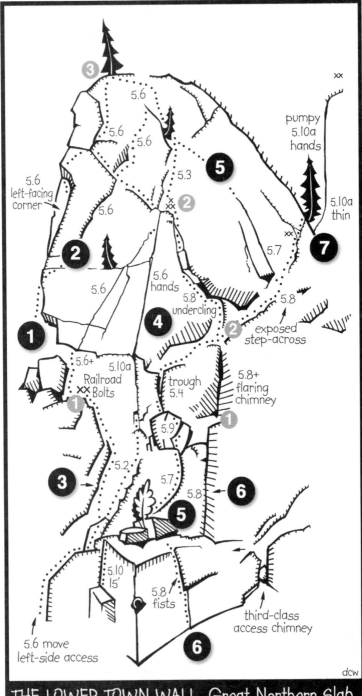

THE LOWER TOWN WALL Great Northern Slab

dcw

with too ambitious back-cleaning. Many stoppers or wireds in the 1/8- to 1/2-inch range, plus a few cams up to a red Camalot. Rappel 120 feet to the ground from the chain anchor.

10. GODZILLA 5.9 ★★★

FA: Don Harder, Don Heller 1972

Perhaps the classic Index crack climb, *Godzilla* has been a milestone for generations of Washington climbers. Traditionally the route starts about 15 feet right of the *City Park* bolt ladder and climbs up and left a bit on some sparsely protected, steep 5.8. A correct stopper placement a dozen feet off the ground makes it reasonable. Climb up and under the obvious flake and either lieback the flake or stem across it to the crack on the left. Continue up the consistently challenging crack/corner until it's possible to step around left (crux, 5.9) and gain the ledges at the top of the *City Park* crack. The *City Park* bolt ladder is often free-climbed directly to the lieback flake at 5.10a. Gear to 3 inches. Rappel down the *City Park* route from bolts and chains.

David Burdick on the Index super-classic, Godzilla

Inner Town Wall

The Inner Town Wall is an appropriate name for a small cluster of climbs located in a canyon that divides the Lower Town Wall from the Lower Lump on the left.

Approach: From the Lower Town Wall a trail leads out to the left, up a short hill past some rocks, and then on up into the canyon on an obvious trail. It'll take 10–15 minutes from the base of the lower wall. Look for the obvious hand cracks on the left wall of the canyon that are *Toxic Shock*.

5.11

Toxic
Shock

optional
belay

Toxic
Shock
crux

TOXIC
SHOCK

5.8 twin
hand cracks

11. TOXIC SHOCK 5.9 ★★★
FA: Steve Strong 1981

An outstanding hand crack that shouldn't be missed. Even though it's a classic it still doesn't get overly crowded. Look for the splitter hand crack in the left wall of a dihedral that's on the left side of the canyon. A 40-foot high pillar with a fixed anchor makes it possible to divide the crack into two short pitches. **Pitch One:** Start on the left, or canyon face, of the pillar with a few short lieback moves (5.9 crux) in a thin crack. Twenty more feet of low fifth class reaches the pillar top. *Variation: 5.8* Start around the corner to the right in a pair of hand and fist cracks that offer somewhat easier climbing than the left start. **Pitch Two:** Move out left from the pillar top to reach the start of the splitter hand crack. Stemming makes the crack manageable, but swing out and use both hands and feet in the crack if you are thinking about a trip to Canyonlands! Gear to 3 inches. Rappel from the big tree.

Pax samples the perfect handcrack on Libra.

12. CORNER FLASH 5.7 ★

Located immediately opposite *Toxic Shock* on the right side of the canyon, this climb is a fun little bit since you are already in there. It's easier than it looks. Gear to 4 inches. Rap from the chains.

Half Moon Crags

These little known crags are located at Stevens Pass, along the flanks of Skyline Ridge (aka Heather Ridge) just opposite the Stevens Pass ski area. Three scattered groups of crags are described briefly here for the adventurous. These are without question the least traveled routes in this guide so be prepared for some exploration in this beautiful setting.

Ramone Rock, closer to the ski area end of the ridge, has received some press in past guidebooks. However, it's never been discussed that the entire ridgeline is composed of granite with cool little outcrops and boulder fields sprinkled across its width. Much of it is exceptionally clean, white stone, but sadly, most of that is fairly short and barely taller than your average gym climb. Of the three groups, Half Moon Crag itself is the best suited for lead climbing, with all the routes being in the 80- to 90-foot range. The boulder wash that descends from the base of Half Moon Crag often has water running in its lower reaches, but near the crags is more often dry.

These climbs provide something new and out of the way, with an added measure of solitude. They include lead climbs, top ropes, and some bouldering. From this lofty viewpoint, US 2 is just a thin ribbon on the far side of the valley; the clean, textured stone at Half Moon is a distinct joy.

Ron Cotman samples the sweet alpine granite of Astroglide *at Half Moon Crag.*

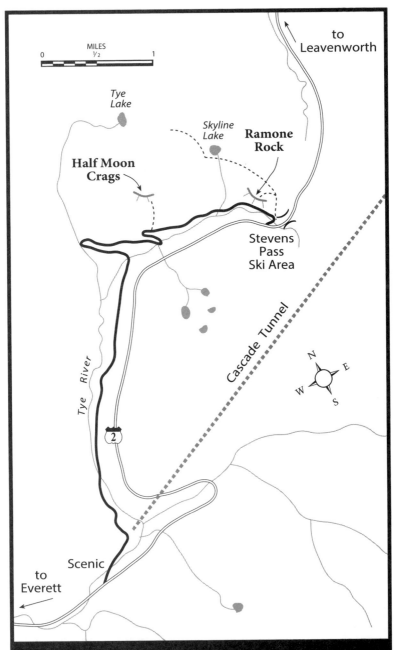

MILES
0   ½   1

Tye Lake

Skyline Lake

Ramone Rock

Half Moon Crags

Stevens Pass Ski Area

to Leavenworth

Tye River

2

Cascade Tunnel

N
W   E
S

Scenic

to Everett

HALF MOON CRAGS

HALF MOON CRAGS BETA

Drive time from Seattle ▲ 1 1/2 hours

Drive time from Spokane ▲ 4 1/2 hours

Approach times ▲ 20 minutes to 1 hour

Getting there: Drive US 2 to Stevens Pass. *Half Moon Group:* From a junction just 100 yards west of the summit sign, locate the old Stevens Pass Highway, which takes off in a northwesterly direction down the drainage. In about 1.4 miles the road makes a large hairpin turn to the left. This is the parking area. Another mile down the road is the Iron Goat Trail, with interpretive signs describing the famous avalanche events of the 1930s. *Ramone Rock and Skyline Area:* Park opposite the ski area and see directions below.

Season: Snow on the old highway dictates the season length. Early June to October is common.

Regulations: Let common sense prevail.

Camping: Car camping at the hairpin turnout on the old highway has been done but proximity to population centers will probably make this a day-use area for the most part. Several campgrounds are located along US 2 between Monroe and Stevens Pass.

Concessions: The Stevens Pass ski area is essentially right across the street (although probably not open). Beyond that, the towns along US 2 have most services.

Climbing type: Traditional, sport, and mixed climbs

Rock type: Granodiorite

Gear: Medium traditional rack with gear to 4 inches. Multiple ropes or single 60-meter, approach shoes, mountain clothing.

Half Moon Group

Half Moon Crag, whose cracks are visible from the US 2, was the first crag to be explored in this group and is home to half a dozen excellent climbs on clean textured granite. Several pieces of gear are required for most of these 85-foot routes, and a centrally located chain anchor is in place for the descent. All the wide cracks have been climbed at around 5.9 and the anchors at the top can be reached by hiking up on the right.

Of special note is a persistent feature of the Refrigerator Crack, the wide crack that comes down the center of the crag. The fissure seems to spew refrigerator-temperature air most of the year, and it's amazing on a hot day to see your breath form clouds inside the 10-inch crack. This is particularly appealing on hot afternoons when thirsty climbers can have an ice-cold beverage of choice after every route.

Approach: From the parking area, look uphill to locate the crags. Half Moon Crag is the larger crag with several wide cracks on its highway face. Enter the older-growth forest just left of an obvious swath of slide alder and vine maple and follow a path up and left. Don't get suckered out to the right into the jungle country! The idea is to reach the boulder wash that descends from the base of Half Moon. Head up and left through the forest until you reach the narrow boulder wash/creekbed, which leads directly uphill to the crags. It's 1000 feet of gain up the boulder wash to reach these gems so you're sure to have the place to yourselves!

THE OBELISK

This is the stunning pinnacle first encountered as you exit the boulder wash and arrive at the Half Moon Group. The Obelisk sits just in front of Half Moon Crag and has no different approach considerations. *Star and Crescent* takes a line near the left edge of the feature and is almost worth the walk by itself.

1. STAR AND CRESCENT 5.10a ★★
FA: Chris Greyell, David Whitelaw 1987
Start at the lower left corner of the rock and work up and slightly right on some fairly sustained and exciting moves. 4 clips.

2. THE ASTEROID CRACK 5.7
FA: David Whitelaw, Chris Greyell 1987
The name is more suggestive of what you might get from hiking up here but this is the fun, 25-foot hand crack on the upper right side of the stone. Enjoy!

HALF MOON CRAG

This is the main crag visible from US 2 and the best of the lead-climbing routes at Stevens Pass are found here. A chain anchor exists at top center, and the top can be reached by walking around on the right.

3. ARCTIC ROSE 5.6 PG ★★
FA: David Whitelaw, Chris Greyell 1987
This one starts on the left-hand end of the crag and climbs easier terrain past some stacked blocks for 25 feet to get started. It's worth it though! As soon as possible move out left and climb the arête to the top. It's just a hair runout in the middle of the arête, but take heart as the rock is excellent. Reliable gear soon appears. Save a 3-inch piece for near the top. At the top a sling on a horn facilitates a directional, as the chain anchors are off to the right. Gear to 3 inches. Rappel *Astral Projection*.

4. ASTRAL PROJECTION 5.9 ★★
FA: Chris Greyell, David Whitelaw 1987
Climb several friendly off-width moves up the Refrigerator Crack until able to step left, passing a bolt, and move on up the face above.

From the last bolt move right a bit and then up easier rock to the top chain anchor. Gear to 3 inches. Rappel the route.

5. ASTROGLIDE 5.9 ★★

FA: David Whitelaw, Chris Greyell 1987

Originally done with just 1 bolt and a handful of brass nuts, the *Glide* seems a bit smoother now with several more bullets! The original start in the thin groove is 5.10a, but moving up the edge of the slab to start is more like 5.8. From bolts at the top, step left to the anchors on *Astral Projection* and rappel. Gear to 2 inches.

6. ASYMPTOTIC 5.10b ★★

FA: Ron Cotman, David Whitelaw 2004

This one arcs left and up the next slab right of *Astroglide*. The crux is bouldering the opening moves although the rest of it isn't a whole lot easier. 5 clips. Rappel.

7. HALF FAST 5.8+ ★

FA: David Whitelaw, Ron Cotman 2004

This is the short route to the right of *Asymptotic*. Climb shallow grooves up and right toward the tree. 3 clips. Rappel.

THE BLUE HOLE SLAB

This is the smallish crag off to the right of Half Moon. Three obvious grooves or crack systems track the face, and a pair of bolts on top serves as an anchor for all three. All the routes require a range of pieces to 2 1/2 or 3 inches. Rappel or walk down on the left.

8. JENNY'S REEF 5.6 ★
FA: David Whitelaw, Chris Greyell 1987
Sneak in from the lower left corner and eventually merge with the center route.

9. THE BLUE HOLE 5.6 ★
FA: Chris Greyell, David Whitelaw 1987
Start just a bit right of the previous route and follow this friendly crack system to the top.

10. THE NORTH FACE OF THE EIGER 5.4
FA: David Whitelaw, Chris Greyell 1987
This is the right-hand of the short routes, and it featured a spot of verglas and a falling pebble one frosty morning.

Ramone Rock

Ramone Rock is the unpretentious looking crag visible just north of the highway and directly across the street from the Stevens Pass ski resort. Its minimal nature probably precludes a special trip. Ramone was the first of the Stevens Pass crags to be explored and remains a tantalizingly brief hint of the local stone. The routes on the left are about 30 feet high and are fairly difficult. Every crack on the rock is a route of some sort, but only a couple of the more obvious ones are worthwhile.

Find a dirt road that takes off from the north side of the summit parking area, opposite the main entrance to the ski resort. Follow the road a short distance as it switchbacks to the right past a number of ski cabins and continue past a microwave station until you reach a gate.

Approach: Park near the gate and proceed on foot up the steep gravel road 100 yards or so until a Washington State Department of Transportation building on the right signals the fairly obvious trail, which takes off uphill on the left. Another 100 yards or so uphill and a cairn marks the left turn for the crag. Routes are described from right to left, as they are encountered.

1. TROUBLE MAKER 5.0
A glorified scramble on the right margin of the rock. Fairly decent rock.

2. THANK GOD FOR BIG JUGS 5.8
This is the steppy dihedral with some greenery en route.

3. PROCTOLOGY 5.8
Not as unpleasant as the name would suggest. It's the corner crack back in a recess. The upper few moves are fun.

4. TEENAGE LOBOTOMY 5.11a
A short, obvious roof problem taking the left exit. It was first done as a top rope.

5. GENTRY'S FACE 5.10 TR ★
The clean white rock on this short little pillar makes another fun top rope.

6. SON OF A PITCH 5.10b ★
This is the short but slightly overhanging finger crack right of the *Troglodyte*. This and the next two routes are 50 to 60 feet left and around the corner from *Gentry's Face*. A single 3/8-inch bolt on top can be backed up with a good large stopper placement.

7. TROGLODYTE IN FLIGHT 5.10a ★
Probably the best route at Ramone. This finger and hand crack is a rather tightly wound little problem. It's pretty hard to do it without using *Sheena* for support somewhere, and at least 5.9 even if you do. A wide spot takes up to a #4 Camalot but it's mostly gear from 3/4 to 2 inches. Big stoppers make a gear belay at the lip.

8. SHEENA IS A PUNK ROCKER 5.9 ★
This is the 8- to 10-inch off-width that is the last crack on the left. You can rock with *Sheena* by reaching out right and stuffing gear into the *Troglodyte*. Fairly cool if you like this kinda thing.

Skyline Area

This area is located about an hour from the car and centers around a number of largish boulders and small pinnacles near the crest of the ridge. Most are in the 25- to 40-foot range, although one is nearly twice that. A number of these features have upper anchors and are commonly done as top-rope problems. The largest of the boulders has a cool south face known as the Skyline Wall with six or seven top ropes in the 5.8 to 5.11 range.

Approach: From the Ramone Rock cairn continue hiking up to Skyline Lake. Beyond the lake numerous trails reach the crest of Skyline Ridge. Hike out along the ridge until you reach a group of quite large boulders beneath a high point known, surprisingly, as The Point.

Leavenworth

Leavenworth. The Bavarian Village. The Worth. It was once almost the entire focus of the sport in Washington, and it remains one of the most extensive attractions for rock climbing in the state. Situated on the eastern slope of the Cascades, this tourist town is ensconced in the center of one of Washington's most concentrated and diverse climbing destinations. Boasting a much drier climate than west-side venues, Leavenworth often offers a sunny weekend when more westerly crags are still shrouded in fog and mist.

Certainly Washington's largest and most diverse climbing area, the blanket term "Leavenworth" really covers about three main areas, each large enough to be a climbing destination on its own: Tumwater Canyon, Icicle Creek Canyon, and the Peshastin Pinnacles State Park. Although primarily a granite climbing area, the Worth also offers sandstone climbing at Derby Canyon and Peshastin Pinnacles to the east of town.

Leavenworth offers a vast and lifelong scope of climbing objectives within a few short miles of each other. Full-on, grid-bolted sport climbs are relatively uncommon in the area, although there are a great many bolted routes to choose from. As you might expect from an area with a nearly sixty-five-year history, the quality routes here are many and quite a few have been pivotal points in local climbing history.

Exciting moves right off the ground are featured at the start of Canary.

Tumwater Canyon, forming the western town boundary, is a long deep trench cut by the Wenatchee River. The canyon is home to countless granite formations. Several of these are on the far side of the river and require significant hikes to reach. Historically, the most popular venues here have been Castle Rock, a popular *Klettergarten* featuring moderate, multipitch trad routes, as well as Midnight Rock higher up the canyon. On the higher end of the difficulty scale, Midnight Rock boasts one of

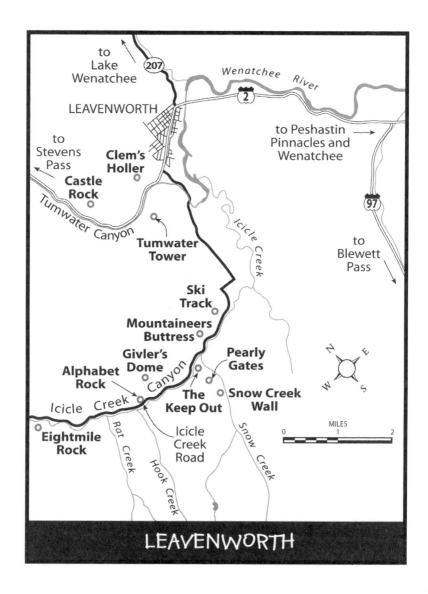

Leavenworth's highest concentrations of quality crack climbs—most in the rather difficult range.

Tumwater Canyon has numerous other rocks with no crowds and exciting adventure climbing in a strikingly beautiful setting. See Victor Kramar's comprehensive *Leavenworth Rock* for details on the more than 1000 routes in the area.

Icicle Creek Canyon, bordering the Enchantment Lakes Region and long protected by a lack of willingness to publicize, is now well documented and perhaps the center of Leavenworth rock climbing. There are huge quantities of rock in this canyon and, over a sixty-year period, much of it has been explored, forgotten, rediscovered, and enjoyed anew. Many first ascents remain and many have been "first ascents" several times. Just southwest of town, on the Icicle Creek Road, the canyon sports several campgrounds and much private property. Where once there was freedom to camp and climb almost anywhere, there are now many private holdings, requiring a greater degree of sensitivity from climbers. Please respect land rights and restrictions when climbing in this canyon.

The Peshastin Pinnacles, east of Leavenworth, consist mainly of moderately angled, bolted sandstone slabs. It was one of the state's first rock climbing areas to feature bolt-protected routes. Not nearly as popular as it once was, Peshastin's easy access, variety of moderate grades, and generally good weather make it a great destination.

LEAVENWORTH AREA BETA

Drive time from Seattle	▲	2 1/2 hours
Drive time from Spokane	▲	3 1/2 hours
Approach times	▲	Roadside to 2 hours

Getting there: Located about 130 highway miles east of Seattle and a dozen miles west of Wenatchee, Leavenworth can be accessed in two ways. One way is to drive US 2 over Stevens Pass, down through Tumwater Canyon, and into town. The other way is to take I-90 out of Seattle and then, at Cle Elum, head north on US 97, which takes climbers over scenic Blewett Pass and down to US 2 roughly halfway between Leavenworth and Wenatchee. This way is somewhat quicker for climbers with plans for Peshastin, while climbers with plans for Tumwater Canyon would better benefit by taking US 2. The I-90 corridor may offer somewhat speedier driving times on congested holiday weekends.

Season: Due to the formation of ice climbs in Icicle Creek Canyon and other drainages, Leavenworth offers climbing possibilities year-round.

Rock climbing is usually possible from March to November. The Peshastin Pinnacles open in April and are usually dry and warm when it's still cold and wet in the other Leavenworth venues.

Regulations: State park regulations and closures apply at Peshastin Pinnacles; the park is closed in winter and bolting is not allowed (call Wenatchee Confluence State Park headquarters at 509-664-6373 for access information). Snow Creek Wall is along the Snow Lakes Trail in the Enchantments, where strict wilderness area regulations apply (day use is permissible, overnight use requires a hard-to-obtain permit and rangers regularly patrol the main trail). There are fee and self-registration kiosks at the parking areas for both Peshastin and Snow Creek Wall. The Northwest Forest Pass is required for parking at the Snow Lakes trailhead (call the Forest Service's Leavenworth ranger station at 509-548-6977 for up-to-date information).

Camping: Eightmile Campground and Bridge Creek Campground, both located in Icicle Creek Canyon are the longtime standard climbers' campgrounds.

Concessions: The entire Bavarian village of Leavenworth is a concession stand.

Climbing type: *Tumwater Canyon:* traditional. *Icicle Creek Canyon:* traditional, sport, bouldering. *Peshastin Pinnacles:* bolted slab.

Rock type: *Tumwater Canyon, Icicle Creek Canyon, Snow Creek Wall:* granodiorite. *Peshastin Pinnacles:* Swauk sandstone

Gear: *Granite areas:* medium traditional rack with gear to 4 inches; extra dark-colored slings/rappel gear, approach shoes, mountain clothing. *Peshastin Pinnacles:* small rack with gear to 3 inches, multiple ropes.

Tumwater Canyon

Tumwater Canyon, forming the western limits of the town of Leavenworth, is the scene of some of the earliest crag climbing in the state's history, which dates as far back as 1948, when Fred Beckey, Wes Grande, and Jack Schwabland made the first ascent of *Midway* on Castle Rock.

Castle Rock is perhaps the most obvious and well traveled of the Tumwater Canyon crags, but the canyon abounds in stone. From the huge features of Jupiter Rock and Waterfall Column at one end of the canyon

Opposite: *The spectacular Castle Rock in Leavenworth's Tumwater Canyon has been an inspiration to trad climbers for over half a century.*

to the striking splinter of Tumwater Tower at the other, the canyon offers quality rock climbing at almost all standards.

Other crags include Midnight and Noontime rocks, reached by continuing up the hillside past Castle Rock, as well as Rattlesnake Rock and Piton Tower, which now sport a number of high-standard sport routes that mostly supercede the older routes found there.

The remote adventure climbs found up near the head of the canyon around Drury Falls are little documented multipitch routes that remain as wild and unknown as ever. The river itself has formed a sort of barrier, and while a good number of climbs have been explored on the "other" side of the river, there is still a wild and unexplored sense about the place just a few miles from town. The classic gendarme of Tumwater Tower, located 1000 up the hillside on the "wrong" side of the river, is one exception of special interest.

Use care parking in the canyon; the road shoulders are narrow but adequate turnouts and viewpoints are plentiful.

CASTLE ROCK

Certainly the "jewel of the canyon," Castle Rock is a dream rock seemingly custom-made for midlevel traditional climbing. Featuring solid, roughly textured rock and high ambiance hundreds of feet above the rushing Wenatchee River, Castle Rock is inspirational, a highlight of climbing in the Leavenworth area.

In his 1969 classic, *Challenge of the North Cascades*, Fred Beckey recounts a bit of the story surrounding the first ascent of the *Midway* route: "Possibly because 1948 was one of the wettest years in northwest history, a number of us began to make regular weekend trips to 'The Canyon,' beginning in late winter. The rock formation I had previously visited quickly acquired the not-so-original name of 'Castle Rock,' and the abutting pillar somehow became 'Jello Tower.' By then several climbing parties had reached the tower's top, but none had completed a route up the main rock's final face. Jack Schwabland, Wes Grande, and I cautiously did this, bestowing the name 'Midway.' Though not really difficult, the exposed step-across from the top of Jello Tower has evoked care ever since that first climb, and has now become a classic move."

Many climbers make some of their first trad leads on the high-quality moderate routes found at Castle Rock, and the broad range of routes keeps them coming back year after year. Another climber with a lifelong history of activity in the canyon is Pete Schoening, who made the first

CASTLE ROCK
(front)

Upper
Castle
Rock

5

4

Jello
Tower

2

4

Logger's
Ledge

16

access

15

Lower
Castle
Rock

17

14

ascent of the *Saber* route back in 1950. *Saber* was not especially ahead of its time in terms of difficulty, although it has long been recognized as a classic entry-level climb on Castle Rock. Schoening, however, would only three years later become legendary in mountaineering history when his quick boot-ax belay on the windswept upper slopes of K2 saved five falling climbers from certain oblivion.

Castle Rock is 2.7 miles west of Leavenworth on US 2, and there's a large parking area below the prominent rock on the east side of the highway.

Approach: The approach to the upper rock is but a 20-minute jaunt up a well-delineated trail, and many climbers complete several two- to three-pitch routes per day on the upper rock. Even closer to the car, the routes on the lower rock are only a little bit more difficult, although the steep lower crag, bristling with overhangs, seems more intimidating than the upper portion. Several classics are found here too. When climbed from bottom to top, Castle Rock offers perhaps five or six pitches of varied and interesting climbing, punctuated by crossing Logger's Ledge.

Upper Castle

The trail to the upper rock leads out of the north end of the parking lot. Climbers will pass a message board, and then a number of switchbacks work on up through the trees. The trail soon swings back toward the rock and leads up to the north end of Logger's Ledge and the upper routes. Logger's Ledge can be traversed all the way around the rock, past the distinctive Jello Tower, until it rejoins the hillside on the south side of the rock and continues as a trail to the summit of Castle Rock.

Descent: The descent is via the approach route, down from the summit off the back side and around the south side of the rock to the southern (extreme right) end of Logger's Ledge.

1. SAINTS 5.8+ ★★
FFA: Steve Marts, Pat Callis 1963

Look for the obvious, capped dihedral just at the junction of the north and highway faces of the rock. Find the obvious short corner about 20 feet left of Angel Crack. **Pitch One:** Climb the corner (crux) and move left to escape the roof that caps it. Continue up and to the left to find a ledge with a spindly tree. **Pitch Two:** Continue out and right, staying right of the arête until another belay can be set somewhat higher than the belay ledge for *Angel*. **Pitch Three:** Continue to the top on progressively easier terrain.

Variation: Short 'n Sassy 5.9+

FA: Jim Yoder 1981

A short, technical crack links the *Saints* dihedral with the *Angel* belay stance. Gear to 1½ inches. Use the standard Castle Rock descent.

2. ANGEL 5.10b ★★

FFA: Fred Beckey, Don Gordon

This climb has traditionally been rated 5.7, as the 5.10 portion is little more than a bouldering start. **Pitch One:** Start with the striking thin crack (crux) and then move left some to find a belay stance. **Pitch Two:** Move up a steepish blocky face to a short, left facing corner and get another belay on a stance with gear. **Pitch Three:** Continue up and slightly right on increasingly easier terrain to the top. Gear to 2 inches. Use the standard Castle Rock descent.

3. DAMNATION CRACK 5.9 ★★

FFA: TM Herbert, Ed Cooper 1960

This is the classic hand and fist crack formed by the left junction of Jello Tower and the main face. Jam or lieback the first 30 feet until you can get onto a stance in the crack. Somewhat (but not much!) easier climbing finishes the upper half of the pitch. Gear to 4 to 5 inches. Rappel.

4. MIDWAY 5.6 ★★★

FA: Fred Beckey, Wes Grande, Jack Schwabland 1948

A watershed route for Leavenworth, this irresistible line marked the first rock climbing in the area and began the long history of Leavenworth climbing. The route ascends the junction between the right side of Jello Tower and the main face of the rock and then makes a dramatic step-across move onto the main face. Several quality variations exist from there. **Pitch One:** Climb the steep, inside corner on the right side of Jello Tower (5.6 near the top) and belay from the mondo bolts atop the tower. **Pitch Two (modern variation):** Suck it up for the exposed step-across move and continue up a few feet before traversing off right on small ledges to the bottom of the obvious chimney. Worm up through the secure chimney, stepping out onto the face when it gets a bit too tight. A comfortable ledge with a 3/8-inch bolt and cracks for gear makes a good stance for the last pitch. **Pitch Three:** Move up from the belay to find the sloping ramps/cracks of the upper face and continue on with less steep but exposed climbing (5.4) past numerous gear options

Barb Thompson nearing the crux final moves on the first pitch of Midway

to the top. Walk off the back side and down the obvious trail on the right, shortly re-gaining Logger's Ledge at its extreme right end (the standard Castle Rock descent). **Pitch Two (original variation):** A recently discovered first-ascent photograph shows that the climbers did not move immediately right into the chimney as is now commonly done, but rather moved up the corner like *Midway Direct* for a few feet before using a right-trending crack to reach horizontal cracks (now with ancient pitons) and a place where a right traverse was made to join the upper portion of the chimney on the (now) standard route.

5. MIDWAY DIRECT 5.6 R ★★
FA: TM Herbert, Eric Bjornstad, R. Neufer 1960

This is a startlingly exposed face climb that forms a variation to the standard *Midway* route. **Pitch One:** Climb the regular start to *Midway* or any of the routes that get one to the top of Jello Tower. **Pitch Two:** Make the famous step-across move and continue straight up the right-facing corner until some face climbing heads left, then up, and finally back right again to an airy ledge. Set up a gear belay. **Pitch Three:** Continue on lower-angled and straightforward rock just about anywhere to the top. Use the standard Castle Rock descent trail around to the right.

6. SOUTH FACE 5.8 ★
FFA: Fred Beckey, D. Collins 1962

This route follows the crack system 10 feet left of *Midway* on the south face of Jello Tower. Kind of harder than it looks, this short route has irritated (or humbled) more than a few who didn't think it looked like much. Continue up Castle Rock and use the standard descent, or rappel from bolts on Jello Tower.

7. CRACK OF DOOM 5.9+ ★★
FFA: Jim Madsen

Scramble up into the alcove above *Old Grey Mare* and fight through the blocky roof above. The climbing to the summit is easier, but exposed and runout. Gear to 3 inches. Use the standard Castle Rock descent.

8. OLD GREY MARE 5.8 PG ★★
FA: Dan Davis

Start in the same place as *Canary* and then climb the sustained prow immediately below *Crack of Doom*. Continue with either *Crack of Doom* or *Canary* to the summit.

Variation: Chicken Little 5.6

From about halfway up the pitch, move a bit more left (5.6) and continue up. Gear to 1½ inches for *Old Grey Mare*. Use the standard Castle Rock descent.

9. CANARY 5.8 R ★★★
FFA: Hank Mather, J. Rupley

Canary is one of Castle Rock's scariest popular routes. Sometimes referred to as *Scary Canary* because of the starting moves on the second pitch. The first pitch climbs a prominent, short dihedral near the left margin of the south face of Castle Rock. **Pitch One:** Start 70 feet right of *Midway*, around the corner and just right of some boulders where Logger's Ledge drops down to a lower level. Several committing sequences lead up to a sloping ledge, from which the dihedral can be climbed directly until just under the roof. A cruxy (5.8) exit right gains *Saber*. **Variation:** From the sloping ledge early in the first pitch climb directly up the right wall of the dihedral to again gain Saber Ledge. This is perhaps just a touch easier than the corner itself. **Pitch Two:** Traverse out left under the roof (5.8, scary) until it can be turned and one of several protection bolts located. Easier climbing continues to an optional gear belay. **Pitch Three:** A last short pitch climbs just about anywhere at about 5.4–5.6. Gear to 3 inches. Walk down the standard Castle Rock descent.

10. CAT BURGLAR 5.6 PG ★
FA: Fred Beckey, Don Gordon, John Rupley 1957

The *Burglar* starts a bit to the right of *Canary*. Locate a spot where a bouldering-type move gains an obvious right-ascending ramp feature. **Pitch One:** Move out right on the ramp and then up discontinuous small

UPPER
CASTLE
ROCK

cracks to reach Saber Ledge near its right margin. **Pitch Two:** The second pitch takes you to the nebulous face and cracks (5.6 PG) just right of Saber Chimney, but most folks just finish with *Saber*. Gear to 2¹/2 inches. From the summit, use the standard Castle Rock descent.

11. DIRETISSIMA 5.7 PG ★

FA: Eric Bjornstad, Ed Cooper 1960

This route starts with the strenuous overhanging crack moves just left of the starting pillar for *Saber*. **Pitch One:** Power through the opening moves with good pro, but watch for rope drag higher up. Climb the left wall of the *Saber* dihedral and reach Saber Ledge. **Pitch Two:** Launch out from the right end of the ledge and climb somewhere to the right of *Cat Burglar* on generally featured rock of decreasing difficulty. Gear to 2 inches. Use the standard Castle Rock descent.

12. SABER 5.4 ★★★

FA: Pete Schoening, Ralph Widrig 1949

Another Castle Rock classic, *Saber* is a grade easier than *Midway* and somewhat less exposed, but it still offers outstanding, interesting, and thought-provoking climbing for its standard. Scramble around Logger's Ledge and identify *Saber* as the large left-facing dihedral near the right margin of the rock. **Pitch One:** Start a bit right of directly under the dihedral and finesse your way up and to the left for a few moves to reach the ledge at the base of the dihedral. Continue up the corner with great opportunities for protection until thinner (5.4) moves lead out left from the corner and up to the right end of Saber Ledge. Odd but apparently adequate homemade bolted anchor systems exist here. Expect climbers to reach this ledge from several other routes as well. **Pitch Two:** Climb straight up the blocky corner/chimney system above the ledge, sometimes climbing on the left and sometimes on the right until the angle eases and 50-meter ropes allow you to just reach the summit rocks. Use the standard Castle Rock descent.

13. CENTURY 5.8 R

FFA: Eric Bjornstad, Ed Cooper 1960

Century has some excellent and rather sustained climbing, but the reliance on fixed pitons in excess of thirty years old is beginning to wear thin. Great climbing here, but it needs some upgrading to stay current. Start just a few feet right of the *Saber* start and climb the rib face above past fixed pins and occasional gear. Use the standard Castle Rock descent.

Lower Castle

Much less traveled than the upper rock, the lower ramparts of Castle Rock offer up some excellent climbing on the intimidating expanses of steep rock and jutting overhangs. Big roof clusters and bright yellow and orange lichen add a lot of drama to this part of the rock! Simply walk a few dozen feet to the right of the car-parking zone and you're there. Although more difficult alternatives exist, the routes featured here all use the obvious *Fault* chimney as an approach pitch.

14. THE FAULT 5.6

FA: Eric Bjornstad, Ed Cooper 1960

Useful primarily as an access route, *The Fault* gives ready access to many of the routes on the lower rock. Find the 2-foot-wide chimney in the middle of the lower wall and climb it until a belay can be made. Right-trending ramps and ledges lead from the top of the chimney to the overhangs of *Idiot's Delight*.

15. CATAPULT 5.8 ★★

FA: Jim Stuart, B. D. Nelson

This is the obvious major weakness through the overhangs, directly above and geologically a continuation of *The Fault*. **Pitch One:** Climb *The Fault* chimney and belay. **Pitch Two:** Move out left, up some steep and exciting ground with excellent steep jams and continue on medium fifth-class climbing until Logger's Ledge is reached just left of Jello Tower. Some climbers belay again before reaching the Logger's Ledge and make a third short pitch. Gear to 2 1/2 inches.

16. THE BONE (AKA PENSTEMON) 5.9 ★★

FFA: Jim Yoder, Paul Christiansen 1979

Pitch One: Climb *The Fault* chimney and belay on stances before it wanders off to the right. **Pitch Two:** Start up *Catapult* and find a place a few moves up where it moves out left. Instead, climb to the right (5.8), around a roof and up to Stoner's Ledge to belay. **Pitch Three:** Climb up through the spectacular roof and easier ground to Logger's Ledge. Gear to 3 1/2 inches.

17. IDIOT'S DELIGHT 5.9 ★

FFA: Eric Bjornstad, Ed Cooper 1960

A couple of exciting overhanging moves are all there is, but it's fun all the same. A reasonable entry-level 5.9. **Pitch One:** Climb *The Fault* chimney and venture out right across ramps and ledges from its top until an obvious way through the roofs becomes visible. Belay right underneath the 'hang. **Pitch Two:** Monkey out around the lip and climb only a short ways above to find a stance with good belay cracks. Making a very short (35-foot) pitch here solves rope-drag problems higher up. **Pitch Three:** Move out and around to the right on easy to mid–fifth class rock to reach Logger's Ledge.

TUMWATER TOWER

Tumwater Tower is the narrow splinter of granite visible on the south side of the Wenatchee River about a mile and a half west of Leavenworth along US 2; parking for the approach is about 2 miles west of town. Despite the demanding approach and short routes, the feature has remained popular for decades. Certainly the commanding position 1000 feet above the river is inspirational.

Approach: Walk across the Wenatchee River Bridge and then follow the river back downstream 0.5 mile along the shore. You can start the combative ascent to the tower from slightly upstream of just below the tower and then angle left across a burnt-tree bench beneath the rocks to finish the approach on the east or downstream side of the formation. Expect a good 2-hour approach from the car for these novelty climbs. A number of routes have been done on and around the base of the lower rock and the obvious wide crack, *Gym Roof* (5.10a), should be visible as you near the tower.

Descent: A single 50-meter rope is more than adequate for the short rappel into the notch behind the tower where the more popular routes start.

1. NORMAL ROUTE 5.6 ★
FA: Fred Beckey, Ralph Widrig, Wes Grande, Joe Heib 1948
From the flat belay platform at the base of the route, move up and right into the obvious deep crack. An ancient bolt (historical interest only!) is found to the right of the initial crack. About halfway up the route a move right reaches a sharp narrow flake and then a couple of balance moves lead up to the summit bolts. Gear to 3 inches. Rappel.

2. UPPER NOTCH ROUTE 5.8 ★
FA: Pete Schoening, Tom Miller 1949
This route starts on the same flat belay rock as the *Normal Route* but then steps off onto the left, or west, face of the tower and works up a short and exposed crack before a difficult move left (5.8) reaches the obvious

TUMWATER TOWER

50′ rappel from
modern bolts

around corner
and up groove

① ②

belay block

curving crack at the notch. Find one of several tricky ways around the corner to the left and into a tight dihedral. Staying in the dihedral to the top is more difficult (5.8) but can be avoided by stepping out right as the first-ascent party did. Rope drag can be an issue on this short but interesting climb and it may prevent problems to belay in the middle, after moving around the corner into the dihedral. Gear to 4 inches. Rappel the *Normal Route*.

3. HIGHWAY ROUTE 5.9

FA: Fred Beckey, Eric Bjornstad 1962
FFA: Rick LeDuc 1973

The only obvious line on the highway side of the rock. Climb small cracks that start near the bottom center/right and lead up and right. Make a short lieback to reach a couple of ancient bolts (due for replacement!). A couple of tricky moves past the bolts brings you into the finishing dihedral of the *Upper Notch Route*. This route would get at least a star with decent bolts. Gear to 3 1/2 inches. Rappel the *Normal Route*.

CLEM'S HOLLER

Clem's is but one of a number of worthy rocks located in the lower Tumwater Canyon vicinity. Clem's features a group of pleasant sport climbs on well-textured stone. The *Playin' Possum* route is notable in that the first two short pitches make a great 5.8 outing if the top 5.10a pitch is excluded. These climbs can be a good choice early in the season, as their south-facing exposure and proximity to the mouth of the canyon allows for maximum sunlight.

To locate the start of the approach, it's easiest to use the junction of US 2 and the Icicle Creek Road as the starting point. Drive west on US 2 from this point for 0.6 mile, or until you see an orange and black "Deer for 7 miles" sign located on a blind curve to the right. Carefully park at the turnout on the river side of the curve.

Approach: A few stacked stones often mark the trailhead, which is several hundred feet upstream from the turnout. The 25-minute hike up the canyon gains about 600 feet of elevation. The climbs are described from right to left, as they are encountered on the approach.

1. OFF RAMP 5.9+ ★

FA: Victor Kramar, Gordon Briody 2000

This 40-foot boulder is located on the right, about two-thirds of the way

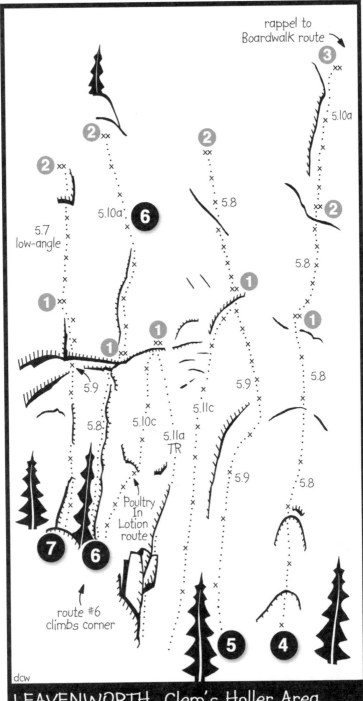

rappel to
Boardwalk route

③ ✕✕

5.10a

② ✕✕

② ✕✕

② ✕✕

5.8

② ✕✕

5.7
low-angle

5.10a

6

① ✕✕

5.8

① ✕✕

① ✕✕

① ✕✕

5.9

5.8

5.8

5.9

5.11c

5.8

5.10c

5.11a
TR

5.9

↑
Poultry
In
Lotion
route

7   **6**

↑
route #6
climbs corner

5   **4**

dcw

LEAVENWORTH Clem's Holler Area

up the trail to Clem's Holler and in an area containing a number of boulders. Look for an especially sharp-topped boulder with a bolted edge immediately beside the trail. 5 clips. Rappel from the obvious shiny chains.

2. KICK START 5.9+

FA: Gordon Briody, Victor Kramar 1996

Perhaps the world's filthiest route! This is the mossy slab at the toe of the rock and is useful primarily as an access route for the *Boardwalk*. The crux is a herky move off the ground and then the grade is substantially less. Follow a cleaner second pitch with gear around to the right to reach the *Boardwalk*. 4 clips plus gear to 2 inches.

3. BOARDWALK 5.6 ★★

FA: Gordon Briody, Ron Cotman 2001

This is a 160-foot friction pitch that stays fairly sustained throughout. Can be reached from either *Kick Start* or the top of *Playin' Possum*. 7 clips. Rappel 160 feet from bolts.

4. PLAYIN' POSSUM 5.10a ★

FA: Ron Cotman, Dave Bale, Gordon Briody, Victor Kramar 2001

This fine climb is made of three short pitches. The first two (5.8) can be climbed as one with a 60-meter rope. The first pitch has some thought-provoking moves and the second is a low-angled slab leading up to the steeper crux pitch. There is a short bit of 5.10a at the fourth bolt on the third pitch. 6 clips. Rappel from bolted stations.

5. NETTLESOME 5.9 ★★

FA: Gordon Briody, Frank Tarver 1997

This engaging gem is found a few feet left of the *Possum* route and follows 10 bolts up around to the right and back left again before a steeper bit brings you to a bolted station with chains. Another much easier and low-angled pitch heads up to the next bolted station. 10 clips. Make two 100-foot rappels.

6. HONKY'S LAMENT 5.10a

FA: Gordon Briody, Ken Eisenberg 1994

This fairly grotty mixed route, the first one established on the cliff, follows a 5.8 crack/flake affair to a stance at the right end of the big roof system. A second pitch climbs the bolted slab above. Can be done as one pitch with a 60-meter rope. 9 clips. Rappel from bolted stations.

7. GUN RACK 5.9 ★★

FA: Pauline Hsieh, Ron Cotman, Gordon Briody 2001

This awesome double-tiered roof is the star of the cliff. Currently it is the leftmost route on the crag. Follow bolts up and left on fairly easy ground until under the roof. A short but sequency crux turns the lip with excellent protection and moves you up to a stance on the low-angled slabs above. Another shallow slab pitch continues up at about 5.6 or 5.7. 7 clips. Rappel from bolted stations.

Icicle Creek Canyon

For decades, the Icicle was a canyon of mystery. Now, however, it has seen several guidebooks come and go, and these days legions of climbers seek out the canyon's rewards more than any other Leavenworth destination. Leading a route on Snow Creek Wall, just a couple of miles up the Snow Lakes Trail and the largest rock formation in the Leavenworth entourage, has long been a milestone for developing climbers. Private holdings have changed the character of the canyon vastly since the 1970s, and the camp-where-you-want ambiance is long gone. Even though heavily posted and sometimes intensively patrolled, the canyon never seems to lack for new routes. Generations of adventure-spirited climbers have found their own challenges and rewards here.

The Icicle is a true climbers' canyon and features attractions that can be enjoyed year-round. Most winters provide some weeks or even months of reasonable ice climbing; check out Jason Martin and Alex Krawarik's *Washington Ice* for details. Sometimes it's kind of odd to be swinging ice tools in the chill when just a few months back you slogged by in 90-degree heat on the way to a rock climb.

The canyon is located just adjacent to the town of Leavenworth and is accessed by driving the Icicle Creek Road, which joins US 2 at the west end of town. It's from this road that both the Snow Lakes Trail and the Stuart and Colchuck lakes trails begin their journey up to the Enchantment plateau. Camp either at Eightmile Campground or deeper in the canyon at Bridge Creek Campground.

Distances related below are measured from the junction of US 2 and Icicle Creek Road. Currently there's a convenient gas station/minimart at the junction as well. Each of the mileages quoted below takes you (more or less) to the spot directly downhill from the actual climb and may or may not be exactly where you park and the hikes begin. Approach directions are included for each formation.

SKI TRACK FORMATION (MILE 3.5)

Approach: The trail to this and other local stones begins near the Fridge Boulder and just across the road from a spacious car park. Begin hiking on an old roadbed and follow it back toward town a bit before the trail heads uphill. A short distance farther is this obvious rock with the parallel hand cracks.

1. SKI TRACK CRACK 5.9 ★★★

Ski Track is certainly one of the finer 5.9 hand cracks in the Icicle. Bouldery moves get you started and then the crack is a cruise. Some think the crux is right at the end when you must leave the crack and make a couple of sporty face moves to reach the tree. Gear to 3 inches. Rap from the tree.

MOUNTAINEERS BUTTRESS (MILE 3.8)

This buttress has been a first experience for legions of climbers over the years and there are still times when classes converge on the friendly cracks. The lower buttress formation has a number of short cracks in the low-fifth-class range, but the routes described below start a bit higher on the feature.

Approach: Located about a half mile toward town from the Snow Lakes trailhead and on the opposite side of the road, there are several parking turnouts immediately beneath the buttress. The hike passes the lower buttress on the right and scrambles up to the base of the main feature.

1. RIGHT CRACK ROUTE 5.2

Start at the lowest toe of the main feature and climb obvious clean cracks for several short, low-angled pitches until you can walk off to the left. Gear to 3 inches.

2. LEFT CRACK ROUTE 5.6 ★

Start 25 feet higher than the previous route and around to the left behind a tree. Several interesting crack bits eventually lead up to where you join the previous route and you can walk off.

3. THE MOUNTIES BIG-O 5.9 ★

Way around the corner on the left is this 4-foot roof with a hand crack through it. A short bit of easier climbing leads up to the crack and then great jams power on through... that's it! Gear to 3 1/2 inches. Walk down to the left.

4. GIBSON'S CRACK 5.5 ★

Scope this one from the road first. Three or four hundred feet right (toward town) of Mountaineers Buttress is this 50-foot crag with an obvious hand crack in a shallow left-facing corner. Gear to 2 inches. Walk off.

SNOW CREEK WALL (MILE 4.3)

Snow Creek Wall is the largest of the established Leavenworth crags and home to several outstanding midlength free climbs at a standard that makes these gems accessible for many climbers. These are multipitch trad climbs, located several miles from the car, so plan on carrying enough gear and clothes for any eventuality.

Outer Space in particular has been a rite of passage for generations of Cascade climbers. Defended by a short bit of 5.9 crack climbing, the legendary 300-foot headwall crack is unbelievably positioned, of moderate standard, and easy to protect. Does it get any finer?

Protection and belays are all built around gear, and the few bolts encountered are likely to be rusting relics from another century. Don't expect any fixed gear on the following routes to be adequate. *Always* back up fixed gear here. *Orbit* and *Outer Space* are highly sought after climbs and it's a rare weekend that doesn't see multiple parties on these routes at once. Please consider another outing if the climb is covered with people.

On weekdays, Snow Creek Wall retains much of the ambiance it had in years past: a quiet place with pushy mountain goats and maybe one other party on a nearby route. The goats (*Oreamnos americanus*) are common in the area and you can expect to find these cloven-hoofed opportunists hanging around both the base and summit area of the wall. They are unmistakable, often have brought their kids, and at more than 150 pounds are big enough to be taken seriously.

What the goats themselves take seriously, however, are the salts and minerals contained in urine. In places that see a lot of human traffic these woolly beasts have made the connection and can be frighteningly brazen. While stressful for humans this can also be disastrous for small alpine plants and turf that the animals will dig up and eat if it has been recently soaked. If possible, try and water the bare rocks and gravel areas in deference to the fragile soils.

Approach: The hike takes a bit over an hour, and leaves from the huge Snow Lakes trailhead parking lot, located a little more than 4 miles into the canyon on your left. From the base of the wall it's still a few more minutes to cross the creek and ascend the hillside to your route. Self-registration is required at this venue and is a simple matter at the kiosk located at the parking area. A Northwest Forest Pass is required to use the lot.

Descent: The descent from the wall is circuitous, and it takes a solid half hour to return to your gear at the base. From the top of the wall, the descent trail leads back to the left, toward the drainage, and then down and around until the wall can be outflanked. Be sure you brought your hiking shoes with you and don't head straight down the loose sandy slabs too soon!

SNOW CREEK WALL (center)

Library Ledge

1

partially hidden

2

1. ORBIT III, 5.9 ★★★

FFA: Ron Burgner, John Marts 1966

Orbit, the other white meat. This is Snow Creek Wall's second most popular route and deservedly so. The 5.9 is minimal and more straightforward than *Outer Space*; it's the next (5.8) pitch that most people find more intimidating! Walk left 200 feet from the start of *Outer Space* and scramble up to ledges beneath the less than obvious starting pitch. **Pitch One:** Head up and left on steepening terrain and find a left-facing, low-angled corner/ramp that leads up the wall. **Pitch Two:** Climb the corner above the belay until a bulge forces some awkward (5.8+) moves to overcome it. Belay a distance higher on easy ground.

Pitch Three: Traverse easily left from the anchors on a ramp/ledge and move up steeper thin cracks at its end. A tricky 5.9 transition from one crack to another leads a few more feet up to the belay beneath a roof. **Pitch Four:** Move out right from the belay and gain a steep slabby corner (lotsa 5.8) that leads on up. From the top of the corner, continuously interesting climbing leads up exposed terrain to a smallish belay from gear and ancient bolts. **Pitch Five:** Climb straight up the corner (5.7+) above the belay until you can swing around to the right and finish the pitch with knobs and buckets and easier terrain. **Pitch Six:** Move a few moves right and climb a steep wall with huge huecos and buckets (5.6) until a belay spot can be reached behind a large flake/block. **Pitch Seven:** Another pitch of minimal difficulty leads toward the upper left edge of the rock. An additional belay may be necessary before the actual top. Medium rack to 2 1/2 inches.

2. OUTER SPACE III, 5.9 ★★★

FFA: Fred Beckey, Steve Marts 1963

This is Leavenworth's great classic route. *Outer Space* is not an especially difficult route; indeed its stunning position and generally moderate demeanor make it an attractive tick for large numbers of climbers. Sadly, tragedies attributable to lack of experience and inattention seem to be a recurring theme here. The crux is kind of squirrelly, totally trad crack climbing, so have your techniques well sorted out before jumping on this one. **Pitch One:** Locate an obvious, low-fifth-class crack and corner system somewhat right of directly underneath the upper shield. Climb about 120 feet or so and belay. **Pitch Two:** Make an easy fourth- and fifth-class traverse an entire rope length to the left to reach a comfortable stance on Two Tree Ledge. **Pitch Three:** From a bit left of center on the ledge, climb up left-facing corners and step out right to find the crux, 1 1/2 inch finger crack that shoots right across big air to easier ground and the belay. **Pitch Four:** Move up from the belay and work left a bit underneath an easy overlap. Eventually cross some exposed big knobs and reach the right side of a small pedestal. Cruxy moves (5.7) up the right side of the pedestal lead to the belay ledge beneath the upper cracks. **Pitch Five:** Step down and left on the ledge and reach one of the sweetest cracks in creation. A few harder (5.8) moves at the start lead to continuous 5.7 crack climbing with plentiful knobs and protection anywhere. Make a belay on Library Ledge. **Pitch Six:** From the extreme right edge of the ledge step out right and work up the thin crack (5.9) a short distance until it

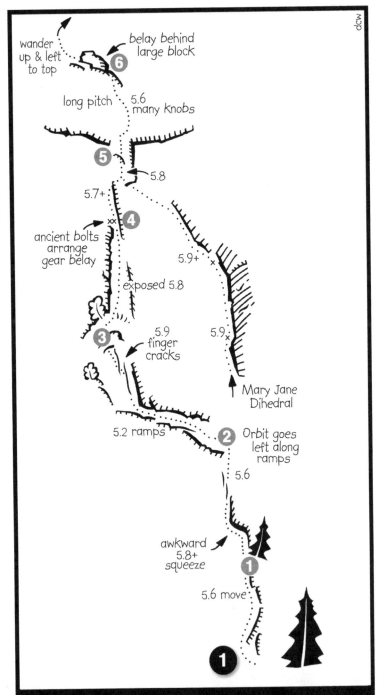

wander
up & left
to top

belay behind
large block

6

long pitch

5.6
many knobs

5

5.8

5.7+

4

xx

ancient bolts
arrange
gear belay

5.9+

x

exposed 5.8

3

5.9
finger
cracks

5.9
x

Mary Jane
Dihedral

5.2 ramps

2

Orbit goes
left along
ramps

5.6

awkward
5.8+
squeeze

1

5.6 move

1

dcw

SNOW CREEK WALL   The Orbit Area

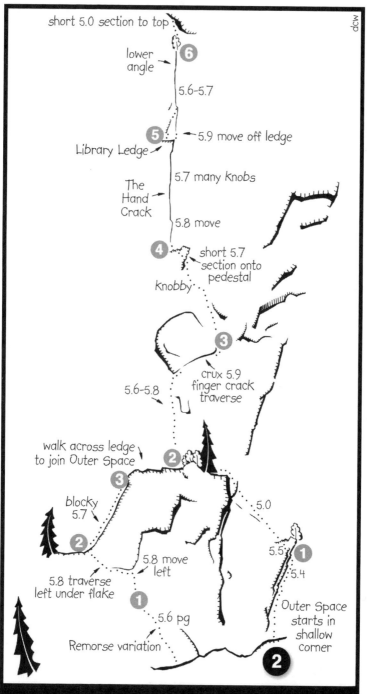

short 5.0 section to top

lower angle

6

5.6-5.7

5 — 5.9 move off ledge

Library Ledge

5.7 many knobs

The Hand Crack

5.8 move

4 — short 5.7 section onto pedestal

Knobby

3

crux 5.9 finger crack traverse

5.6-5.8

walk across ledge to join Outer Space

2

3

blocky 5.7

5.0

2

5.8 move left

5.5

1

5.4

5.8 traverse left under flake

1

5.6 pg

Outer Space starts in shallow corner

Remorse variation

2

dcw

Snow Creek Wall   Outer Space

Paul Warner miles above the valley on the last pitch of Outer Space

widens and resumes its previous character. Continue until difficulties ease. One more belay may be required depending on rope length. ***Variation:*** It may be slightly easier to climb the wider cracks directly off Library Ledge and then move right about 20 feet up to reach the main crack. Medium rack to 31/2 inches.

PEARLY GATES (MILE 4.3)

The Pearly Gates are located 40 fairly steep minutes up the Enchantment side of Icicle Creek Canyon near the "back side" of Snow Creek Wall. Considered by some to be one of the finest crags in the Icicle, the totally clean rock is as good as it gets.

Quite a few excellent routes exist here in pretty much all grade ranges. The routes on the left side are some of the sweetest hand and

170

finger cracks to be found; the right-side routes are more sport oriented and are also excellent climbs. A shining white friction slab on the right margin of the rock offers several friendly slab routes, all on the finest stone.

Approach: Start as per the well-traveled Snow Lakes Trail, which requires self-registration at the trailhead kiosk. Further, a Northwest Forest Pass is now required for the long-traditional use of the parking lot. Shortly after crossing Icicle Creek and traveling 100 yards on an old roadbed, the trail reaches a bridge spanning the irrigation aqueduct. Just beyond the bridge the Pearly Gates way trail branches off to the right and in a short distance crosses Snow Creek on logs. A well-defined path leads uphill, mostly just left of a rocky/grassy rib, and eventually reaches the Gates at their left margin. Two short 5.7 cracks are found on either side of a dirty chimney and the rest of the routes start lower and around to the right.

1. CELESTIAL GROOVE 5.9+ ★★★
FA: Ron Cotman, Pauline Hsieh 2001
This is the leftmost of the cool crack lines at the Gates. Steep and pumpy opening moves lead into a shallow dihedral/ramp and then up a short left-facing corner with a great crack. A bolted station is at the top. Sustained and strenuous with great gear. Gear to 21/2 inches. Rap from bolts.

2. CLOUD NINE 5.9+ ★★★
FA: Ron Cotman, Victor Kramar 2001
Located a bit right of center on the big crack wall, *Cloud Nine* is an outstanding 5.8 hand crack followed by a short bolted sport line for a second pitch. **Pitch One:** Steep moves with locker jams (5.8) lead off the ground and over a bulge to the main face. Easier jamming finishes the crack and a short slab leads up to the bolts. **Pitch Two:** A short bolted pitch leads straight up (minimal 5.9+) above the belay and then angles off left to the anchors. Gear to 31/2 inches, although clever climbers can do it all on small Aliens and wireds. Rappel from bolts at the end of either pitch.

3. NO ROOM FOR SQUARES 5.8 ★
FA: Dave Bale, Ron Cotman 2001
Just right of *Cloud Nine* is a somewhat contrived line with 2 bolts. *No Room* is the first crack to the right of the bolted route and is an excellent short finger and hand exercise that leads to a ledge with a bolted anchor. Gear to 21/2 inches. Rappel the route.

4. LOST SOULS 5.9 ★

FA: Ron Cotman, Darren Frink 2001

This is the crack immediately right of *No Room for Squares*. Climb straight up the central crack and finish at the same ledge and anchors as the previous route. Gear to 2½ inches. Rappel the route.

5. GOLDEN DELICIOUS 5.8+ ★★

FA: Ron Cotman, Victor Kramar 2002

You may have to poke around to find this one but it's worth looking for. Walk past the crack climbs as though heading off to the right-hand group of climbs, then double back and sneak up behind a big block to find the start of this route. Bolted anchors are on a ledge in the middle but it can be done as one long pitch. Gear to 2 inches. Rappel the route

6. LOAVES OF FUN 5.8 ★★

FA: Dave Bale, Gordon Briody 2001

This route is located another 100 feet or so along the cliff past an area of roofs and overhangs. A big flat boulder large enough for several people to sit around on is situated immediately at the base of this route.

Follow an up-and-left-trending double crack system characterized by chockstones and unique rounded features locked in between them. Turn an overhang on the right and pass 2 bolts on the slab above. 2 clips plus gear to 2 1/2 inches. Rappel 100 feet from chains.

7. MILKY WAY 5.10b ★★

FA: Ron Cotman, Gordon Briody, Pauline Hsieh, Mike Croswaite 2001

This two-pitch slab route has a steep first bit that is 5.10b and somewhat awkward. **Pitch One:** From near the bottom left of the slab find a 15-foot-high left-facing corner. Two bolts protect the crux corner and then a 10-foot, 5.8 traverse left reaches the line of bolts coming down the slab. From there 5.9 climbing finishes the pitch at the bench. **Pitch Two:** The second pitch is often reached by climbing to the bench area via *The Dog Ate My Topo*. From a 2-bolt anchor, climb past 9 bolts on the left margin of the slab. There is a bit of 5.9+ between the third and fourth bolts, but generally the pitch is easier. 9 clips. Make two 100-foot rappels from bolts.

8. THE DOG ATE MY TOPO 5.7 ★★

FA: Victor Kramar, Ron Cotman 2001

Perhaps the one case in history where the dog actually did munch the paperwork! Tina did it… On the far right side of the crag is a small rounded buttress down low with bolts and sweet texture. Friendly and fun 5.7 on incredible rock lead up to a bolted anchor on the broad bench. Recommended to move the belay 50 feet left and continue with any of the routes on the upper slab. 8 clips. Rappel 100 feet.

9. THE SCENE IS CLEAN 5.8 ★★

FA: Dave Bale, Ron Cotman, Pauline Hsieh 2001

From the bench reached by *Milky Way* and *The Dog Ate My Topo*, find an obvious short flake near the start with a bolt to its right. From there, continue up on similar terrain to reach a bolted anchor. 7 clips. Rappel 100 feet.

10. THE REFLECTOR 5.8 ★

FA: Gordon Briody, Dave Bale 2001

This trad line takes on the thin flakes and seams between *Milky Way* and *The Scene Is Clean*. Gear to 1 1/2 inches. Rappel from bolted anchors above.

THE KEEP OUT (MILE 4.7)

The Keep Out is named for the obvious sign and creekside waterworks development that make a tempting way to cross the creek directly in front of this crag. Modern sensitivities suggest accessing this crag from the Snow Lakes or Pearly Gates trails on the back side.

Approach: Bushwhack over from one of these trails, skirting around the skanky pond, and walk around the rock on its left. Several ho-hum, moderate cracks also exist, but the whole point is the *Tongue in Cheek* crack, shooting right up the middle and unlike any other.

1. TONGUE IN CHEEK 5.8 ★★
FA: Reilly Moss 1974

A totally unique curiosity! What this really is a 5-inch crack with a quartz dike running down the middle of if forming two parallel cracks. The implications of protecting along the brittle quartz dike are worth considering. Still, it's quite fun! Gear to 4 inches. Walk down.

BRUCE'S BOULDER/BARNEY'S RUBBLE (MILE 5.6)

This less than appealing looking boulder group just off of Icicle Creek Road has nearly as much local history as Eightmile Rock does. Once again, generations of climbers have top-roped and soloed all over these stones.

BRUCE'S BOULDER

5.2　5.11　5.11　5.10　5.9　5.7

The steeper, river face of Bruce's has great problems and there are also a number of fun mid–fifth class problems on the south face of the boulder (the side visible from the road).

Barney's, located across the road from Bruce's, has been the scene of much low-stress top-roping and bouldering for many years. See photos for offerings.

ALPHABET ROCK (MILE 6.0)

This popular roadside crag is privately owned these days, but a respectful situation still allows climbers access. Parking exists on the opposite side of the road, several hundred feet farther up the canyon.

1. Z-CRACK 5.10c ★

This is the left of the two cracks on the main face and it starts from an obvious cave. The difficult and cruxy starting sequence is short and the rest of the crack is fairly straightforward and no harder than 5.10a. Usually top-roped. Gear to 2 inches.

Givler's Dome

ALPHABET ROCK

Givler's Crack

Dogleg Crack

Meat Grinder

2. MEAT GRINDER 5.9+ ★

The *Grinder* is a good hand and fist exercise with a tricky crux slot. Some get frustrated trying to apply technique and just lieback the crux section. Fairly scary on the lead though! Gear to 3 1/2 inches.

3. DOGLEG CRACK 5.8+ ★

Dogleg is a short but popular hand crack located 50 feet to the right of *Meat Grinder*. The awkward bit in the lower third is the crux. Gear to 2 1/2 inches. The bolted face to the right is 5.10a.

GIVLER'S DOME (MILE 6.0)

Perhaps the most popular crack climb in the Icicle, with the possible exception of *Classic Crack* on Eightmile Rock, Givler's height above the canyon offers great views and a little extra daylight time as the canyon below plunges into afternoon shadow. The rock is named for Al Givler, a friendly and talented Washington climber who did much to develop local standards in the 1970s. His death in Alaska with Dusan Jagersky left a sadness felt by many and it's fitting that this popular destination carries his name.

High-standard face routes like *Timson's Face* (5.10c) and steep cracks like *Bo Derek* (5.10b) make up some of the other classic routes up here. However, for most climbers, *Givler's Crack* is the reason to make the uphill slog. The trail begins to the right of Alphabet Rock and passes several other stones along the way. Plan on hiking 45 minutes.

1. GIVLER'S CRACK
5.8 ★★★
FA: John Marts

Just barely 5.8, *Givler's* is an exciting step for leaders first venturing out at this standard. There is a way to avoid the bottom moves by working around on a ledge to the right, but reaching the crack from there really isn't much easier. **Route:** Start in the shallow corner (5.8) at the bottom and make several strenuous moves up and onto the face. Trend a bit left to reach the crack and follow it a few moves up to a gear belay at a flake/stance. Continue up the spectacular crack until it lies back and a gear anchor can be constructed. Gear to 3 inches. Walk off to the left.

Barb Thompson enjoying the day on Givler's Crack

EIGHTMILE ROCK (MILE 7.6)

This has long been one of the traditional hangouts in the Icicle. We are fortunate indeed that the owner of this feature continues to allow our presence. Many a Washington climber has bruised and shredded his hands learning to jam here, and the routes continue to be a gathering place for those keeping traditional skills alive. Parking is available along Icicle Creek Road, just above the rock. Please do not use the private road leading across the bridge near the climbing face.

1. TWIN CRACKS 5.8 ★

The left-hand crack system on the wall. Short crux is about two-thirds of the way up. Belay behind a block and walk down and around to the left. Gear to 3 1/2 inches.

2. CLASSIC CRACK 5.9 ★★★

One of the sweetest hand cracks in the Icicle, and a learning experience for generations of local climbers. Because *Classic Crack* is considered to be the standard for 5.9, many practiced till they could reliably jam up and down it several times before considering themselves ready for more remote challenges. Gear to 4 inches. Scramble off to the right from bolt anchors above the route.

3. MICKEY MANTEL 5.7 TR

This popular top rope is on the blunt, right-hand arête and to the left of *Deception*.

4. DECEPTION 5.9+ ★

This is the waving crack just around the corner from *Mickey Mantel* on the right. A great many have thought it looked much easier than it is. What do *you* think? Gear to 2 1/2 inches.

Peshastin Pinnacles

The Peshastin Pinnacles, although currently somewhat underappreciated, were one of the first Washington rock climbing areas to feature bolt-protected routes. Once the nursery area for nearly everyone who learned to climb in Washington, the easy access and variety of moderate routes continues to offer good climbing, and there's reliable weather throughout a long season. Many come to Peshastin in early and late season when other areas, even the nearby Icicle Creek Canyon, are still suffering from inclement weather. Indeed the only limiting factor to the climbing season is a political one, as the state park closes for the winter between October 15 and March 15.

The park is 4 miles east of the junction of US 2 and US 97. From Leavenworth, continue east on US 2, pass the junction, turn left on North Dryden Road, and reach the park in a little less than a mile. There is ample parking, and a great grassy picnic area with benches and outhouses. Considerable trail work has mostly arrested the erosion that once endangered many of the approach slopes, and the new trails seem to be working well. Please try to remain on constructed trails and respect the fragile nature of this unique sandstone area. The park closes at dusk each day and does not provide potable water or telephone service.

The Peshastin Pinnacles are comprised of Swauk sandstone. The pinnacles themselves are but one aspect of a stone formation that exhibits outcrops all over the state. Climbing here tends to consist of moderately angled sandstone slabs with bolts and occasional gear for protection. Since the state park was created, many of the original anchors have been replaced and upgraded; however, climbers should be aware that old, vintage hardware may still be found on some of the less-traveled routes. The days of new-route pioneering are probably over for Peshastin, and climbers should be aware that drilling, bolting, or gluing is prohibited in the park without approval from the advisory committee.

These are bolted routes from before the days of sport climbing—traditionally bolted routes if you will—and as such they tend to be a little bit more runout than modern bolted sport routes. Generations have

enjoyed themselves here, however, and while the angle usually isn't too steep, the climbing is definitely fun and rewarding.

It's possible to come to the Pinnacles and climb only bolt-protected routes where a rack of quickdraws will be all that's needed. There are many routes where a modest rack is still useful however, and it's a good

Sarah Doherty on the crux second pitch of Potholes

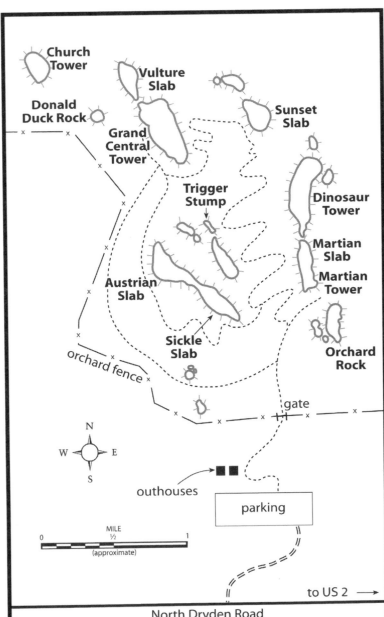

Church
Tower

Vulture
Slab

Donald
Duck Rock

Sunset
Slab

Grand
Central
Tower

Dinosaur
Tower

Trigger
Stump

Martian
Slab

Martian
Tower

Austrian
Slab

Sickle
Slab

Orchard
Rock

orchard fence

gate

N
W   E
S

outhouses

parking

MILE
½
(approximate)
0   1

to US 2 →

North Dryden Road

PESHASTIN PINNACLES

idea to carry some gear and keep the options open. Typically a Peshastin rack might include the following:

- ▲ One 60-meter or two 50-meter ropes
- ▲ 3–5 medium stoppers
- ▲ 2–3 TCUs/Aliens
- ▲ 3–4 cams to 3 1/2 inches
- ▲ 10 quickdraws

ORCHARD ROCK

Orchard Rock is the first rock visible on the right, immediately beyond the gated fence. The route names tend to be generally descriptive of the climbs themselves and several of the climbs are good warm-ups or introductory climbs for novices.

Descent: The routes included here finish at the higher summit from

ORCHARD ROCK

behind pillar

route goes deep between pillars

route starts on east side

which an 80-foot rappel down the parking-lot side of the rock reaches the ground. Alternatively, the rappel can be made less intimidating for new climbers by rappeling to a second bolted anchor at the end of the *Scramble* traverse and making a second rappel, less exposed than the first, from there.

Chris Greyell soloing The Tunnel *circa 1975*

1. THE GULLY 5.0 PG ★★

Long underrated, in the author's view, there just aren't many other routes of this standard with such quality moves and an exciting finish. Contrary to some printed material, the rock isn't any worse than other Peshastin routes. The route ascends the large cleft on the east side of the rock until a balancey sequence gains the top. Gear to 1 1/2 inches. Rappel 75 feet from bolts.

2. THE CRACK 5.7 ★

This short crack is a reasonable variation to *The Gully*. There are a couple of full-on steep jamming moves before you pull over. Start up *The Gully* and then step left, around the corner where holds and protection are obvious. Some years the crack features a lot of yellow hornet activity, beware! Gear to 2 inches. 60 feet.

3. THE TUNNEL 5.6 PG ★★

This used to be kind of a rite-of-passage climb for beginning leaders. Its unique nature has made it a fun excursion for generations. Climb cracks a short ways up and through the tunnel and then scramble a few feet up an alley before making a committing and somewhat unprotected (5.6) move out of the alley and up onto the main formation on the right. Exciting climbing leads up a bit to some thoughtful exit moves and the summit bolts. Gear to 21/2 inches. 80 feet.

4. THE SCRAMBLE 5.0 PG

Just a plaything really, the *Scramble* really doesn't have enough pro to recommend it as a beginner's lead and the lack of pro combined with a big traverse make it problematic as a route to lead a novice on. Still, it's kinda fun and shares the final, exposed moves of the *Gully* to reach the top. Gear to 11/2 inches. 80 feet.

MARTIAN TOWER

The next crag immediately uphill from Orchard Rock, Martian Tower is the steepish craglike formation on the lowest end of Martian Slab. From its top, questionable anchors exist for a rap off the right side, or you can continue up the ridge beyond until you reach the top anchors of the *Martian Direct* route. From there a rappel is possible off either side.

1. BUTTER BRICKLE 5.8+ R

FFA: Bill Sumner

The *Brickle* climbs up the wide crack/flake on the steep face of Martian Tower. Above the wide crack the difficulties ease some, and an amazing array of museum junk is bolted onto the crag for protection. Once a strenuous test piece, it certainly needs some updating of gear. Rappel.

2. CATACOMBS 5.8 ★

FA: Dan Davis, Dick Springate, Dave Beckstead, Errin Duncan

Another fairly neglected route that's actually a pretty cool climb. Bluster up a short steep wall passing one cruxy move and enter a scoop/chimney affair with big huecos. Make a belay back in the recesses of the cave and follow an easier short pitch up the chimney to the top. Gear to 2 inches. Rappel.

MARTIAN SLAB

Martian Slab is characterized by its most prominent feature: the Martian *Diagonal* route. Most of the other routes on this rock intersect it to some

MARTIAN TOWER
(Catacombs)

②

degree and descent is usually accomplished by either rappeling the individual routes or joining the *Diagonal* route and following it to its end at the upper-left notch. From there a homemade but burly anchor serves for the 15-foot rappel to walking terrain.

1. MARTIAN DIAGONAL 5.6 ★★
FA: Dave Beckstead, Fred Stanley

While many starts are possible, the original line reaches the left-slanting crack at its lowest point. **Pitch One:** Reach the diagonal crack as soon as possible and follow it to the higher of the two mid-slab belay stations. **Pitch Two:** Climb up the long, slanting ramp that leads up and left. Belay at an obvious bolted station on the ramp. **Pitch Three:** Mostly third class, this short bit reaches the upper terminus of the rock from which a 15-foot rappel leads down to walking terrain. Gear to 3 inches.

2. DIAGONAL DIRECT 5.8 PG ★★★
FA: Pat Callis, Dick McGowan

This excellent multi-pitch route starts immediately right of a largish bush at the lower end of the slab and about 25 feet left of the standard *Diagonal* start. Many do the first pitch and either rappel or finish with the standard route. **Pitch One:** Follow a striking line of grooves and pockets (5.6) directly to the higher of the mid-slab anchor stations. The crux is at the last clip before the belay niche that is shared with the standard *Diagonal* route. 10 clips, 35 meters. **Pitch Two:** Climb out right from the belay to pass a bolt and reach the pocketed crack/seam. Interesting climbing up the crack (some 5.8 PG) leads to an airy belay on the ridge crest. 6 clips. Traditionally this pitch is done with a couple of additional pieces of gear. Gear to 3 inches.

3. BASEBALL NUT 5.9 PG ★★
FA: Jeff Ball, Stefan Swoboda 1996

This line is immediately left of *Diagonal Direct* on the upper slab of rock. **Pitch One:** Climb any of the routes that reach the upper of the two mid-slab anchor stations. **Pitch Two:** Instead of working out right to the *Direct* route, climb up and somewhat left to find the line of bolts that parallels the upper pitch of the *Direct* route. 6 clips, rappel from the same anchor as the *Direct*.

Nutty Buddy *offers some slightly runout but classic Peshastin slab climbing. (Sarah Doherty)*

4. MARS ROVER 5.4 ★★

Start on the uphill (left) side of the big bush mentioned on the *Diagonal Direct* and climb the short route to the lower of the two mid-slab anchor points. 6 clips.

5. GALILEO 5.6 ★★

Galileo is about 15 feet uphill and to the left of the previous route. Pass 5 clips and share the lower of the mid-slab belay stations with *Mars Rover*. It's about 5.6 to continue to the upper set of anchors.

6. NUTTY BUDDY 5.9 PG ★★

This is an excellent short route that follows an indistinct seam up and right of the *Serpent*. Start in the same place as *Serpent* only work out right a bit on a ramp to pick up the first bolt. It's a little runout but clever routefinding keeps it reasonable. 4 clips.

7. SERPENT 5.8 PG ★★★

FA: Ed Vervoort

The *Serpent* goes straight up from the same starting spot as *Nutty*

Martian Tower

Butter Brickle

Martian Slab

MARTIAN SLAB FORMATION

Buddy. Interesting huecos, friction moves, and varied techniques make for an excellent climb if only just a little runout here and there. Climbers may want to rappel somewhat to the left where the ground is higher. 30 meters, 6 clips.

8. VOYAGER 1 5.8+ ★★★

FA: Ed Vervoort 1980

Follow the park trail up another switchback from the *Serpent* route to reach the start of *Voyager* routes. *Voyager 1* starts a dozen feet right and downhill of *Voyager 2*. Work out right a couple of moves behind the bush to reach the first bolt. Clever Peshastin slab dancing works up and slightly left. The upper half of the route goes straight up across easier terrain to reach a modern anchor in the slanting groove 20 feet below the *Martian Diagonal* route. 8 clips, 30 meters.

9. VOYAGER 2 5.8 ★★★

FA: Ed Vervoort 1980

This route starts underneath the obvious big bathtub hueco. Climb a fun Peshastin seam to reach the lower right side of the bathtub. An awkward move gets one into the hole and then the route continues from the upper left side of the hole. 30 meters. 8 clips to the anchor shared with *Porpoise* in the groove underneath the *Diagonal*. **Variation:** Climb out right from the third clip on *Voyager 2* and join the upper and easier half of *Voyager 1*.

10. PORPOISE 5.4 ★

Porpoise takes the obvious left-facing corner just uphill from the *Voyager* starts. The short crack offers a few good places to play with gear and then after the bolt the route moves up and right to finish at the *Voyager 2* anchor. Gear to 2 inches, rappel as per *Voyager*.

11. HARPOONIST 5.10B R

FA: Jim Yoder

Immediately left of the *Porpoise* corner with little to recommend it. 3 clips.

12. GREY WHALE 5.8+ R

FA: Bill Sumner, Al Givler

Very short with a couple of scary moves to reach the first bolt. 2 clips.

DINOSAUR TOWER

Potholes

to parking lot

to Sunset Slab

Chris Greyell cruises the 5.8 sandstone classic, Windward Direct
on Sickle Slab.

DINOSAUR TOWER

Dinosaur Tower sits astride the highest ridge at Peshastin and aside from the archeological theme offers some of the area's more classic difficult routes. One perennial classic at a moderate standard is the Potholes route which takes the impressive face up and left from the lone tree still growing near the saddle.

1. POTHOLES 5.8 ★★★
FA: Fred Beckey, Ed Cooper 1958
A long-standing area classic and a multipitch route. **Pitch One:** Rack your gear at the highest saddle between Dinosaur Tower and the Trigger Stump, and climb cracks and buckets out and left until an airy belay stance is reached with an assortment of fixed hardware. **Pitch Two:** Climb out and left from the belay, passing a cruxy (5.8) bulge on the way up into the slot leading to the summit. A medium cam can be placed on the left as you enter the rounded slot finishing the route. Gear to 2 1/2 inches. Rappel.

SUNSET SLAB

Just north of Dinosaur Tower and across a small drainage is the ever-popular Sunset Slab. Sunset's collection of mostly fairly easy and now well-protected routes makes it a great place for warm-ups or first-time sand travelers. Sunset can be reached by hiking up and over the hill past Martian Slab and Dinosaur Tower or by taking the perimeter trail around to the west and then following the switchbacks up the hillside behind Grand Central Tower.

1. SUNRISE 5.6 ★★★
FA: Dan Davis, Dick Springate
This is the leftmost route on the slab and a good warm-up route after long hours in the car. Start in the same place as the *Sunset* route, only work up and left a bit and follow good rock and obvious protection. 6 clips.

2. SUNSET 5.4 R ★
FA: Fred Beckey, Steve Johnson
Use the same start as the *Sunrise* route and at the second clip climb up and right to use the well-worn little crack or groove. Climb past a bolt to finish at a good ledge with multiple anchors. Some may climb to the

SUNSET SLAB

third bolt on *Sunrise* and then step right to get back on route and avoid the runout. 3 clips and a few optional pieces of small gear.

3. THE 5.5 ROUTE 5.5 PG ★

Follow a line of 4 bolts a few feet right of the *Sunset* groove. Finish at the same ledge as *Sunset*. 4 clips.

4. BOOBY VINTON 5.6 ★★★

Downhill and about 10 feet to the right of the *5.5 Route*, *Booby* takes a great line of pockets and short grooves up the middle of the slab to finish at an obvious pair of belay chains on a steep white block of rock. 7 clips.

5. NATIONAL VELVET 5.6 PG ★

FA: Don Harder

This route takes a more old-school line immediately right of the *Booby*. At the diagonal groove near the top of the pitch move left, clip a bolt, and finish left at the same anchor as *Booby Vinton*. 5 clips.

6. VELVET ELVIS 5.8 ★★★

FA: Jim Yoder

Start just left of the obvious bush growing at the base of the slab from a series of broken and gravelly steps. Follow the obvious line of bolts straight up. Near the top continue past the diagonal groove to a modern anchor and rappel or lower. 30 meters exactly. 10 clips.

7. GREEN VELVET 5.8+ R ★★

FA: Al Givler

This is the right-most route in our text. There have been other routes explored up and to the right. Some of these bolts may still be visible. Green Velvet starts to the right of the bush and works up thru a somewhat difficult start past two bolts before wandering left to another bolt and then up to the mid-slab anchor. Better to join the Elvis route and follow that to the higher anchors. 3 clips to reach the mid-slab anchor.

GRAND CENTRAL TOWER

The west face of Grand Central is the largest exposed face in the Peshastin Pinnacles. Unfortunately the quality climbing is somewhat limited as a good bit of this expanse of stone is just too crumbly for reliable

100′ rappel
75′ rappel
Vertigo
Empire State
GRAND CENTRAL TOWER (east)

climbing. While many sandy, difficult, and decomposing routes have been pioneered, only a couple are worth repeats and those are of very high quality.

The generally overhanging uphill or east side of the formation, just opposite Sunset Slab, is about 80 feet tall and the home of several classic

Chris Greyell cranking through the overhanging moves at the start of Empire State

Peshastin crack climbs. The east face gets sun fairly early and then passes into the shade for most of the day. On summer days it's cooler here, and on chilly spring mornings early risers can find some sun when the rest of the pinnacles are still locked in cold and shadow.

1. EMPIRE STATE 5.9 ★★
FA: Fred Beckey, Dick Springate, Norm Webber

This east-face route climbs overhanging rock out of the big cave just right and somewhat lower than the *Vertigo* start. Shimmy up the crack from the bottom and pass a bolt in the cave. Lieback out of the cave to the right and continue with the odd off-width crack past bulges and holes. The crux is exiting the cave, and beyond that ledges and edges ease the strain. Gear to 4 inches. Make an exciting, free-hanging 75-foot rappel from bolts into the sandy gully.

2. VERTIGO 5.8 ★★★
FFA: Fred Beckey, Charlie Bell

One of Peshastin's steeper and most classic routes, complete with

The author working through the steep jams at the start of Vertigo. *(Scott Jouppi)*

its sandbag bouldering start and exceptional and varied moves with exciting exposure. From the highest notch with the hillside on the "back" of Grand Central Tower, *Vertigo* climbs a steep finger and hand crack to reach the big chimney above. **Route:** Several sequency and specific bouldering moves (probably 5.9+) get your feet off the ground and get you started on the technical finger and hand crack above. Climb 20 feet up the classic left-facing corner (5.8) and traverse around to the right to reach the bottom of the big chimney. You can either thrutch up the chimney (easier) or move a bit left after the bolt and climb the shallow corner past a fixed pin to the anchors in the notch. ***Variation:*** From the top of the hand crack, instead of moving around to the right, continue up the slightly decomposing flake directly above. Better than it looks (5.9). Gear to 3 1/2 inches. Rappel back to the start, 100 feet.

3. WEST FACE 5.8 ★★★
FFA: Fred Beckey and party

This route originally went all the way to the shared summit notch with *Vertigo*. Occasionally adventuresome parties still make the journey, but for most people, most of the time, only the first pitch is really considered of value. It's probably one of the more heavily bolted pitches at Peshastin and as such is a common choice for a first lead at this standard. **Route:** Move up past some large potholes to reach the first bolt. The first tricky moves are just above it. Then trend way left to reach a rounded crack feature and more bolts. Follow the bullets up the shallow right-facing corner until several cruxy slab moves lead up and right to the belay. Quickdraws. Rappel from the industrial-strength anchor.

4. LIGHTNING CRACK 5.9 R ★★★
FA: Fred Beckey, Dick McGowan 1960

A long sought after and classic Peshastin climb, the zigzagging crack of the second pitch offers delightful climbing at about 5.7. The original first pitch is somewhat notorious, with significant potential for a fall onto the lower-angled slabs below. Many climbers now avoid the first pitch (and the crux) in favor of using *West Face* start. For the record, the original climb starts in a corner formed by the right side of Madsen's Buttress. Part of the way up the corner surmount a difficult (5.9) bulge and commit to 25 feet of runout but easier climbing to reach the anchors. For a fun and less risky route consider the following prescription. **Pitch One:** Climb

GRAND CENTRAL TOWER
(west)

75' rappel
off back

Upper
Lightning
Crack

Potholes

Lightning Crack
original start
(5.9 R)

West Face
route

Victoria Wentz on the popular West Face *of Grand Central Tower*

the first pitch of *West Face* (5.8) as detailed above. **Pitch Two:** Make a long, horizontal pitch (5.2) to the left using some sparse gear placements until you reach the anchors underneath the second pitch of *Lightning Crack*. **Pitch Three:** Work some airy moves up from the belay and over a slightly decomposed overlap to find a short bolted slab (5.8), which leads left until you are able to reach the crack. Enjoyable 5.7 crack climbing follows until you reach the big ledge shared with *Empire State*. Gear to 2½ inches. A 75-foot rappel down the overhanging east face makes a spectacular finish for this route.

AUSTRIAN SLAB

Austrian Slab is located due west of Dinosaur Tower, although it's somewhat lower on the hillside. Trails lead to this destination by walking down and north from the saddle at Dinosaur Tower or by following the perimeter trail around to the left (west) from just inside the gate. Austrian Slab hosts an excellent collection of the more difficult routes at Peshastin. These are exciting routes with more modern protection and are currently some of the best for their grade in the park.

1. MEXICAN FIESTA 5.7 ★★
FA: Dave Whitelaw, Bill Enger, Carl Delica
This is the left-most route on the slab. Start just above an obvious bush 25 feet left and uphill from *Slender Thread*. A slippery move to the right at the overlap is the crux. 7 clips to its own anchor.

2. SLENDER THREAD 5.9+ ★★★
FA: Rich Doorish
This was one of the original classics at Austrian Slab. Continuously difficult climbing and clever moves work up the obvious seam/groove to a second slippery crux near the top. 10 clips.

3. FAKIN' IT 5.10A R ★★
FA: Mark Weigelt, Mead Hargis
From the base of the big tree climb about 12 feet up to the horizontal ledge and get the first bolt. Then move out and left a bit to follow sparse holes and sustained small features directly up the middle of the slab. 5 clips.

4. CAJUN QUEEN 5.10B R ★
FA: Pat Timson, Mead Hargis
Maybe just a bit harder than *Fakin' It*, *Cajun Queen* has some unique and technical moves in the first half. Share the same start and the same first clip on *Fakin' It* but then trend up and right, making use of an obvious small hole. Many find their way back over to *Fakin' It* to avoid the easier but huge runouts higher on the original pitch. 3 clips.

5. AUSTRIAN SLAB 5.8 ★★★
FA: Fred Beckey
Start about 15 feet up and right of the big tree at the base of the slab

AUSTRIAN SLAB AND
SICKLE SLAB

and follow this, the original line on the slab, up a great collection of pockets and grooves directly to an independent anchor. 12 clips.

6. BUCKET LIST 5.9+ ★★★

FA: Dave Whitelaw, Wes Bevens

Bucket List starts in the shallow groove (crux) immediately right of the *Austrian Slab* route and then climbs up and right into a series of large huecos. Interesting buckets and slab moves lead to a shared anchor with *Slakin'*. 9 clips.

7. SLAKIN' 5.9 ★★★

FA: Don Brooks, Ric LeDuc

Another 20 feet uphill and to the right of *Bucket List* is an amazing alignment of big holes and huecos angling up and somewhat to the right. It gets interesting when the buckets run out and a series of cruxy and clever moves back to the left get one to the anchor shared with *Bucket List*. 9 clips.

SICKLE SLAB

Sickle Slab is located uphill and right of Austrian Slab on the next ridge to the west of Martian Slab. In effect it is an uphill extension of Austrian Slab. From the big tree at the base of Austrian Slab follow the trail as it switchbacks up the hill to the ridge crest. One branch leads over to the base of the slab and the other heads back downhill toward the parking lot and is itself another approach to this rock.

1. WINDWARD DIRECT 5.8 PG ★★
FA: Dan Davis, Curtis Stout
Still a Peshastin classic, this route follows an obvious line of grooves, seams, and pockets up from the highest point of the sandy bench beneath the slab. There are a reasonable number of bolts but the route may be a little sporty by modern standards. Near the top move to the left across several seams to reach the anchors. 6 clips. It's suggested to belay the second from the top and then rappel. Some may choose to bring a few pieces of optional gear but it is commonly led on just the bolts.

2. WINDWARD 5.6 PG ★★
FA: Eric Bjornstad, Pat Callis
It's actually a pretty fun route for its standard. Use the same start as *Windward Direct* only head out right at the obvious ledge/ramp. Follow the easy ramp about 30 feet nearly to the right before passing a bolt and moving upwards across some fun and exposed 5.6 to reach the ridge. There are several places on the last portion of the route where most will want to place some traditional gear. Several stoppers and gear to 2 inches. Belay the second from the top and then rap from chains at the ridge.

3. WINDSONG 5.8 ★★★
FA: Dave Whitelaw, Bill Enger
Incorrectly shown as the *Windcave* route in some publications, this picturesque route takes a varied and interesting line directly up and into the large wind cave located 60 feet off the ground on the extreme right-hand edge of the formation. 7 clips, rappel from chains at the lip of the cave.

Opposite: *Natalie Merrill belays her daughter Katherine on* Windsong, *Sickle Slab.*

Exit 38

Exit 38 on I-90 is becoming one of the most visited rock climbing venues in the state. While the more obvious of these crags have been looked at and scratched over for many decades it was not until the advent of sport climbing that the forces of the cosmos aligned in a way that made climbing here user-friendly. Bryan Burdo was one of the first to recognize the modern potential of climbing in the Snoqualmie Valley and many of the routes here are a testament to his hard work and commitment. The Exit 38 road itself was once an earlier incarnation of I-90, back in the days of two-lane interstates. Prior to that it was originally part of the old wagon road over Snoqualmie Pass.

The area comprises quite a number of far-flung crags, boulders, and walls that generally fall into the three main areas: Deception Crags, the Far Side, and Mount Washington. Only the first two are covered in this volume. There is a large amount of stone in this corridor of the Snoqualmie Valley and new routes and rocks are sure to be developed as this book is in production. Special thanks are due Leland Windham not only for his new route production but also for helping me sort out the conflicting information that exists for some of the Exit 38 routes.

The Deception Crags are actually two state parks: Ollalie State Park and Iron Horse State Park. Parking can be in either of these,

On the lower portion of the Far Side classic, Endless Bliss

but the Deception Crags climbs in this guide all start near the trestle of the Iron Horse Trail, formerly the old Milwaukee Railroad. Ollalie State Park is located 0.25 mile past the Deception Crags trailhead and has a picnic area, toilet, and telephone.

The Far Side climbing areas are accessed by driving to the end of the Exit 38 road and hiking varying distances up the hillside to reach the assorted stones. There are nine separate destinations at the Far Side, although this book discusses only the three more popular ones that fit the selection criteria. Presenting a generally sunny exposure, the Far Side routes are good candidates for early and late-season climbing.

Sadly, a recurrent theme at some of the Exit 38 parking locations

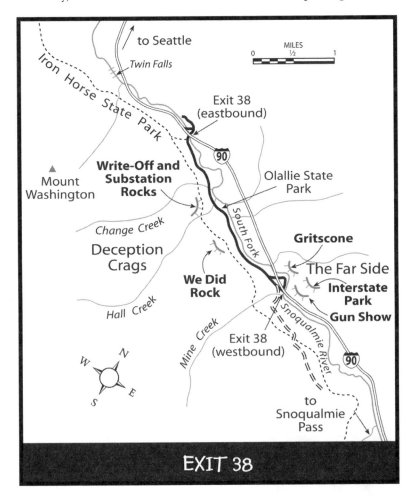

has been one of car break-ins and even theft of credit-card information. It's probably best not to leave anything visible in cars parked at these locations.

EXIT 38 BETA

Drive time from Seattle ▲ 45 minutes
Drive time from Spokane ▲ 3 1/2 hours
Approach times ▲ 10–40 minutes

Getting there: What a great idea to name a freeway exit after a climbing area! Drive I-90 (passing Issaquah and North Bend if coming from Seattle); keep a watch on those exit signs and take the one marked 38. These numbers correspond to the distance from the start of I-90 in Seattle near Safeco Field, and (obviously) exit 38 is the magic number. Access trails to the crags exist all along the 2-mile length of the road.

Season: Something can be found here virtually any time of year that the sun is out for half a day, but generally April to early October is about all anyone can hope for.

Regulations: The climbing in the state parks is day use only.

Camping: There is no camping in the state parks. The closest state-operated campground is the Tinkham Campground located at exit 42, which is 4 miles east of the climbing areas. The campground is generally open from the middle of May to the middle of September.

Concessions: I-90's exit 31, located just 7 short miles west of the climbing area, offers fast food, gourmet coffee, traditional groceries, and factory outlet stores.

Climbing type: Sport

Rock type: Metamorphosed basalt, affectionately referred to as "rhinostone"

Gear: Rope, quickdraws. A very few routes require gear and are so noted in the text.

Deception Crags

Deception Crags are possibly the most popular of the Exit 38 climbing choices. The access is a very short jaunt up a forested mountainside and the routes are easy to find. With a good number of good moderate climbs these areas are almost always busy. Actually, it's probably not the best climbing in the area but it is the easiest to reach.

Leave I-90 at exit 38 and make a right at the intersection at the bottom of the off-ramp. About a half mile after the exit, a large parking area is on the left.

Approach: Immediately across the street from the parking area, step over the guardrail to start the approach. The obvious trail works up the right side of Change Creek a little distance before turning up into the woods and passing underneath the trestle.

SUBSTATION ROCK

For many, this is the first rock seen at Exit 38. There are several good introductory climbs here and a unique ambiance, as the rusting bulk of the Iron Horse trestle looms overhead.

Climbs on the left-hand portion of this rock tend to be more difficult. The routes described here start with those on the moderate slab in the center and continue rightward a short distance to the *Glom Don* route located at the margin of the real rock and the concrete. All routes feature rappels from fixed anchors.

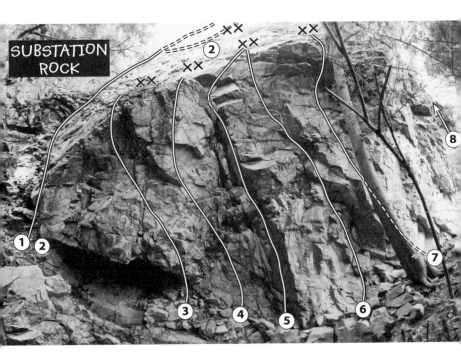

1. HOMO ERECTUS 5.6 ★
FA: Bryan Burdo
Starts left of a low cave and angles up and right. 6 clips.

2. RUG MONKEY 5.7 ★
FA: Bryan Burdo
Move out right after starting with the previous route. 6 clips.

3. PRIMORDIAL BLUES 5.9 ★
FA: Bryan Burdo
Reaches anchors to the right of *Rug Monkey*. 2 clips.

4. CHAIN SMOKIN' 5.10c ★
FA: Dale Fleshman, Curtis Gibson 2001
3 clips.

5. HURLY-BURLY 5.9 ★★
FA: Bryan Burdo
This one takes the highly featured fracture. 4 clips.

6. SUBLIMINAL 5.10b ★
FA: Bryan Burdo
4 clips.

7. SUBVERSIVE 5.10d ★
FA: Brian Burdo
4 clips.

8. GLOM DON 5.8 ★★
A unique climb that is a combination of climbing real rock and concrete. Go ahead and yard on the crack between the rock and concrete but don't put gear in the crack… cement ain't real rock and the gear won't hold. The variation out to the left is about the same difficulty. 4 clips.

WRITE-OFF ROCK

Write-Off Rock has become a first climbing experience for legions of Seattle sport climbers. The short access and pleasant views combined with good novice routes can create a bit of a scene here but it's usually pretty

Micah Lambeth crankin' the concrete on Glom Don

friendly in any case. Write-Off Rock is located up and around the corner from the Substation and at the level of the Iron Horse Trail.

The routes tend to be fairly straightforward leads, although the top of the rock can also be reached by hiking around and over the top from the left side of Substation Rock below. If scrambling along here to set top ropes, be aware of the real danger of kicking rocks loose that will tumble down the routes at Substation. It's entirely possible, after hiking all the way around, to find that someone has started to lead the route you were planning to top-rope. Patience is important at such a popular venue!

1. FLAMMABLE PAJAMAS 5.5

FA: Bryan Burdo

This is the leftmost route on the slab. Most of it is substantially easier than 5.5. 2 clips.

2. KNIFE IN THE TOASTER 5.9

FA: Bryan Burdo

Just a few feet right of *Pajamas* and in the middle of the feature is this easy slab, which leads up to a steeper headwall and a one-move crux. 5 clips.

3. MOM, THERE'S PINK IN MY BURGER 5.6 ★

FA: Bryan Burdo

Just a bit right of the *Toaster* route and following a rather indistinct prow formation. This route climbs up past the visible chains on *Bottoms Up* and uses the higher of the two top anchors. 4 clips.

4. BOTTOMS UP 5.7 ★

FA: Jean Pierre Banville

The rightmost route on the rock, *Bottoms Up* tends to look easier than its neighbor to the left but is actually the slightly more interesting of the two. You can pass the anchor and finish at the higher set of bolts if they are not occupied. 5 clips.

DECEPTION WALL

Deception Wall is the name tacked onto the largish, scruffy-looking section of cliff just past the big trestle. While there are a number of routes that can be accessed in various precarious ways, the two climbs that follow have the most relevance to this book and are conveniently accessed from the concrete trestle itself. There's no shoulder to the trail here so please try to keep your belay tidy, as bicycles and even the odd state parks truck are likely to pass this way.

1. UNDERGROUND ECONOMY 5.9 ★

FA: Bryan Burdo

This route starts from the concrete trestle at the third support structure from the end. A couple of eyebolts screwed into the timbers provide an anchor for the belayer perched on the bridge structure. The route tends to look easier than it is, but the unusually polished stone is deceptive. 5 clips.

2. JIFFY POP 5.7 ★
FA: Mike Orr

Jiffy starts right at the end of the concrete trestle and immediately steps off to the right making for some instant exposure before the first bolt is reached. 4 clips lead up and right to a burly-looking, chain-link anchor.

WE DID ROCK

We Did Rock is divided into right and left portions, separated by a short bit of scruffy cliff. We Did Right is a short blob of somewhat more compact material located on the right, just past *Jiffy Pop* and the end of the trestle. The first four routes described below are on this feature and are described from right to left, as they are encountered. We Did Left is the larger smooth slab, also on the right, and about 200 feet farther along the trail. The defining characteristic of the We Did area, aside from the popularity of the climbs, is the joke associated with the nomenclature. The idea is to tack the words "We Did" onto the beginning of each route name...

1. EASY STREET 5.6 ★
FA: Curtis Gibson
3 clips.

2. YOUR SISTER 5.7
FA: Bryan Burdo
3 clips.

3. MY EX-WIFE 5.10a ★
FA: Curtis Gibson
4 clips.

4. THE JOKE 5.10c ★
FA: Mike Orr
4 clips.

WE DID ROCK

Climber on the popular Sobriety, *We Did Rock*

5. THE BLOCKHEAD 5.10a ★
FA: Mike Orr

The Blockhead is the first route encountered at We Did Left and is the steep, blocky climb immediately right of the main slab. Some looseness and odd bolt locations may cause distraction. 6 clips.

6. SOME DRUGS 5.9 ★★
FA: Bryan Burdo

This one's a bit more demanding than the ones to the left. There are some thought-provoking sequences to reach the upper slabs. 6 clips.

7. ABSOLUTELY NOTHING 5.9– ★★
FA: Bryan Burdo
Many find this one just a touch easier than its neighbors. 6 clips.

8. SOBRIETY 5.9 PG
FA: Brent Kertzman
A clone of *Absolutely Nothing* but with poorly positioned bolts. 6 clips.

9. THE BLACK CABOOSE 5.10a ★
FA: Curtis Gibson, Jim Yoder
The short roof affair on the lower portion is cruxy but can be skirted on the left... sorta. 6 clips.

The Far Side

Climbing at the Far Side has quite a different flavor than at Deception Crags. Located on the opposite side of the freeway and oriented with a more southerly aspect, the small crags tend to provide warmer temperatures on chilly spring and fall days. The ambiance here is *almost* idyllic; certainly the views of the valley, McClellan Butte, and beyond are beautiful enough to inspire many, but road noise from the freeway 500 feet below is pervasive and tends to impede communication.

The rock at the Far Side generally presents a more monolithic face than the road cuts at Deception Crags, and the plentiful edges and delightfully clean, weathered textures are wonderful experiences. The routes here tend to be short, most of them in the 35- to 50-foot range, and almost all routes are protected with quickdraws only.

There are nine distinct rocks that comprise the Far Side venue, although only three of them are detailed here. Further, there is plentiful untouched rock, and new crags are being developed even as this guide goes to press. A number of trails lead to the different crags and visitors are advised to allow a bit of extra time to sort out the various approaches if they haven't been here before.

At the bottom of the exit 38 ramp, make a right and drive on the exit 38 road for 2 miles, passing most of the other climbing venues in the process. Pass underneath I-90 and find the parking area just beyond at a big hairpin turn with ample turnouts.

Approach: From the parking area, walk up the paved road for several hundred yards, passing a sign for the State Fire Training Center and eventually reaching a large concrete bridge across the Snoqualmie River. The hiking trail takes off to the right immediately after the far end of the bridge. Step over the guard rail and after one hundred feet or so reach the signed and obvious old Pacific Telephone and Telegraph trail that angles up the hillside above the river.

To reach the Gritscone, Gun Show, and Interstate Park, follow the main trail about 15 minutes until you reach a Y in about 0.75 mile. Take the right fork. The left fork leads up another 5 minutes to the Overhaul Wall, which has over thirty routes at all levels, though mostly rather difficult.

Some 50 feet after taking the right fork, and stepping through a perpetually muddy area, you'll see the Gritscone Boulder to the right, several hundred feet off the main trail. To reach Gun Show and Interstate Park, continue up the main trail another quarter of a mile past numerous underground cable signs until you reach another fork just a few yards past the "Bonnie and Clyde" sign (a particularly gunshot-wounded cable warning sign). Take the right fork again and in about 5 minutes or so come upon a large, horizontal, downed log on the right side of the trail. From the middle of this log you can step over and hike downhill for about 100 feet to reach the Gun Show area. Continuing on the main trail past the log another 5–10 minutes takes you out of the woods and to a small clearing underneath the Headlight Point formation in the Interstate Park area.

THE GRITSCONE

The Gritscone is a glacial erratic, a large sandstone conglomerate boulder left stranded on a moraine by the last glacier that lived in these parts. The routes are short, but with remarkable texture. Sadly the 'Scone is just a bit too short to be a real destination, but its unique qualities make for fun play at all standards.

All but the overhanging 5.11 route in the middle can be readily top-roped, and a Sunday afternoon here may see senior citizens on one route and eight-year-olds on the next. A full range of grades makes the Gritscone a pretty fun, low-key place, with afternoon sun filtering pleasantly down through the trees.

1. NEEDLE MAGNET 5.7
FA: Bryan Burdo, Leland Windham, Sarah Leonard 1999
This is the short, bolted crack visible on the left margin of the rock as you walk in. 3 clips.

2. MAGNETIC ANOMALY 5.9

FA: Bryan Burdo

There are only a couple of moves on this short bite which starts 5 feet right of *Needle Magnet*. Super sticky rock texture! 2 clips.

3. LUCKY ARMS 5.6 ★

FA: Bryan Burdo, Leland Windham, Sarah Leonard 1999

This is the rampy affair just left of the big roofs. 3 clips.

4. SNAFFLE BAFFLER 5.7 ★

FA: Bryan Burdo, Leland Windham, Sarah Leonard 1999

The *Baffler* is on the left side of the big roof and provokes some impressive positions for a 5.7. It's a bit chossy at the end though. 2 clips.

5. CHICA RAPIDA 5.10a ★★

FA: Bryan Burdo, Sarah Leonard

The Gritscone's entry-level 5.10. The last bolt is a bit oddly placed and makes for an interesting but still safe crux. 4 short clips and it's over.

6. 99 GRIT 5.9 ★★

FA: Bryan Burdo

A highly textural experience with cool moves. 3 clips.

7. PETE'S POSSUM PALACE 5.7 ★★

FA: Bryan Burdo, Leland Windham, Sarah Leonard 1999

Probably the best of the easier routes here with positive edges throughout. 3 clips.

8. SO FUNNY I FORGOT TO ROPE UP 5.7

FA: Bryan Burdo, Leland Windham, Sarah Leonard 1999

These last two routes push the envelope on worthiness but are here to sample. 2 clips.

9. SO EASY I FORGOT TO LAUGH 5.5

FA: Bryan Burdo, Sarah Leonard 1999

This one is a candidate for the least worthy route in this guide. Still, the rock is solid and the bolts are sound. 2 clips.

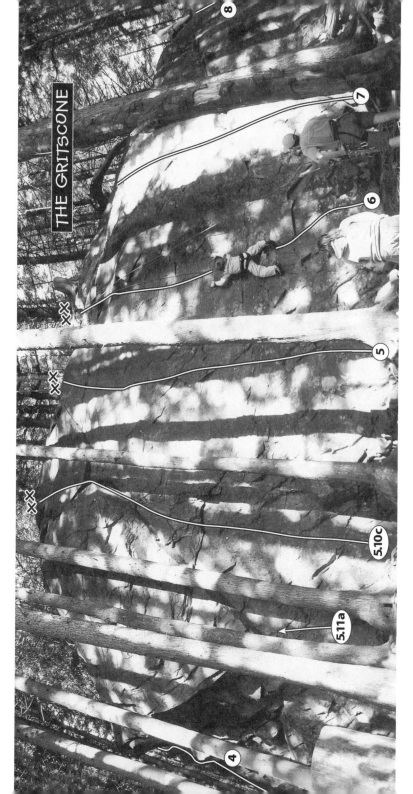

THE GRITSCONE

David Whitelaw checking out the great textures on Chica Rapida.
(Jennifer Keller)

INTERSTATE PARK

I-Park is a 30- to 80-foot cliffband on the north side of I-90 and about 400 feet above the road. The climbing happens on three different lobes of rock, all with sunny exposure and high-amplitude freeway noise. The rocks, as one encounters them on the approach, are Headlight Point, Eastern Block, and the Squishy Bell.

Headlight Point
The Headlight is the first small outcrop encountered at I-Park and offers several very short and generously bolted entry-level routes on excellent rock. The routes tend to be a little contrived but many fun variations are possible.

1. SWERVE 5.6 ★
FA: Bryan Burdo
The first route encountered, and a good warm-up with 3 clips and chains.

2. IN THE MIDDLE AGAIN 5.7 ★
FA: Bryan Burdo
Pretty much the same thing as *Swerve* with a slightly harder move right at the end. 4 clips.

3. LIGHT-HEADED AGAIN 5.7 ★
FA: Bryan Burdo
A little contrived, but fun moves if you stay exactly on the bolt line. 4 clips.

4. NOCTURNAL REMISSION 5.8 ★★
FA: Bryan Burdo
Pleasant surprises all the way up. Hidden bolts and hidden buckets! 6 clips.

5. SWARM 5.7 ★
FA: Bryan Burdo
Fairly nondescript with some large rest areas. Look for an obvious triangular roof about 25 feet right of *Nocturnal* and move up, staying left of the roof until past it. 5 clips.

HEADLIGHT
POINT

6. CARNAGE BEFORE BEDTIME 5.10a ★

FA: Bryan Burdo

A good 5.10 sampler and easy to top-rope from the *Swarm* anchor. Climb the initial moves on *Swarm* and then power out right and tackle the roof directly. 6 clips.

7. EATING ROCKS 5.6

FA: Bryan Burdo

Follow the trail past the preceding routes a short distance and up a few scramble moves until the large chasm that divides Headlight Point

Sarah Trebwasser on Swerve, *Headlight Point*

from the Eastern Block is visible above. The smooth slab of *Impartial Eclipse* will be almost in front of you at this point, and a 30-foot way trail leads back left to where the routes start beneath an obvious corner and crack. 3 clips.

8. EATING DUST 5.6 ★
FA: Bryan Burdo
Very much like the rock-eating version to the left except not so hard on the teeth. 3 clips.

EATING ROCKS
AND
EATING DUST

9. INSOMNIAC 5.8 ★★

FA: Bryan Burdo

Climb either *Eating Rocks* or *Eating Dust* to get to the start of this one, then take the obvious corner to the right of the crack and finish up with the cool arête. 10 clips.

10. BICYCLING TO BELLINGHAM 5.10b ★★

FA: Bryan Burdo

Again use either *Eating Rocks* or *Eating Dust* to reach the bolted stance beneath *Insomniac*. From there find a crack out left that curves back right and crosses *Insomniac* as a ramp. Move around to the right where another crack takes you to a small roof with a bolt and a short crux. 5 clips plus gear to 3 1/2 inches.

Eastern Block

The Block is really just a continuation of Headlight Point and separated from it by the fault that is the cave area. Beyond that and around to the right is the main portion of the Eastern Block Wall with a number of steep and overhanging 5.10s and 5.11s. At its right margin the Block retains its vertical aspect but the quantity of huge jugs and interlocked blocks makes a couple of great, steep routes with moderate grades.

1. DELIGHTFUL CACOFFINY FUNNELED WITHIN 5.8 ★★

FA: Leland Windham, David Wolfe

Scramble up into the bottom of the cave and find this as the left of the two routes on the right wall. Climb up through the coffinlike "tunnel" and exit right, up a short easy face to the anchors. 5 clips. Rappel straight down *Phone Threats* to exit.

2. PHONE THREATS 5.10a ★

FA: Leland Windham

This is the right-hand of the two cave routes and is almost as cool as the tunnel. Easily top-roped from the anchors on the *Delightful Cacoffiny*. 6 clips.

3. IMPARTIAL ECLIPSE 5.8 ★★

FA: Bryan Burdo

The *Eclipse* is located around the corner to the right of the cave, on the left edge of a smooth slab. Slither up a small left-trending ramp and then follow the bullets back right past a ledge and up. 6 clips.

4. ATTACK OF THE BUTTER KNIVES 5.8 ★
FA: Bryan Burdo

This and the next route start at the right side of the Eastern Block, several hundred feet beyond *Impartial Eclipse*. There are a number of more

KISS OF THE CROWBAR

⑤

Jennifer Keller on Kiss of the Crowbar

difficult climbs between these two. Start to the left of *Kiss of the Crowbar* and then angle up and right to join it. 8 clips.

5. KISS OF THE CROWBAR 5.7 ★★★
FA: Bryan Burdo

The *Kiss* is an excellent steep route with super jugs and big exposure for such a moderate grade. 7 clips.

Squishy Bell

Squishy Bell is a short little crag located to the right of the Eastern Block formation. Hike past all the previous routes and then follow a short uphill section to this brief encounter. There are chains above all four of the routes and the top can be reached by hiking around on the left.

1. CATATONIC 5.6 ★
FA: Jeff Forister, Carrie Akerstrom
On the left. Two quick clips and it's gone.

2. WINTER RUSHING IN 5.8 ★
FA: Leland Windham, Steve Martin
Follow highly textured jugs up and right. 4 clips.

3. NOVEMBER GLAZE 5.9 ★★
FA: Leland Windham, Steve Martin
Pump through a small roof and then up the textured, steepish slab above.

4. SUMPTUOUS BITS 5.5 ★
FA: Steve Martin, Jeff Forister, Carrie Akerstrom
On the right. Another 2-clip wonder. Good beginner lead though.

GUN SHOW

Gun Show exists on a band of cliffs about 100 feet beneath the Interstate Park area and has been the scene of some excellent new route development during this book's production.

There are a good number of liberally bolted moderates here, of which the most well known is probably *Endless Bliss*, the gorgeous 40-meter slab near the right margin of the area. The short route ending just right of the *Bliss* is called *Super Squish* and is around 5.10c.

Follow the trail to Interstate Park as detailed above and step over the horizontal log as described. The trail loses about 100 feet of elevation and a great view of *Endless Bliss* presents itself as soon as you exit the trees. Routes here are set up to be workable with a single 60-meter rope.

1. ENDLESS BLISS 5.9– ★★★
FA: Leland Windham, Dave Wolfe
There's often an endless stream of climbers trying their hand at this area classic. Generously bolted, the climb is just barely 5.9 at one spot and the rock texture feels almost like Velcro! Chains in the middle allow you to rappel off with a single 60-meter rope. 135 feet, 16 clips.

2. SINKERVILLE 5.9

FA: Leland Windham, Dave Wolfe

Immediately left of *Bliss*. The gymnastic crux sequence at the bottom gets you going. 65 feet, 6 clips.

3. ELATION AT THE END OF ETERNITY 5.10– ★★★

FA: Leland Windham, David Wolfe

Elation takes the steep and fractured-looking wall 25 feet left of *Sinkerville*. The route can be led in one long pitch, but many break it into two at the midway station. The upper half is a sweet, Velcro-textured slab like *Endless*. 135 feet, 16 clips.

4. CLOSENESS TO FOREVER AS THE SOIL BLEEDS BLACK 5.8 ★

FA: Leland Windham, David Wolfe, David Argento

Fairly easy climbing leads up through a distinctive, foot-wide slot and up to a steep headwall with a one-move crux right at the end. 95 feet, 9 clips. A variation out left from the fifth bolt is 5.10d.

GUN SHOW

5. ABYSS BEHIND THE GAZE OF HUMANITY 5.10d ★★

FA: Leland Windham, David Wolfe

Mostly this one's included here for orientation, but it's an excellent two-pitch climb with 7 bolts on the first pitch and 4 bolts on the second, both 5.10d. It is located 12 feet left of *Closeness to Forever.*

6. JERRY WAS A RACE CAR DRIVER 5.7 ★

FA: Leland Windham, Vince Bailey, David Wolfe

Start a bit uphill and left of the other routes near an old stump and angle up and right on a ramp, passing bolts and optional gear. It's easy to set up a top rope on *Abyss* from this climb. 90 feet, 6 clips.

7. HANGING ON A STRING THEORY 5.7 ★

FA: Leland Windham, Keith Johnson

Features a short right-facing corner sequence that allows access to the upper slab. 70 feet, 7 clips.

8. BAPTIZED IN THE RIVER BLACK 5.7

FA: Leland Windham, David Wolfe

A bulge at the same height as the open book on the adjacent route makes the short crux on this textural offering. 60 feet, 4 clips.

Opposite: *Leland Windham at the crux of* Closeness To Forever

Tieton River

Climbers have been visiting these crags for almost forty years now, but it has been primarily in the last fifteen that this area has seen the growth of any real climbing population. It has, however, advanced at a constant rate, and recent trail rehabilitation fostered in part by the Access Fund has helped alleviate some of the more pressing concerns.

Issuing from the Goat Rock Wilderness, the Tieton River winds its way down through several climatic zones before merging with the Naches River near Yakima. Several forks of the river converge at Rimrock Lake, a reservoir east of the summit of White Pass and from which irrigation projects distribute the water to crops in the Yakima Valley.

The lava that eventually formed the andesite columns we climb on at the Tieton spewed forth from what is estimated to have been a 16,000-foot volcano almost a million years ago. The flow, which was hundreds of feet thick and insulated to a degree by the quickly cooled top layer, or entablature, took its sweet time cooling and the result is the thousands of standing columns and the continuous cracks we climb on.

Located near Yakima on the eastern slope of the Cascades, the Tieton area is a true desert with an annual precipitation of only about 7 inches. This makes for reliably dry days, although wind and cold can be a

Chris Carlsten demonstrating textbook lieback style on First Blood

235

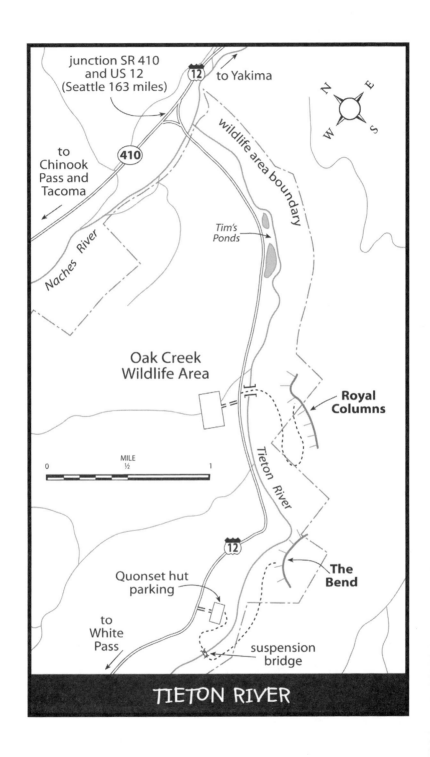

junction SR 410
and US 12
(Seattle 163 miles)

to Yakima

12

wildlife area boundary

N
E
W
S

410

to
Chinook
Pass and
Tacoma

Naches River

*Tim's
Ponds*

Oak Creek
Wildlife Area

**Royal
Columns**

Tieton River

MILE
½
0   1

12

**The
Bend**

Quonset hut
parking

to
White
Pass

suspension
bridge

TIETON RIVER

deterrent in the spring and fall. The cliffs typically tend to face west, so morning sun is not something to count on.

The rock at the Tieton looks similar to Vantage rock, although the similarities end there. While bolted routes do exist and have become more common, the quality and quantity of the local cracks has made traditional climbing much more the status quo than it has at its more northerly neighbor. The ratings are stiff here! The sustained nature of the crack climbs particularly accentuates this perception and many find themselves climbing more moderately rated climbs here than in other areas.

Most routes are approximately half a rope length, or 75–80 feet long, and are descended via rappels from various descent stations located along the cliff tops. Prudent climbers are advised to have a few assorted bolt hangers, nuts, descending rings, and bits of sling available in case these anchors have been vandalized. The Washington Department of Fish and Wildlife (WDFW) advises that any permanent installation of new hardware on its lands requires written permission from the Oak Creek Wildlife Area manager. Replacement of existing hardware must be of a color and design that integrates into the natural landscape.

Typically the top layer of stone (the entablature) is profoundly shattered and loose. Some routes stop short of this hazard and others climb through it to reach the top. Climbers should be extremely aware, wear helmets, and consider the lives of those below when traversing this zone of potentially lethal rubble.

Climbing at the Tieton exists due to a somewhat arduously worked out set of access parameters. It is important to remember that these rocks are entirely under the jurisdiction of the WDFW, whose primary concern is to maintain a safe and viable habitat for the natural residents.

TIETON RIVER AREA BETA

Drive time from Seattle ▲ 2½ hours
Drive time from Spokane ▲ 3½ hours
Approach times ▲ 10–30 minutes

Getting there: From I-90 at Ellensburg, exit south onto US 97 and continue to Yakima on I-82/US 97. From Yakima follow SR 410 west for 18 miles to the junction with US 12. A left turn onto US 12 finally puts you alongside the Tieton River and on the road to the climbs. The Royal Columns are located 2 miles up this road and across the highway from

---

the Oak Creek Wildlife Area headquarters. Parking at the Quonset hut for the Bend routes is 3.5 miles from the turnoff onto US 12.

Season: The Tieton is a desert area that receives little precipitation. Climbing has been done every month of the year, but April to October is the norm. Many of the climbs face west and can be chilly on spring and fall mornings.

Regulations: WDFW enforces an annual seasonal closure February 1 through April 1 for the Tieton River Trail and climbing areas to allow wildlife, particularly golden eagles, to establish nesting territories undisturbed. The Bend and Royal Columns are closed during this time, but climbing areas upstream from the suspension bridge at the Quonset hut parking area remain open. Check with the Oak Creek office if unsure of the status at the Royal Columns and other features. Parking permits are required to park at the wildlife area across the highway from the Royal Columns and at the Quonset hut parking area for the Bend. Climbers are required to access the cliff face at the Royal Columns by utilizing a climbing trail that travels upriver after crossing the steel Tieton River footbridge. Climbers need to go through the pedestrian gate in the elk fence near the bridge.

Camping: Windy Point Campground, located 6 miles into the canyon, is the most convenient for climbers. Climbers often share the sites with parties of boaters and rafters who have come to enjoy the Tieton River itself. Late-night arrivals may find a closer, legal place to toss their bags out at the Tim's Pond turnout, located about 1.5 miles from the SR 410/US 12 junction on the left and just before the Oak Creek Wildlife Center (509-653-2390). Northwest Forest Pass required for Tim's Pond. The U.S. Forest Service Ranger Station in Naches (509-653-1400) can provide information about campgrounds in the area. Be aware that fire danger is extreme in eastern Washington in the dry months and that state agencies often prohibit open fires of any type. Please check local regulations carefully.

Concessions: All things can be found in Yakima. Naches businesses also have most services and supplies including groceries, auto repair, and lodging.

Climbing type: Primarily traditional crack climbing, although bolted arêtes do exist.

Rock type: Columnar andesite

Gear: Medium traditional rack with gear to 4 inches. Sometimes the variable columnar cracks require added finesse to protect realistically. Extra dark-colored slings/rappel gear, approach shoes, mountain clothing.

Royal Columns

The Columns have been the longest running feature at the Tieton show, although there are now several other great venues as well. At the Columns you can expect generally excellent rock, great protection, and afternoon sunshine.

Rattlesnakes and other nonpoisonous serpents can be found here and you should be vigilant for them. Mostly these are shy, reclusive creatures with no taste for confrontation. Please respect their right to exist in their natural state. Ticks are another story however, so read up on how to correctly remove them and be on the lookout for these blood-suckers in the spring.

Descent: Descent is by numerous rap stations located along the cliff tops. Or you can exit the routes by hiking uphill to the left a bit and then walking down and around the cliffs on the left perimeter.

Judicious stemming solves the crux on Inca Roads *for climber Chris Carlsten.*

1. NIMROD'S NEMESIS 5.5 ★

Climb an appealing set of double cracks up past an obvious roof and on up to a belay stance on the left. A fixed pin in the upper part of the climb may or may not be present. Gear to 3 inches. 60 feet.

2. CONTRACTION ACTION 5.9 ★

Climb scary-looking cracks past roofs to reach a flaring squeeze. Don't thrash too much and you'll trend left to the top. Gear to 3 inches. 65 feet.

3. RENDER US WEIGHTLESS 5.9+ PG ★

FA: Jamie Christiansen 1976

A local test piece that works through a roof with some scary brass

nuts and continues up the crack in the pillar's left face. The crack ends a few feet below the top and the crux is 10 feet of 5.9+ to the anchors. Gear to 2½ inches. 90 feet.

4. INCA ROADS 5.10a ★★★
FA: Dale Farnham, Paul Boving, April 1974

This long, strenuous hand crack is one of the most aesthetic in the area. There are excellent jams the whole way, but don't forget to be creative and stem your feet if you want your forearms to last! Gear to 3½ inches. 90 feet.

5. LITTLE-KNOWN WONDER 5.7 ★

This very fun route takes advantage of two great cracks and you jam and stem your way to wonderment. Gear to 3 inches. 90 feet.

6. MUSH MAKER 5.7+ ★★

Perhaps a bit of sandbag, this long, aesthetic hand crack is not to be missed! Gear to 3 inches. 70 feet. Rappel from bolted station.

7. FIRST BLOOD 5.8 ★★

Sustained and pumpy, there probably aren't any 5.9 moves here but almost all of them are 5.8! It's a classic fist crack with good pro but few good rests. Several pieces to 4 inches. 70 feet.

8. WILD CHILD 5.7 ★

Find the largest roof on the crag about two thirds of the way along the base from the game gate on the right margin. Double cracks lead up to the roof and some exciting and awkward moves turn the big roof on its left. Construct a gear anchor and then move right several columns to the right to find an appropriate rappel station.

Variation: Slash 5.8+ ★★

From the roof level, step out left and lieback and jam an airy left-facing flake. Gear to 4 inches. 75 feet.

9. LEVEL HEAD 5.6 ★

Just right and around the pillar from *Wild Child* is a short bolted arête with rap hangers about 40 feet off the ground. Just right of this is a pair

of cracks in a recess that passes two large, flat ledges on climber's right. Climb the cracks and take gear to 2½ inches. Construct a gear belay at the top and then move right to a bolted rappel station.

10. GOOD TIMER 5.4 ★

Look for the roof on *Slacker* and then move one crack system to the left. A fairly substantial tree lives at the top of this fun and easy climb. Gear to 2½ inches.

11. SLACKER 5.4 ★

Big holds, good pro, and exciting position lead up past a big overhang. Gear to 3 inches. 60 feet.

12. RAP ROUTE 5.5 ★

This one's a bit shorter than many, but still a fun climb. Move left about midway and follow the left-hand crack. Gear to 2½ inches. 50 feet.

13. ROUGH BOYS 5.5 ★

Use the same start as the previous route, only continue straight up the original crack line. Gear to 2½ inches. 50 feet.

ROYAL COLUMNS
(center left)

14. WESTERN FRONT 5.3 ★★★

You usually just don't get clean and aesthetic climbing at this
standard. Great for a first lead or for just enjoying the stone even if you
can climb harder. Gear to 2½ inches. 50 feet.

15. THE CUTTING EDGE 5.7 ★★★

Like climbing the blade track on a huge guillotine! This steep and
picturesque climb is an area must-do. Although a guidebook fifteen years

ago warned that the cleaver had loosened, the author has not noticed any recent changes. Cleverly work the finger and hand crack and then (just to be safe) gingerly climb over/by/around the glistening blade. Gear to 2½ inches. 60 feet.

16. X-FACTOR 5.7+ ★★★

Located immediately right of *The Cutting Edge* and of more or less the same standard (perhaps a touch harder), the *Factor* is a strenuous jamming experience in a cool corner. Gear to 2½ inches. 60 feet. (The big left-facing chimney on the right is worthwhile and about 5.6.)

17. CROSS-EYED AND PAINLESS 5.9 ★★

This is the cool hand and finger crack that is the first crack right of the off-width on the right side of the detached column. There are steep, technical moves the entire way—keep your wits and stem when you can.

Opposite: *Working out the sequences on the surprisingly pumpy* Mush Maker

Keep some gear to back up the anchor. Gear to 2½ inches, have some medium stoppers and TCUs too. 65 feet.

18. THRILLER PILLAR DIRECT 5.9+ ★

FA: Ed Mosshart, Andy Fitz 1989

You'll need some experience here to think this is 5.9. Still, they are exciting moves with incredible position. Several pieces to 1½ inches plus 4 clips. 80 feet. (The dihedrals on either side of the pillar can also be climbed at 5.6 and 5.7.)

19. CACTUS LOVE 5.9 ★

FA: Andy Fitz, Ed Mosshart 1987

Sustained and physical, this great finger and hand crack stays in your face then drags you over a roof till its done. Gear to 2½ inches. 80 feet.

Opposite: *Sarah Doherty gliding up the track on* The Cutting Edge

20. JAM EXAM 5.9 ★★

A sort of full-body-workout type of experience. This one tests how many ways you know to cram body parts into a crack. Gear to 3 1/2 inches, plus TCUs. 70 feet.

The Bend

The Bend is one of the outstanding destinations of the Tieton area. The higher standards at the Bend mean that many outstanding routes are not within the scope of this book, but several stellar exceptions do exist. The Bend features two different aspects: the Bend North and the Bend West. This book includes only a small sampling from the western venue.

Park at the WDFW Quonset hut (Northwest Forest Pass required) and follow clear footpaths down to the suspension bridge across the river. The WDFW seasonal restriction begins at the downstream side of this bridge. Once across the bridge, a short hike downstream on the Tieton River Trail takes you to where an obvious trail branches off to the right and uphill to the rock.

1. PEACE, LOVE AND ROPE 5.8+ ★★
FA: Ed Mosshart, John Ohrembreck, Jeff Main 1989
This one requires making a fourth-class traverse in from higher ground on the right. Once there, a bit of ho-hum rock leads to this hand-jam and lieback adventure. Gear to 3 1/2 inches.

2. ED'S JAM 5.8 ★★★
FA: Ed Mosshart, Andy Fitz 1987
One of the finest cracks at this grade anywhere, and the pitch just goes on and on. Look for the obvious, mostly right-facing hand crack with a sling-festooned tree on it some 70 feet up. Shady oaks at the base provide a place to leave your pack, and a short (50-foot, 5.2) approach pitch leads up and left to a stance and a place for a gear anchor. Start up the thin crack (5.8) and move left at the tree to reach the main crack. Gear to 3 1/2 inches. 140 feet. Rappel from bolted anchors on top.

3. SALMON SONG 5.10a ★★★
FA: Ed Mosshart, Andy Fitz 1988
A Tieton classic and an intimidating looking one at that! The crack,

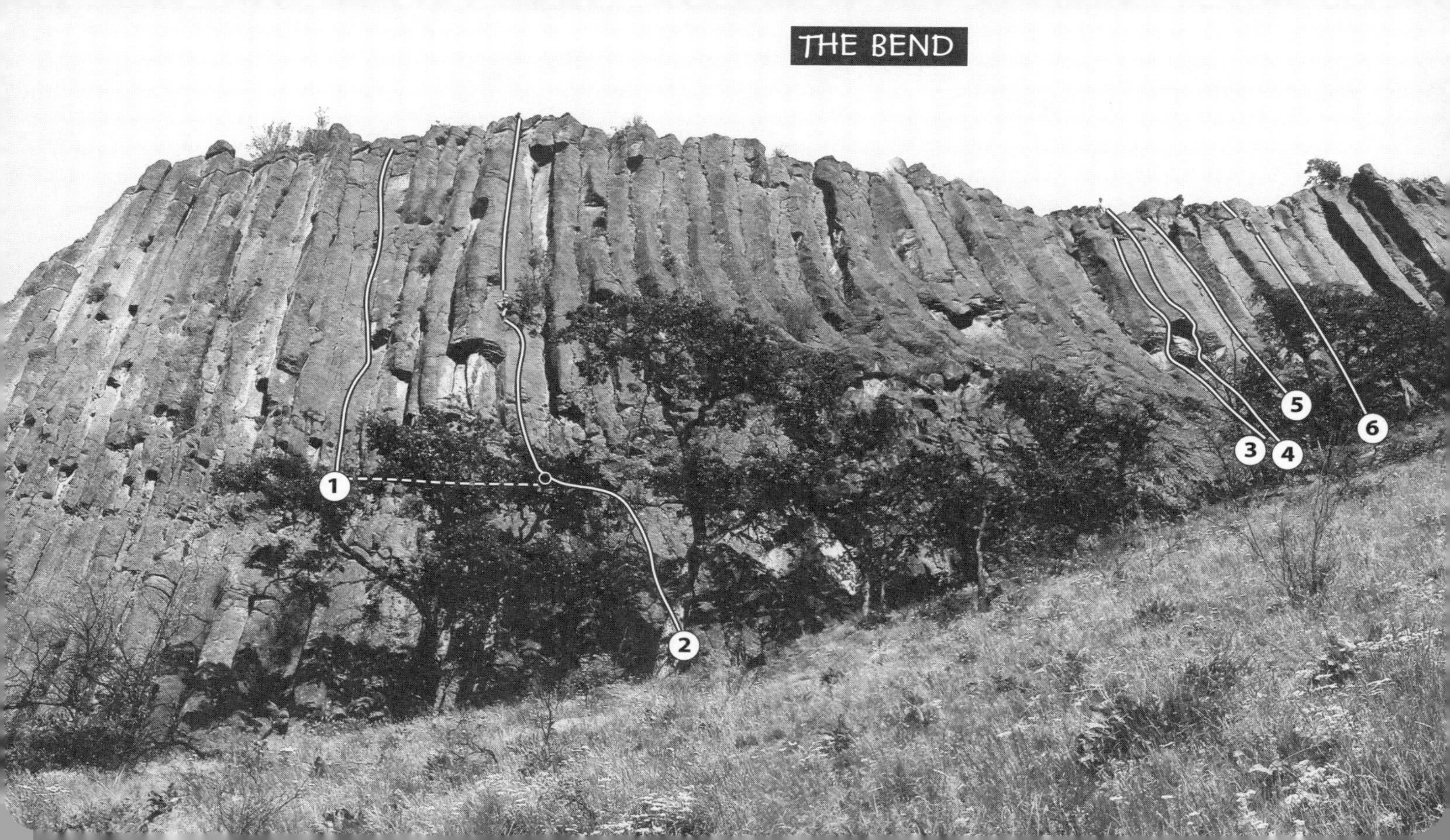
THE BEND
1
2
3
4
5
6

Climbers starting up the main crack of Ed's Jam

however, is truly excellent and goes from fingers to hands after pulling the double-tiered roof. Gear to 2½ inches.

4. TIERS 5.9 ★

FA: Andy Fitz, Ed Mosshart 1987

This is the line immediately right of *Salmon Song*. It's a pumpy but good hand and fist crack going through the double-tiered roof and up the wider crack above. Gear to 3½ inches.

wide 5.9 5.8 twin cracks

THE BEND WEST
(right)

5. CRUEL HARVEST 5.8+ ★

FA: Andy Fitz, Matt Christensen 1988

Stem up the middle between this steep pair of striking thin cracks. Gear to 2 inches.

6. HALLOWED GROUND 5.8+ ★★

FA: Andy Fitz, Ed Mosshart 1987

There is everything from thin fingers to hands on this quite fine sampling. Gear to 2¹/₂ inches.

Frenchman Coulee

Frenchman Coulee is about classic basalt columns. Dozens of sweet cracks alongside exciting sport climbs characterize the climbing found here. Located a couple of easy driving hours east of Seattle, this area may boast the state's longest climbing season. Sometimes referred to as Vantage, the Coulee is a great venue in spring and fall before soaring summer temperatures erode climbers' ambitions.

Climbing at Frenchman Coulee has seen several periods of tremendous growth in the last dozen years and it appears that many of the highest quality climbs have been discovered and documented. Additionally, an attempt has been made to develop climbs at all standards, and worthwhile easy to moderate climbs are numerous at the Coulee. More than 500 climbs have been described for this popular area and climbers in search of more comprehensive information are referred to Marlene Ford and Jim Yoder's guidebook, *Frenchman Coulee: A Rock Climber's Guide.*

The Feathers, Sunshine Wall, and its satellite crags make up the bulk of the areas described here and offer numerous choices with respect to both difficulty and solar orientation. Climbers overly baked by the dry summer heat can find a boat launch and convenient swimming access on the

Linda Sears belays Doug Walker on the Sunshine Wall classic Party In Your Pants.

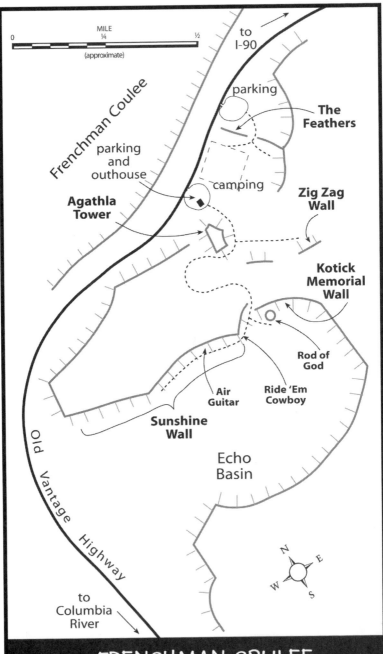

Columbia River, just a few more miles down the Old Vantage Highway.

A common problem in the past has been the practice of top-roping and lowering off the fixed anchors at the tops of these climbs. Ropes coated with desert dust are surprisingly abrasive under load, and hangers and chains can get worn through rather quickly due to this practice. **Please** only use quickdraws or locking biners of your own to top-rope and lower from. The chains themselves are *only* for rappel. Responsible parties have tried to stay on top of this situation, but be aware that worn gear can still sometimes be found at the tops of popular routes.

Protecting traditional routes at Frenchman Coulee poses some different conditions than are commonly found on granite. The undulating and changing dimensions of the fissures at the Coulee sometimes result in cracks that are wider inside than they are at the surface. This condition can make it possible for cams to "walk" into wider sections of the crack where they may not fit well or might fall out. It's thought that this may have been a factor in at least one recent tragedy. The bottom line is to examine and understand your gear fully if you are going to trad climb here or anywhere.

FRENCHMAN COULEE BETA
Drive time from Seattle ▲ 2 1/2 hours
Drive time from Spokane ▲ 2 hours
Approach times ▲ Roadside to 30 minutes

Getting there: Drive I-90 to exit 143, labeled for the Gorge Amphitheater and Wanapum Lake. (From Seattle it's a straight shot east on I-90: pass the town of Vantage, cross the Columbia River, and in a few miles start to look for exit 143.) From the bottom of the exit, turn left onto Silica Road and in 0.8 mile look for the intersection of Silica and the Old Vantage Highway. Make a left on the Old Vantage Highway and begin the descent into the coulee. At 1.3 miles from the intersection you'll reach the parking lot for the Feathers on the left, and about a quarter mile beyond is the entrance to the campground and the main climbers' parking area.

Season: The place receives only about 8 inches of rain a year so the season is more dictated by temperature and wind velocity than wetness. During some winters the local waterfalls freeze enough to allow ice climbing. Warm sunny days can occur any time of year but March to November represents a good bit of the climbing. Average midsummer temperatures into the 80s and 90s often suggest other destinations or shady climbs early in the day.

Regulations: Parking permits are required both at the Feathers and the main climbers' parking areas. Permits can be purchased for $12.00 in the town of George at the Colonial Market (207 West Montmorency Street; 509-785-3231). Look for the big red brick building on the right.

Camping: Camping in the area seems to be stabilized after a period of flux. Currently it is restricted to an area between the climbers' parking lot and the south side of the Feathers. There are no facilities and the camping is free. Two Access Fund–provided toilets are located at the climbers' parking lot and reader board. Open fires are prohibited from May 15 through October 15. There is a KOA campground located in Vantage, 10 miles from the climbing area.

Concessions: The nearest concessions are located either in Vantage or George, both about 10 miles from the climbing area. Climbers traveling to and from the Seattle area will be more likely to stop at Vantage for the small country store, gasoline, and burgers.

Climbing type: Sport, traditional

Rock type: Columbia River basalt

Gear: Sport climbing/traditional crack climbing gear. To minimize frightening wear on the anchors always use your own carabiners when top-roping and lowering.

The Feathers

Located within feet of the Old Vantage Highway, the Feathers is a single fence of basalt columns—all that remains of the dividing zone between two waterfall plunge basins formed during the Missoula Floods of 12,000 years ago. Conveniently for us, the east-west orientation provides shade on one side and sun on the other, and the narrow walk-through in the middle of the formation makes for easy access to both sides.

This area features the highest concentration of moderate to easy routes at Frenchman Coulee, and many of the examples here are excellent candidates for first leads. Almost all the Feathers climbs are bolted sport routes. While the Coulee has many truly classic crack climbs, almost none of these are found at the Feathers. The northeast portion of the group features a detached block known as Satan's Pillar, and the first five routes described below are on this interesting and popular formation.

THE NORTH SIDE

This is the side of the Feathers most people see first, and the car park just underneath makes it a roadside attraction. Remember, parking permits are required, and they *do* come around writing tickets fairly often.

1. SATAN'S LITTLE HELPER 5.9 ★★
FA: Leland Windham 1991

This is a fun climb on the parking-lot face of the block. Staying to the right at the top keeps it at 5.9. 5 clips and anchors.

SATAN'S PILLAR

2. SATAN'S WAGON 5.10b ★★★
FA: Bob Buckley, Kevin Kurtz
Thought by many to be the best offering for its grade at the Feathers. Very pumpy. 7 clips and anchors.

3. BLOOD BLISTER 5.10a ★★
FA: Mack Johnson, John Alving
Sort of a gym-inspired squeeze job, but good moves throughout. 5 clips and anchors.

4. JESUS SAVES 5.8 ★★
FA: Kevin Kurtz, Jeff Ball
Moderate and fun. 5 clips and anchors.

5. NOTCH ROUTE 5.6 ★
FA: Gene Prater, Bill Prater 1948
Another of the old-time Frenchman's climbs, this one was pretty much a free-solo until retrobolted to protect the innocent. Climb the back side of the pillar from the notch. 3 clips and anchors.

6. SHIN SMASHER 5.9 ★
FA: Jason Prinster, Kevin Pogue
This one is just behind the Satan's Pillar formation and features 3 clips on a pillar with a small roof between the first and second bolts.

7. ALTAR OF SACRIFICE 5.7 ★
FA: Leland Windham, Kurt Greenbaum 1991
Another route that has sprouted a few more bolts... probably for the best in this case. Look for 4 clips on a small face just opposite Satan's Pillar. 4 clips and anchors.

8. DESERT SHIELD 5.10a ★★
FA: John and Gina Eminger
This is the route immediately left of *The Uprising* and was for some time a runout offering with only 2 bolts. It now features 6 and some think that adds up to it feeling more like 5.9. Share anchors with *The Uprising*.

9. THE UPRISING 5.8 ★★★
FA: Jeff Ball, Bob Buckley, Kevin Kurtz
Those who climb 5.10 often cite *Satan's Wagon* as the best route

at the Feathers, but this one is at least as good for its grade. 4 clips and anchors. (The large crack to the right of this feature is called *Porthole* on the north side and *Mirror* on the south. Both are 5.8 and only marginally interesting.)

10. SHAKE IT DON'T BREAK IT 5.5 ★
FA: Kevin Pogue, Elisa Weinman
This is one of the easier Feathers offerings. 3 clips and chains on top.

11. MANDATORY SUICIDE 5.4 ★★
FA: Mike Hylland, Kevin Pogue, Craig Dodson
Another quality easy one. Look for the top anchor on the pillar to the right. 4 clips and anchors.

12. GET THE PEVER FEVER 5.5 ★
FA: Jessica and Jim Pever
The *Fever* is fairly similar to the last route but with 3 clips and its own top anchor.

THE FEATHERS
(north, center)

13. BECKEY ROUTE 5.7 ★★
FA: Kevin Pogue, Elisa Weinman
Five clips make this moderate route a popular one.

14. WHERE THE SIDEWALK ENDS 5.1 ★
FA: Marlene Ford, Jim Yoder
Still the Feathers' easiest climb, although recently upgraded to 5.1.
A good first lead in any case. 3 clips and anchors.

15. RUFFLED FEATHERS 5.7 ★
FA: Marlene Ford, Jim Yoder
Short and fun... but that's the Feathers! 4 clips and anchors.

16. FEATHER IN MY CAP 5.6 ★
FA: Marlene Ford, Jim Yoder
The is the rightmost route at this part of the Feathers. 3 clips and
anchors.

THE SOUTH SIDE

People in the camping area to the south often walk directly uphill to the south-side routes, but most park to the north and access these climbs via the obvious gap (or walk-through) in the middle of the ridge.

17. SO FUNNY I FORGOT TO LAUGH 5.9 ★

FA: Leland Windham, Paul Schenkenberger 1992

Follows the left edge of a block and has been upgraded to 5 clips and anchors.

18. MEDICINE MAN 5.10a ★★

FA: Jim Yoder, Dick Cilley

This was the original route on this side of the block. It originally had 4 clips… Then some rock broke off and it had 3. Currently rejuvenated with 4 clips again.

19. FRAGGLED PICKLE 5.10a ★

FA: Jean Pierre Benville, Lyne Benville

This route is a bit of a squeeze job and requires a thoughtful approach to not block the walk-through. 6 clips and anchors.

20. DON COYOTE 5.8 ★★★

FA: Kevin Pogue, Elisa Weinman

Another route that seems to be evolving. It has been upgraded from 4 clips to 5 and is often thought to be pumpy. Good footwork is the ticket. 5 clips and anchors.

Don Coyote *is a fine 5.8 requiring judicious footwork.*

21. OLD CRACK 5.7

While not especially popular these days, this crack was one of the original routes in the entire Frenchman Coulee area. Use the *Don Coyote* anchors to finish. Gear to 4½ inches.

22. DANCE OF THE SHAMAN 5.10b ★

FA: Bob Buckley, Kevin Kurtz

This is a pretty short one. Three cruxy clips and you're up!

23. HARDENING OF THE ARTERIES 5.10c ★★

FA: Leland Windham 1991

This short test piece sees much traffic. One of the more difficult routes here even if it is very short. 4 clips and anchors.

24. RING PIN CRACK 5.6 PG ★

FA: Gene Prater 1955

Crack climbing at the Feathers isn't generally so hot, this one's okay though, and historic! Gear to 6 inches.

262

25. WINDWALKER 5.10a ★★

FA: Elisa Weinman Pogue, Mike Hylland

This one's only 5.10a if you strictly avoid anything to do with the crack. 4 clips and anchors.

26. NIGHTBIRD 5.10a ★★

FA: Kevin and Elisa Weinman Pogue, Craig Dodson

Just around the corner to the right of *Windwalker*, this is a pumpy one with 4 clips and bolted anchors.

27. SKIING @ 49 NORTH 5.10b ★

FA: Jim Yoder, Marlene Ford

Skiing has been the scene of several different routes over the years. It'll hopefully remain like it is for a while. 6 clips and anchors.

28. ME TOO 5.9 ★

FA: Marlene Ford, Paul Strauss, Jim Yoder

A surprising bit of variety on this one. 4 clips and anchors.

Hardening of the Arteries *is one of the more difficult routes located at the Feathers.*

29. UPDRAFTS TO HEAVEN 5.5 ★★

FA: Paul Strauss, Jim Yoder, Marlene Ford

The *Draft* is one of the better easy routes at the Feathers. Start around the corner to the right from *Me Too* in an obvious chimney. 4 clips and anchors.

Zig Zag Wall

Zig Zag has seen steady improvements over the last few years and is certainly worth a visit even if it's not as grand as the King Pins area of Sunshine Wall. The advantage is that the Zig Zag is shady and cooler when the Pins are melting in solar radiation.

Approach: From the reader board and outhouses at the main climbers' parking area, hike up over the rise and pass Agathla Tower and the trail to Sunshine Wall on your right. Continue a short distance straight ahead (southeast) until the short wall is apparent.

1. SCISSOR MAN 5.9 ★
FA: Jim Yoder, Bill Robins, Marlene Ford, and others
Located near the left margin of the cliff, this route climbs a bolted orange pillar. 5 clips and anchors.

2. SECRET PASSAGE 5.10b ★
FA: Jim Yoder, Marlene Ford
This is another short, bolted pillar, somewhat similar to *Scissor Man*. A bit of groping is often required to find the "secret." 6 clips and anchors.

3. STARLESS IN VANTAGE 5.9 PG ★
FA: Marlene Ford, Jim Yoder
Generally pretty well bolted, the center section has a bit of a runout on less than optimal rock, which is fortunately the easier portion of the route. The lower section is the good part, however. 6 clips and anchors.

4. UNFINISHED BUSINESS 5.8 ★★
FA: Elisa Weinman, Kevin Pogue, Barbara Jones
This is a fairly popular climb near the center of the cliff, despite being rather short. It doesn't seem to be bolted correctly, but there are enough clips to keep it sane. 5 clips and anchors.

5. SOMEWHERE ON EARTH 5.7
Pretty much a variation, really. This is the short but interesting-looking open book capped by a roof that is immediately left of *Edge of Mistakes*. Climb a few feet of chossy but easy rock to reach the white

ZIG ZAG WALL

Micah Lambeth locked on target on Orangekist

finger crack and climb it a short distance to the roof. Step right, around the corner and use the 2 protection bolts on *Mistakes* to finish. 2 clips plus TCUs; anchors.

6. EDGE OF MISTAKES 5.6 ★

This is the fun, thinner crack just left of *Orangekist*, although it may take some local experience to find the most solid gear placements. Climb the crack/corner for 30 feet or so, then move up onto the left face to find 2 protection bolts. 2 clips plus gear to 2½ inches. Rappel from the fixed anchor on the ledge above.

7. ORANGEKIST 5.8 ★★

FA: Marlene Ford, Jim Yoder

The *'Kist* is a short little gem with some of the better rock at the Zig Zag. Obvious chains about 40 feet up mark the route. 4 clips, with the crux between the second and third; anchors.

8. THE JAGGED EDGE 5.7 ★★

FA: Joe Gribnau, Kevin Pogue

Six clips make this one pretty popular. Steep climbing at the bottom leads to huge edges on the upper part of the climb. Obvious rap anchors are in place.

Kotick Memorial Wall

The Kotick Memorial Wall is located immediately east of the walk-down chimney that leads to Sunshine Wall (see the Sunshine approach, below). As soon as you are through the corridor, hang a sharp left and find the first route on the freestanding pillar about 200 feet to the east of you. *The Rod of God* is an exciting climb on the pillar and well worth the experience. With windy days fairly common in eastern Washington, it's good to know the Kotick Wall sometimes offers protection from the main blasts. Some of the pillar tops may have multiple slings tied through the bolts for rappel stations. Have some extra webbing on hand in the event these look overly dried out.

1. THE ROD OF GOD 5.8 ★★

FA: Kurt Schmierer, Bob Buckley, Keven Kurtz, Jeff Ball

An excellent route on the right side of the pillar. Reported to be loose, but really only minimally so. The freestanding pillar is quite popular. 4 clips with a 3-bolt anchor and slings on the pillar top; use extra runners for top-roping.

2. CRACK IN THE BACK 5.6

FA: Jim Yoder, Bill Robins

This is the only crack climb featured in this group, although most of the cracks and chimneys along this stretch have been climbed. Fairly secure-feeling climbing leads up the recess to a finish on the *Well Preserved* anchors, from which the crack can be top-roped if desired. Take some large pieces to 4 inches or more. Rappel *Well Preserved*.

3. WELL PRESERVED 5.10b ★

FA: Jim Yoder, Marlene Ford, Bill Robins

The hardest part of this route is trying to understand how to use the cruxy, sloping holds at the start. Good climbing though, and not quite so hard once you get going. 6 clips and anchors. Rappel.

4. WILD THING 5.10a ★★
FA: Marlene Ford, Jim Yoder, Bill Robins
The majority of the sequences on this climb are less than 5.10, but the last move to the chain is certainly a "wild thing." 5 clips and anchors.

5. SILHOUETTES 5.10a ★★
FA: John Eminger, John Kittel, Gary Kock
This is an excellent and really rather moderate 5.10a, although some find the first couple of clips a little scary. Reputed to be the best route at Kotick, others think *The Rod* gets higher marks for uniqueness. 5 clips and anchors.

Doug Walker on The Rod of God

6. A GAME OF INCHES 5.9
FA: Mike Brown, Scott Schaff, Marlene Ford, Jim Yoder

Pretty scruffy rock at the bottom. Local wisdom is to make the first few moves of *Silhouettes* and step right to get onto this route as the rock improves. 5 clips and anchors.

Sunshine Wall

Sunshine Wall is probably the second biggest draw at Frenchman after the Feathers. Classic hand cracks proliferate alongside radical sport arêtes and the place draws them all. Beasts, babies, boom boxes, and all the bustle of a train station are sometimes the rule here, and still, at other times the crowds are surprisingly few and then the sinuous columns can take on a quiet glow in the afternoon light. Cool spring and fall temperatures are mitigated by the southern exposure and the lineup of outstanding climbs at all grades is hard to beat.

Approach: From the main climbers' parking area, walk up the remains of the road past the hulking Agatha Tower and take the first right after the tower. The trail crosses the flats and then works up through the terraces to the mesa rim. Once you reach the mesa top, the trail moves off to the south and eventually comes to a walk-down chimney that allows access to the south-facing columns and cracks of Sunshine Wall.

Sunshine Wall is divided into several sections, with the Near End being the first encountered. Walking along the base of the wall in a westerly direction takes you to the King Pins area, and a bit farther to the Tilted Pillars. Just past the Tilted Pillars a walk-down gully allows for easy descents.

1. PAT'S CRACK 5.9 PG ★

This is a pretty good crack that demands solid jamming skills. Look for the obvious widening hand crack five cracks to the right of *Ride 'em Cowboy*. The route doesn't get much traffic and the exit moves through the entablature are rather loose, so use caution. Gear to 4 inches. Walk back down through the access chimney.

2. RIDE 'EM COWBOY 5.9+ ★★★

Ever-popular classic bolted pillar that features a "saddle" for a no-hands rest at the second bolt. 9 clips and anchors.

3. PARTY IN YOUR PANTS 5.8 ★★★

The entry-level classic for Sunshine Wall, the *Party* follows double cracks all the way to the rim. Judicious stemming keeps the route from getting too strenuous, and a new 3-bolt anchor and chains add to the security of this extremely popular route. It's fairly long, so take many pieces up to 3 inches.

4. JUSTIFIED ANCIENTS OF MU MU 5.8 ★★

FA: Kevin Pogue, Mike Hyland

This climb is set up as two short pitches but is sometimes run together as one. The first half takes on a short pillar, then the climb moves to the right and up again. 9 clips.

5. THROBBING GRISTLE 5.9 ★★★

FA: Kevin Pogue 1994

Still another exposed column arête with amazing position and a moderate grade. There's often a group of people standing around waiting

Desert ambiance and a climber on Ride 'em Cowboy

for a turn on this one. Sell your car and buy more quickdraws, there are 13 clips!

6. STROKIN' THE CHICKEN 5.6 ★★

FA: Bill Robins, Paul Certa 1989

This one's pretty good and of moderate grade. A good crack for hands, and pro and pillars to stem from, makes *The Chicken* a good example of its grade. Gear to 3¹/₂ inches.

Scott Buzan cruising the arête on Whipsaw

7. WHIPSAW 5.9 ★★★

FA: Kevin Pogue

Ground zero for bolt wars, this route was chopped and rebuilt three times before the fires cooled. *Whipsaw* is nonetheless a great climb up a striking arête and at a standard that's sure to bring smiles. 10 clips. Rappel.

8. PONY KEG 5.10a ★★★

FA: Max Duffard, Dante Leonardi 1985

Just an arm span left of *Whipsaw* and ostensibly the reason behind the bolt chopping. *Pony Keg* ranges from hands to slightly wider and still gets led traditionally despite the bolts being within reach. The *Whipsaw*

SUNSHINE WALL (overview)

King Pins

Tilted Pillars

Preying Mantel

The Chossmaster

Air Guitar

Vantage Point

George and Martha

Peaceful Warrior

5 4

KING PINS
(Air Guitar Area)

bolts do make a sort of safety valve, though, and more than one gripped leader has thankfully reached over and made some clips. Gear to 4 inches. Rappel.

9. AIR GUITAR 5.10a ★★★
FA: Max Duffard, Dante Leonardi 1985
Air Guitar has become a somewhat notorious classic Vantage crack, some argue *the* classic Vantage crack. The crack starts quite thin and works through fingers, to hands and fists, and even a few, short off-width moves at the top. Gear to 4 1/2 inches. Double chain anchors are in place beneath the plaque.

10. CROSSING THE THRESHOLD 5.8 ★★
FA: Bill Robins, Paul Certa 1988
This is the hand and fist crack in a recess immediately right of *Clip 'em or Skip 'em*. Comfortable stems across to the right side may help mitigate stress. Gear to 4 inches. Use the anchors on *Clip 'em* to rappel.

11. CLIP 'EM OR SKIP 'EM 5.8 ★★
FA: Kevin Pogue 1991
Surprisingly pumpy for its moderate grade, but plenty of bullets keep it all in perspective. Like the name suggests, there are 10 clips to keep you from sweating. Rappel.

12. VANTAGE POINT 5.8 ★★
FA: Kevin Pogue, Brian Bidduck, Paul Hornbeek 1997
Way out on the front face of a big pillar and pretty sustained 5.8. 11 clips and anchors. Rappel.

13. GEORGE AND MARTHA 5.10a ★★★
FA: Karl Birkenkamp 1986
One of the best at Sunshine Wall without question. Probably not a lot more difficult than *Air Guitar*, but certainly longer... it just goes and goes... and then it gets wider. Gear to 4 1/2 inches or so is a drag to carry, but useful on the final wide bit. Rappel.

14. PEACEFUL WARRIOR 5.6 ★★
FA: Kevin Pogue 1990
Outstanding exterior moves, amazing buckets, and lots of clips give

Micah Lambeth nearing the finish line on the super-classic Air Guitar

this "chimney" plenty of excitement for its grade. Don't touch the shaky chockstones about midway up the route though! 7 clips, all cleanly out on the right; climbing the bolted line without the chimney is 5.10 and easily top-roped. Rappel from chains.

15. TANGLED UP IN BLUE 5.9 ★★

FA: Bill Robins, Charlie Edmunds 1988

Start on the 7-foot-high pedestal that is 20 feet right of *Seven Virgins* and climb the splendid hand crack on the left side of a recess. Killer jams and rest stems keep it from getting extreme. Gear to 4 inches. Rappel from anchors on the bolted line immediately left (*Narlux*, 5.10c, three stars).

KING PINS
(George and Martha Area)

Narlux
(5.10c)

15

14

13

16

climb faces left

Sunlight streams through from behind the pillar on Seven Virgins and a Mule. *(Jennifer Keller)*

16. SEVEN VIRGINS AND A MULE 5.7 ★★

FA: Bill Robins, Pete Rieke, Paul Hunt 1991

Another outstanding chimney route, only this one requires getting totally inside. There's a perfect gear crack in the back of the undulating recess that ranges from thin fingers to hands. Several steps up and back from the top of the chimney you can find cracks to construct an anchor. Be sure and use several *different* cracks. Gear to 3½ inches. Scramble down the narrow gully several hundred feet to the west.

17. THE CHOSSMASTER 5.7 ★★

FA: Kevin and Elisa Pogue, Craig Dodson 1992

This is a great beginner lead and 14 clips keep it manageable all the way. Climb the pillar on the left side of the big crack and then move right, past a set of intermediate anchors and continue on up.

18. PREYING MANTEL 5.10a ★

FA: Kevin Pogue, Ian Krueger 1993

This attractive route features a short section of steep climbing near the bottom and then the pillar lies back some and the standard eases considerably. A short second pitch leads to the rim but doesn't offer the quality of the first. Rappel from either pitch.

Banks Lake

Perhaps better known as a winter ice-climbing destination, the granite crags around the northern end of Banks Lake provide a unique opportunity for granite cragging in the desert. While basalt is usually thought of as the predominant stone in eastern Washington, the coulees in some cases have been scoured down to reveal the granite bedrock beneath. Running from east to west and crossing the north end of the lake, these granite formations provide good climbs accessible from traditional walking approaches as well as by canoe. (A popular approach has been to arrive with a canoe, secure a place in one of several campsites, and venture forth each day to climb, paddle, swim, and explore directly from the boat.)

A number of difficult sport routes have been established around the area, most notably on Roadside Rock and in nearby Northrup Canyon. Much of the rock visible west of this area has been explored in past ages.

The Banks Lake area, being just about in the center of the state geographically, is quite arid and bad weather often consists of high wind and scudding grey clouds with little actual precipitation. Rattlesnakes are fairly common, however boating to climbs instead of walking minimizes the exposure. Be alert on crag tops and anytime you're walking around. Personal watercraft are much more of a presence here than in earlier years, and on major holidays the once awesome quiet has been transformed by the whine of two-cycle engines and the pop of opening beers.

Still, narrow channels amid flooded orange

Leland Windham finding out all details on Bassomatic

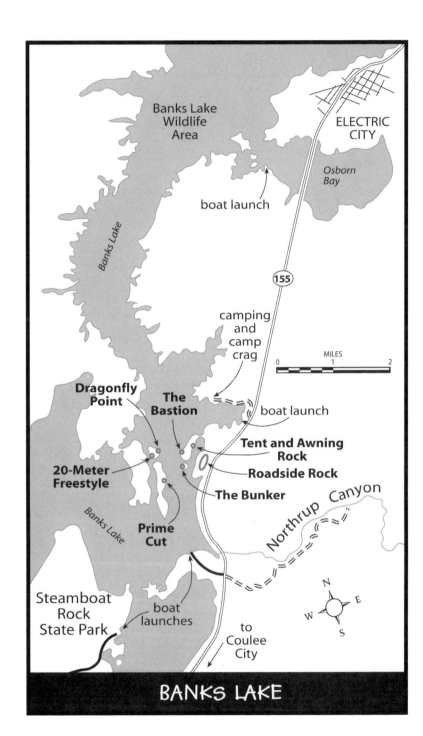

Banks Lake
Wildlife
Area

ELECTRIC
CITY

Osborn
Bay

boat launch

Banks Lake

155

camping
and
camp
crag

MILES
0   1   2

**Dragonfly
Point**

boat launch

**The
Bastion**

**Tent and Awning
Rock**

**20-Meter
Freestyle**

Roadside Rock

The Bunker

Banks Lake

Northrup Canyon

**Prime
Cut**

Steamboat
Rock
State Park

boat
launches

to
Coulee
City

N
W   E
S

BANKS LAKE

crags, secluded beaches in little stone bays, water comfortable enough to swim in, and great granite to climb on: it's all here at Banks Lake!

BANKS LAKE BETA

Drive time from Seattle ▲ 4 hours

Drive time from Spokane ▲ 1 3/4 hours

Approach times ▲ 15–30 minutes by canoe

Getting there: Signs for the Grand Coulee Dam (just north of Banks Lake) mark the entire route north from I-90. From I-90, 2 miles east of George, take SR 283 northeast toward Ephrata. At Ephrata it becomes SR 28, which you still follow in a northeasterly direction until its junction with SR 17 at Soap Lake. SR 17 continues to the northeast, traveling up the Lower Grand Coulee and passing the spectacular Dry Falls just south of Banks Lake itself. SR 17 joins US 2 at the southwest corner of the lake; follow US 2 across the earthen dam and into Coulee City. From Coulee City take SR 155 north toward Electric City and Grand Coulee Dam. When you see signs for Steamboat Rock State Park and Northrup Canyon you will be close. One of the campgrounds and a boat launch are just a couple of miles south of Electric City, to the west of the highway.

Season: Precipitation is rare here, and bad weather usually means cold temperatures and high winds, which can be frightening in a canoe. The area contains some of the Washington's more outstanding ice climbing in the winter months. Rock climbing is possible from April to late October, although midsummer is staggeringly hot.

Regulations: The campgrounds require a modest fee.

Camping: There are two campgrounds north of Steamboat Rock. Both are accessed to the left (west), just north of Roadside Rock. The southern one is the boat lauch and is often noisy; the second one (shown on map) is preferred. Another campground is located 2 miles farther north at Osborn Bay and may be the only one open in early season.

Concessions: Electric City and Grand Coulee immediately to the north provide all services, including lodging.

Climbing type: Traditional cracks, mixed routes, and sport climbs. Many are accessible only with a canoe or boat.

Rock type: Granite

Gear: Medium traditional rack with gear to 4 inches. Extra dark-colored slings/rappel gear, 2 ropes or one 60-meter rope, 16- to 18-foot open canoe, cooler, mask, fins, snorkel.

The Bastion

This area offers some of the best examples of canoe-based climbing and is also the only boat-in area that is also accessible on foot. Tent and Awning Rock is located just across the isthmus that leads out to the Bastion and is also accessible by walking. The routes are presented from left to right across the face and around into the cut between the Bastion and the Bunker.

Descent: Bolted anchors exist at the top of *Bassomatic*, *Half-Bassed*, and *Bucolic Bass*, allowing for rappels back into your canoe from all these routes.

1. HOOK, LINE AND SINKER 5.10a ★★
FA: David Whitelaw, Dick Erb 1984

A thought-provoking climb on the left margin of the rock. Climb out of the boat and up through a wedge-shaped niche. Pass an overhang and continue straight up to a spectacular series of technical moves that pass a bolt and finish the route. 3 clips plus gear to 2 1/2 inches. Rappel.

2. BASSOMATIC 5.9 ★★★

FA: Chris Greyell, David Whitelaw 1984

The obvious crack line, straight up the middle of the slab, *Bassomatic* is a great climb that shouldn't be missed. On the first ascent, Greyell trapped a sleeping bat in a pocket with a #2.5 Friend, providing quite a surprise for his second as the cam got removed! Gear to 3 inches. Rappel.

3. HALF-BASSED 5.8 PG ★★

FA: David Whitelaw, Chris Greyell 1984

Another sweet line. Climb some committing moves with rather tricky

pro to reach the crack. From there it's a romp and gets bigger the higher you go. Gear to 3½ inches. Rappel.

4. PERFECT BASSER 5.11b ★
FFA: Steve Risse, Dave Tower 1984
Not really in the scope of this book, the route's generally sustained at 5.10a/b with a super cruxy finish.

5. BUCOLIC BASS 5.9+ ★★
FA: Dave Whitelaw, Chris Greyell 1984
Around the corner several hundred feet right of the previous routes, the *BB* climbs a narrow, reddish buttress of rock that almost reaches the water. Climb out of the canoe just right of the buttress bottom and climb a committing series of moves some distance to the first bolt. Clever use of slings gains natural pro at midheight and a couple of bolts protect the last exposed and cruxy moves up and right. Take several pieces of gear to 2 inches and extra slings to hitch the horn. Rappel.

Tent and Awning Rock

This is the small, clean blob of rock located in the narrow bay that almost separates the back side of the Bastion from the mainland. In fact, older maps show the Bastion as an island, although now a swampy isthmus connects it to the shore. These two short climbs on great rock make for a fun excursion in the quiet little bay; a respite from the whine of watercraft is welcome. To reach Tent and Awning paddle most of the way into the bay and find this rock on the left (west) bank.

1. THE VESTIBULE 5.7 ★
FA: Dave Whitelaw, Chris Greyell 1997
Balance up the eerie edge past 2 clips and savor the brevity of it all. There are bolts at the top, but please walk down and avoid leaving slings.

2. AFTER THE GOLD RUSH 5.10b ★★
FA: Chris Greyell, Dave Whitelaw 1997
This is the short bundle of joy up the striking gold wall adjacent to

Leland Windham on After The Gold Rush

TENT AND AWNING

The Vestibule. Features steep hauling on "killer flatheads." 4 clips, rap hangers at the top.

The Bunker

This is the small, blocky island just south of the Bastion. The climbs are located on the west face, near the southern tip.

1. THE EMERGENCE OF MAN 5.9
FA: Don Brooks, Dick Erb, Chris Greyell, David Whitelaw 1984
This follows the obvious multisized (wide) crack/chimney at the back of the short waterway. Somewhat technical and harder than it looks. Gear to 4 1/2 inches. Rappel to boat.

2. CHRIS AND DAVE'S 5.10a ★★
FA: Chris Greyell, David Whitelaw 1986
This climb is 20 feet right of the previous route and features exciting

moves up seams and cracks before it picks up a few bolts. It then powers up and left, around the roof, with some athletic, exterior moves. Gear to 2¹/2 inches. Rappel to boat.

Prime Cut Area

This striking rock is visible across the water west of Roadside Rock. An obvious, shallow, right-facing flake/corner shoots up the wall to a bolted anchor, making for one of the sweetest crack climbs at Banks. Beach the canoe near the bottom of the route and belay in standard fashion, i.e., on the ground beneath the route.

1. PRIME CUT 5.10a ★★★
FA: Don Brooks, David Whitelaw

This is exterior, athletic, Yosemite-style crack climbing. Make a few lieback and undercling moves up and right past a big cam placement (crux) to reach somewhat easier ground, and then jam and stem the remaining distance to the bolted anchors. Gear to 4 inches. Rappel.

Leland Windham and Jennifer Keller on the cruxy start of Prime Cut

Dragonfly Point

Dragonfly is the rounded, reddish bluff forming the northern corner of the channel that leads in to the 20-Meter Freestyle Area. Beach the canoe about 40 feet right (north) of the climb and hike over to a standard-style climb that starts on the slabs just above the water. There are great views across the lake to the basalt cliffs from here.

1. DRAGONFLY IN AMBER 5.8 ★
FA: David Whitelaw, Jennifer Keller, April 2003

Beach the canoe and carry your gear 40 or 50 feet left to the start of this one. Crux is near the bottom. Pass 4 or 5 bolts to a chain anchor. Rappel.

20-Meter Freestyle Area

Paddle west past Dragonfly Point several hundred feet into the narrow channel and locate this inviting crag on the right. Direct sunshine can make the Freestyle a blast furnace in some conditions, but the shallow waters and small rock islands below make for outstanding swimming and lounging. All the routes on this crag are pretty high-quality crack climbs and none of them has any bolts save the anchors at the top.

20-METER FREESTYLE AREA

1. THE SPITZ MARK 5.9 ★

FA: Dave Whitelaw, Chris Greyell 1986

This is the leftmost crack system on the rock. Step out of the canoe and find a ledge about 5 feet above the water to belay from. Climb the crack, up and right, to some large cracks and then move back left to cracks that reach the top. Gear to 3¹/2 inches. Rappel.

2. BUTTERFLY CRACK 5.10a PG ★

FA: Don Brooks, David Whitelaw 1984

Follow the right-trending crack till it peters out a bit shy of the top. Gear to 4 inches. Rappel.

3. DON'S CRACK 5.10a ★★

FA: Don Brooks, Chris Syrjala, David Whitelaw 1984

This was the original route on the crag, straight out of the boat and up the middle. Fairly sustained and requiring all manner of technique from wide to small. Gear to 4 inches. Rappel.

4. 20-METER FREESTYLE 5.10a PG ★★★

FA: David Whitelaw, Steve Scott 1985

This intimidating climb requires thoughtful gear placements and has technical sequences all the way up. Small brass pieces provide protection near the finish of the climb. Gear to 2¹/2 inches including small wireds and perhaps a screamer or two for added security. Rappel.

Roadside Rock

Roadside Rock is the most obvious of all the granite formations, although the novelty factor of other more obscure rocks made it among the last to see any development. The rock seems to mark the demarcation line between east and west. East of this point most development has been by Spokane climbers and west of it much has been done by groups from Seattle. There are more than forty routes at Roadside, many of them at higher grades. What follows is just a sampling of lines on the south end of the rock.

Park about 4 miles south of Electric City, on the west side of the road and more or less right in front of the rock. Wander over to the left to reach the featured climbs. All the Roadside Rock routes are accessed on foot.

(bolts not shown)

ROADSIDE ROCK

1. RED ARÊTE 5.9 ★★

High-quality textured stone and super position on the obvious arête makes this an area classic. The bolts seem oddly positioned but there are enough to keep it sane. 10 clips and rap station.

2. CARROT TOP 5.9 ★★

Just left of the *Red Arête* is an ominous off-width with a bolted 5.12 route leading out of the left side of it. Around the corner to the left is a pretty orange face with two routes. *Carrot Top* takes an exciting line near the right edge of the slab. Six clips lead to open cold-shuts. It is strongly advised to run your rope through the shuts and then move 8 feet left and finish with the real anchor at the top of *Reflecting Depths*. Rappel.

3. REFLECTING DEPTHS IMBIBE 5.9 ★★

FA: Leland Windham
Start just left of *Carrot Top* and work your way up the fabulous stone past 6 clips. Rappel from the chains.

4. RED HOT 5.8 ★

Cross a scree gully left of the *Red Arête* area and look for a shining white slab just behind a large pine tree. Rather brief... but fun! 3 clips to rap anchor.

CULTURE CLUB

Technically this is part of the west face of Roadside Rock although it is the only part of the rock that is best accessed using boat-in climbing strategies. From a point beneath the large tree in front of the *Red Hot* route a nasty looking chimney/gully leads down west to the water. On the water face of the rock immediately north of the bottom of the gully are three well-bolted 5.9ish/10a routes (*Peace, Love,* and *Harmony*) that are very fun and more easily reached from the comfort of your watercraft.

Appendixes

A. EMERGENCY MEDICAL FACILITIES

Anacortes (Mount Erie)
Island Hospital
1211 24th Street
(360) 299-1300

Concrete (Washington Pass)
East Valley Medical
Main Street in Concrete
911 or (360) 853-8183

Leavenworth
Cascade General Hospital
817 Commercial Street
(509) 548-5815

Grand Coulee (Banks Lake)
Coulee Community Hospital
411 Fortuyn Road
(509) 633-1753

Monroe (Index and Static Point)
Valley General Hospital
14701 179th Avenue SE
(360) 794-7497

Mount Vernon (Darrington)
Skagit Valley Hospital
1415 East Kincaid
(360) 428-2165

Quincy (Frenchman Coulee)
Quincy Valley Medical
908 10th Avenue SW
(509) 787-3531

Snoqualmie (Exit 38)
Snoqualmie Valley Hospital
9575 Ethan Wade Way SE
(425) 831-2300

Wenatchee
Central Washington Hospital
1300 Fuller Street
(509) 662-1511

Yakima (Tieton River)
Yakima Valley Memorial Hospital
28th and Tieton Drive
(509) 575-8000

B. WILDERNESS FIRST-AID INSTRUCTION

Wilderness Medical Associates: *www.wildmed.com*
SOLO Wilderness Medicine: *www.soloschools.com*
Sirius Wilderness Medicine: *www.siriusmed.com*

C. ROUTES BY DIFFICULTY

5.0–5.3
The Gully 5.0
Right Crack Route 5.2
The Scramble 5.0
Trouble Maker 5.0
Western Front 5.3
Where the Sidewalk
    Ends 5.1

5.4
Black Jack
Good Timer
Mandatory Suicide
Mars Rover
The North Face of the
    Eiger
Porpoise
The Right Stuff
Saber
Slacker
Sunset

5.5
The 5.5 Route
Flammable Pajamas
Get the Pever Fever
Gibson's Crack
Leaning Crack
Lust For Dust
Nimrod's Nemesis
Rap Route
Rough Boys
Shake it Don't Break It
So Easy I Forgot to
    Laugh
Sumptuous Bits
Updrafts to Heaven

5.6
Archies
Arctic Rose
Beckey Route (Liberty
    Bell)
The Blue Hole

Boardwalk
Booby Vinton
Cat Burglar
Catatonic
Crack in the Back
Diagonal
Easy Street
Eating Dust
Eating Rocks
Edge of Mistakes
The Fault
Feather in My Cap
Galileo
The Great Northern
    Slab
Homo Erectus
Jenny's Reef
The Joker
Left Crack Route
Level Head
Lucky Arms
Midway
Midway Direct
Mom, There's Pink In
    My Burger
National Velvet
Normal Route
Notch Route
The Open Book
Peaceful Warrior
Ring Pin Crack
South Arête II, (SEWS)
Strokin' the Chicken
Sunrise
Swerve
The Tunnel
Velvasheen
Windward

5.7
Altar of Sacrifice
The Asteroid Crack

Baptized in the River
    Black
Beckey Route
    (Frenchman)
Big Tree Two
Bottoms Up
The Chossmaster
Corner Flash
The Crack
The Cutting Edge
Diretissima
The Dog Ate My Topo
Ground Hog Day
In the Middle Again
The Jagged Edge
Jerry Was a Race Car
    Driver
Jiffy Pop
Hanging on a String
    Theory
Kiss of the Crowbar
Lasting Impression
Light-Headed Again
Little-Known Wonder
Mexican Fiesta
Mickey Mantel
Needle Magnet
Old Crack
Pete's Possum Palace
Psycho
Ruffled Feathers
Rug Monkey
Seven Virgins and a
    Mule
Snaffle Baffler
So Funny I Forgot to
    Rope Up
Somewhere on Earth
Swarm
Tyndall's Terror
Under the Boredwalk

The Vestibule
Wild Child
Your Sister
Zig Zag
5.7+
Mush Maker
North Face (Concord Tower)
X-Factor
5.8
American Warrior
Attack of the Butter Knives
Austrian Slab
Big Tree One
Black Fly
Canary
Catacombs
Catapult
Cave Route
Century
Clip 'em or Skip 'em
Closeness to Forever as the Soil Bleeds Black
Crossing the Threshold
Delightful Cacoffiny Funneled Within
Diagonal Direct
Don Coyote
Dragonfly in Amber
Ed's Jam
False Impression
Finishing Touch
First Blood
Givler's Crack
Glom Don
Half-Bassed
Impartial Eclipse
Insomniac
Jack of Diamonds
Jesus Saves
Justified Ancients of Mu Mu

The Lizard
Loaves of Fun
No Room for Squares
Nocturnal Remission
The Nose
Old Grey Mare
Orangekist
Overexposure
Party in Your Pants
Patriot Crack
Potholes (Peshastin)
Proctology
Rappel Grapple
The Rash
Ray Auld Memorial Route
Red Hot
The Reflector
The Rod of God
The Scene Is Clean
Serpent
South Face
Spring Fever
Thank God for Big Jugs
Tongue in Cheek
Touching the Sky
Tree Shadow
Twin Cracks
Unfinished Business
Upper Notch Route
The Uprising
Vantage Point
Velvet Elvis
Vertigo
Voyager 2
West Face (Grand Central Tower)
West Face/Southwest Rib (SEWS)
Windsong
Windward Direct
Winter Rushing In
5.8+
The Blueberry Route

Butter Brickle
Cruel Harvest
Dogleg Crack
Golden Delicious
Grey Whale
Half Fast
Hallowed Ground
King of Diamonds
Magic Bus
Peace, Love and Rope
Queen of Diamonds
Saints
Voyager 1
5.9
A Game of Inches
Absolutely Nothing
Astral Projection
Astroglide
Baseball Nut
Bassomatic
The Bone
Cactus Love
Carrot Top
Charlie Chan's Number One Suspect
Classic Crack
Contraction Action
Cross-Eyed and Painless
Damnation Crack
Direct East Buttress (SEWS) (5.9 A1)
The Emergence of Man
Empire State
Endless Bliss
Godzilla
Green Velvet
Gun Rack
Highway Route
Hurly-Burly
Idiot's Delight
Jam Exam
Knife in the Toaster
The Kone

Lightning Crack
Lost Charms
Lost Souls
Magnetic Anomaly
Me Too
Mistress Jane's Chains
The Mounties Big-O
Nettlesome
New Creation
99 Grit
Northwest Corner
  (NEWS)
November Glaze
Nutty Buddy
Orbit
Outer Space
Pat's Crack
Primordial Blues
Princely Ambitions
Red Arête
Reflecting Depths
  Imbibe
Safe Sex
Satan's Little Helper
Scissor Man
Sheena Is a Punk
  Rocker
Shin Smasher
Sinkerville
Ski Track Crack
Slakin'
So Funny I Forgot to
  Laugh
Sobriety
Some Drugs
The Spitz Mark
Springboard
Starless in Vantage
Tangled Up in Blue
Taurus
Throbbing Gristle
Tiers
Till Broad Daylight
Toxic Shock

Underground Economy
Westward Ho!
Whipsaw
5.9+
Bucket List
Bucolic Bass
Celestial Groove
Cloud Nine
Crack of Doom
Deception
Dirt Circus
Dreamer
Kick Start
Meat Grinder
Northwest Passage
Off Ramp
Redemption
Render Us Weightless
Ride 'em Cowboy
Scarface
Silent Running
Slender Thread
Thriller Pillar Direct
5.10a
Air Guitar
American Pie
Big Tree 2000
The Black Caboose
The Blockhead
Blood Blister
Breakfast of
  Champions
Butterfly Crack
Cajun Queen
Carnage before
  Bedtime
Chica Rapida
Chris and Dave's
Cornucopia
Cowboys Don't Cry
Desert Shield
Don's Crack
Elation at the End of
  Eternity

Fakin' It
Fraggled Pickle
Freedom Fighter
Fuddhat
Gentry's Face
George and Martha
Honky's Lament
Hook, Line and Sinker
Inca Roads
Intimidator
Libra Crack
Medicine Man
My Ex-Wife
Nightbird
No Holds Barred
On Eagles Wings
Phone Threats
Playin' Possum
Pony Keg
Potholes (Erie)
Preying Mantel
Prime Cut
Revolver
Salmon Song
Silhouettes
Stance or Dance
Star and Crescent
Troglodyte in Flight
20th Century Clock
20-Meter Freestyle
West Face (NEWS)
  (5.10/1A)
Wild Thing
Windwalker
5.10b
After the Gold Rush
Angel
Asymptotic
Bicycling to
  Bellingham
The Cashman
Dance of the Shaman
Harpoonist
Luke 9:25

Milky Way
On Line
The Pillar
Pucker Up
Satan's Wagon
Secret Passage
Skiing @ 49 North
Son of a Pitch
Subliminal
Terminator
Total Soul

Well Preserved
5.10c
Chain Smokin'
Hardening of the
 Arteries
The Joke
Penny Lane
Z-Crack
5.10d
Abyss behind the Gaze
 of Humanity

Lethal Weapon
Subversive
5.11
Direct East Buttress
 (SEWS)
Teenage Lobotomy
West Face (NEWS)
5.11b
Perfect Basser

D. ROUTES BY TYPE

SLAB ROUTES
American Pie 5.10a
Baseball Nut 5.9
Big Tree One 5.8
Black Fly 5.8
The Blueberry Route
 5.8+
Bucolic Bass 5.9+
Cajun Queen 5.10a
The Cashman 5.10b
Charlie Chan's Number
 One Suspect 5.9
Diagonal 5.6
Diagonal Direct 5.8
Dirt Circus 5.9+
Dragonfly in Amber 5.8
Endless Bliss 5.9–
Fakin' It 5.10a
The 5.5 Route 5.5
Fuddhat 5.10a
Green Velvet 5.8+
Grey Whale 5.8+
Harpoonist 5.10b
Hook, Line and Sinker
 5.10a
The Kone 5.9
Luke 9:25 5.10a/b
Magic Bus 5.8+
National Velvet 5.6
The North Face of the

Eiger 5.4
Northwest Passage 5.9+
Nutty Buddy 5.9
On Line 5.10a/b
Perfect Basser 5.11b
The Pillar 5.10b
Porpoise 5.4
Potholes 5.8
 (Peshastin)
The Rash 5.8
Revolver 5.10a
Safe Sex IV, 5.9
Serpent 5.8
Silent Running 5.9+
Stance or Dance 5.10a
Star and Crescent 5.10a
Sunset 5.4
Till Broad Daylight 5.9
Total Soul 5.10a/b
Under the Boredwalk
 5.7
Voyager 1 5.8+
Voyager 2 5.8
West Face 5.8 (Grand
 Central Tower)
West Face (NEWS)
 5.10 A1
Westward Ho! 5.9
SPORT ROUTES
A Game of Inches 5.9

Absolutely Nothing
 5.9–
Abyss behind the Gaze
 of Humanity 5.10d
After the Gold Rush
 5.10b
Altar of Sacrifice 5.7
American Warrior 5.8
Asymptotic 5.10b
Attack of the Butter
 Knives 5.8
Austrian Slab 5.8
Baptized in the River
 Black 5.7
Beckey Route
 (Frenchman) 5.7
Bicycling to
 Bellingham 5.10b
The Black Caboose
 5.10a
The Blockhead 5.10a
Blood Blister 5.10a
Boardwalk 5.6
Booby Vinton 5.6
Bottoms Up 5.7
Bucket List 5.9+
Carnage before
 Bedtime 5.10a
Catatonic 5.6
Chain Smokin' 5.10c

Carrot Top 5.9
Chica Rapida 5.10a
Clip 'em or Skip 'em 5.8
The Chossmaster 5.7
Closeness to Forever as the Soil Bleeds Black 5.8
Cowboys Don't Cry 5.10a
Dance of the Shaman 5.10b
Delightful Cacoffiny Funneled Within 5.8
Desert Shield 5.10a
The Dog Ate My Topo 5.7
Don Coyote 5.8
Easy Street 5.6
Eating Dust 5.6
Eating Rocks 5.6
Edge of Mistakes 5.6
Elation at the End of Eternity 5.10–
Endless Bliss 5.9–
False Impression 5.8
Feather in My Cap 5.6
Finishing Touch 5.8
Flammable Pajamas 5.5
Fraggled Pickle 5.10a
Freedom Fighter 5.10a
Galileo 5.6
Get the Pever Fever 5.5
Glom Don 5.8
Golden Delicious 5.8+
Gun Rack 5.9
Half Fast 5.8+
Hallowed Ground 5.8+
Hanging on a String Theory 5.7
Hardening of the Arteries 5.10c
Heartbeat 5.9
Homo Erectus 5.6

Hurly-Burly 5.9
Impartial Eclipse 5.8
In the Middle Again 5.7
Insomniac 5.8
Intimidator 5.10a
The Jagged Edge 5.7
Jerry Was a Race Car Driver 5.7
Jesus Saves 5.8
Jiffy Pop 5.7
The Joke 5.10c
Justified Ancients of Mu Mu 5.8
Kiss of the Crowbar 5.7
Knife in the Toaster 5.9
Lethal Weapon 5.10d
Light-Headed Again 5.7
Lucky Arms 5.6
Magnetic Anomaly 5.9
Mandatory Suicide 5.4
Mars Rover 5.4
Me Too 5.9
Medicine Man 5.10a
Mexican Fiesta 5.7
Milky Way 5.10b
Mistress Jane's Chains 5.9
Mom, There's Pink in my Burger 5.6
My Ex-Wife 5.10a
Needle Magnet 5.7
Nettlesome 5.9
New Creation 5.9
Nightbird 5.10a
99 Grit 5.9
No Holds Barred 5.10a
Nocturnal Remission 5.8
November Glaze 5.9
Off Ramp 5.9+
On Eagles Wings 5.10a
Orangekist 5.8
Peaceful Warrior 5.6

Pete's Possum Palace 5.7
Phone Threats 5.10a
Playin' Possum 5.10a
Potholes (Erie) 5.10a
Preying Mantel 5.10a
Primordial Blues 5.9
Pucker Up 5.10b
Red Arête 5.9
Red Hot 5.8
Redemption 5.9+
The Reflector 5.8
Ride 'em Cowboy 5.9+
The Rod of God 5.8
Ruffled Feathers 5.7
Rug Monkey 5.7
Satan's Little Helper 5.9
Satan's Wagon 5.10b
Scarface 5.9+
The Scene Is Clean 5.8
Scissor Man 5.9
Secret Passage 5.10b
Shake it Don't Break It 5.5
Shin Smasher 5.9
Silhouettes 5.10a
Sinkerville 5.9
Skiing @ 49 North 5.10b
Slakin' 5.9
Slender Thread 5.9+
Snaffle Baffler 5.7
So Easy I Forgot to Laugh 5.5
So Funny I Forgot to Laugh 5.9
So Funny I Forgot to Rope Up 5.7
Sobriety 5.9
Some Drugs 5.9
Starless in Vantage 5.9
Subliminal 5.10b
Subversive 5.10d
Sumptuous Bits 5.5

Sunrise 5.6
Super Squish 5.10c
Swarm 5.7
Swerve 5.6
Terminator 5.10b
Throbbing Gristle 5.9
Touching the Sky 5.8
Underground Economy 5.9
Unfinished Business 5.8
Updrafts to Heaven 5.5
The Uprising 5.8
Vantage Point 5.8
Velvet Elvis 5.8
The Vestibule 5.7
Well Preserved 5.10b
Where the Sidewalk Ends 5.1
Whipsaw 5.9
Wild Thing 5.10a
Windsong 5.8
Windwalker 5.10a
Winter Rushing In 5.8
Your Sister 5.7

CRACK CLIMBS

Air Guitar 5.10a
The Asteroid Crack 5.7
Bassomatic 5.9
Breakfast of Champions 5.10a
Butter Brickle 5.8+
Butterfly Crack 5.10a
Cactus Love 5.9
Celestial Groove 5.9+
Classic Crack 5.9
Cloud Nine 5.9+
Contraction Action 5.9
Corner Flash 5.7
The Crack 5.7
Crack in the Back 5.6
Crack of Doom 5.9+
Cross-Eyed and Painless 5.9

Crossing the Threshold 5.8
The Cutting Edge 5.7
Damnation Crack 5.9
Deception 5.9+
Dogleg Crack 5.8+
Don's Crack 5.10a
Ed's Jam 5.8
Empire State 5.9
First Blood 5.8
George and Martha 5.10a
Gibson's Crack 5.5
Givler's Crack 5.8
Godzilla 5.9
Good Timer 5.4
The Great Northern Slab 5.6
Idiot's Delight 5.9
Inca Roads 5.10a
Jam Exam 5.9
Leaning Crack 5.5
Level Head 5.6
Libra Crack 5.10a
Lightning Crack 5.9
The Lizard 5.8
Loaves of Fun 5.8
Lost Souls 5.9
Meat Grinder 5.9+
The Mounties Big-O 5.9
Mush Maker 5.7+
No Room for Squares 5.8
Northwest Corner III, 5.9
Old Crack 5.7
Party in Your Pants 5.8
Patriot Crack 5.8
Pat's Crack 5.9
Pony Keg 5.10a
Prime Cut 5.10a
Princely Ambitions 5.9
Proctology 5.8

Psycho 5.7
Rap Route 5.5
Rappel Grapple II, 5.8
Ray Auld Memorial Route 5.8
Rough Boys 5.5
Salmon Song 5.10a
Seven Virgins and a Mule 5.7
Sheena Is a Punk Rocker 5.9
Ski Track Crack 5.9
Somewhere on Earth 5.7
Son of a Pitch 5.10b
Strokin' the Chicken 5.6
Tangled Up in Blue 5.9
Taurus 5.9
Teenage Lobotomy 5.11a
Thank God for Big Jugs 5.8
Tiers 5.9
Tongue in Cheek 5.8
Toxic Shock 5.9
Troglodyte in Flight 5.10a
Twin Cracks 5.8
Velvasheen 5.6
Vertigo 5.8
Western Front 5.3
Wild Child 5.7
X-Factor 5.7+
Z-Crack 5.10c
Zig Zag 5.7

TRAD ROUTES

Angel 5.10b
Archies 5.6
Arctic Rose 5.6
Astral Projection 5.9
Astroglide 5.9
Beckey Route (Liberty Bell) 5.6

Big Tree Two 5.7
Big Tree 2000 5.10a
Black Jack 5.4
The Blue Hole 5.6
The Bone 5.9
Canary 5.8
Cat Burglar 5.6
Catacombs 5.8
Catapult 5.8
Cave Route 5.8
Century 5.8
Chris and Dave's 5.10a
Cornucopia 5.10a
Cruel Harvest 5.8+
Direct East Buttress
   (SEWS) 5.9 A1
Diretissima 5.7
Dreamer 5.9+
The Emergence of Man
   5.9
The Fault 5.6
The Gully 5.0
Half-Bassed 5.8
Highway Route 5.9
Honky's Lament 5.10a
Jack of Diamonds 5.8
Jenny's Reef 5.6
The Joker 5.6
Kick Start 5.9+
King of Diamonds 5.8+
Lasting Impression 5.7-
   5.10
Left Crack Route 5.6
Little-Known Wonder

5.7
Midway 5.6
Midway Direct 5.6
Mountaineers Route
   5.2
Nimrod's Nemesis 5.5
Normal Route 5.6
North Face (Concord
   Tower) 5.7+
Notch Route 5.6
Old Grey Mare 5.8
The Open Book 5.6
Orbit 5.9
Outer Space 5.9
Overexposure 5.8
Peace, Love and Rope
   5.8+
Penny Lane 5.10c
Render Us Weightless
   5.9+
Right Crack Route 5.2
The Right Stuff 5.4
Ring Pin Crack 5.6
Saber 5.4
Saints 5.8+
The Scramble 5.0
Slacker 5.4
South Arête (SEWS) 5.6
South Face (Castle
   Rock) 5.8
The Spitz Mark 5.9
Springboard 5.9
Southwest Couloir
   (SEWS)

Thank God for Big Jugs
   5.8
Thriller Pillar Direct
   5.9+
The Tunnel 5.6
Tree Shadow 5.8
20th Century Clock
   5.10a A2
20-Meter Freestyle
   5.10a
Tyndall's Terror 5.7
Upper Notch Route 5.8
West Face (NEWS)
   5.11a
West Face/Southwest
   Rib (SEWS) 5.8
Windward 5.6
Windward Direct 5.8

TOP ROPES

Gentry's Face 5.10
Lasting Impression
   5.7–5.10
Mickey Mantel 5.7
The Nose 5.8
Queen of Diamonds
   5.8+

SOME AID

City Park C1
Direct East Buttress
   (SEWS) 5.9 A1
20th Century Clock
   5.10a A2
West Face (NEWS)
   5.10 A1

E. ROUTES BY QUALITY

★★★

Air Guitar 5.10a
Austrian Slab 5.8
Bassomatic 5.9
Beckey Route (Liberty Bell) 5.6
The Blueberry Route 5.8+
Booby Vinton 5.6
Breakfast of Champions 5.10a
Bucket List 5.9+
Canary 5.8
Celestial Groove 5.9+
City Park C1
Classic Crack 5.9
Cloud Nine 5.9+
The Cutting Edge 5.7
Direct East Buttress (SEWS) 5.9 A1
Don Coyote 5.8
Dreamer 5.9+
Ed's Jam 5.8
Elation at the End of Eternity 5.10–
Endless Bliss 5.9–
Fuddhat 5.10a
George and Martha 5.10a
Givler's Crack 5.8
Godzilla 5.9
The Great Northern Slab 5.6
Inca Roads 5.10a
Kiss of the Crowbar 5.7
The Kone 5.9
Libra Crack 5.10a
Lightning Crack 5.9
Lost Charms 5.7 A0 (or 5.9)

Midway 5.6
On Line 5.10a/b
Orbit 5.9
Outer Space 5.9
Party in Your Pants 5.8
Pony Keg 5.10a
Potholes 5.8 (Peshastin)
Prime Cut 5.10a
The Rash 5.8
Ride 'em Cowboy 5.9+
Saber 5.4
Salmon Song 5.10a
Satan's Wagon 5.10b
Serpent 5.8
Silent Running 5.9+
Ski Track Crack 5.9
Slakin' 5.9
Slender Thread 5.9+
Sunrise 5.6
Throbbing Gristle 5.9
Total Soul 5.10a/b or 5.11a
Toxic Shock 5.9
20-Meter Freestyle 5.10a
The Uprising 5.8
Velvet Elvis 5.8
Vertigo 5.8
Voyager 1 5.8+
Voyager 2 5.8
West Face (Grand Central Tower) 5.8
West Face/Southwest Rib (SEWS) 5.8
Western Front 5.3
Westward Ho! 5.9
Whipsaw 5.9
Windsong 5.8
X-Factor 5.7+

★★

Absolutely Nothing 5.9–
Abyss behind the Gaze of Humanity 5.10d
After the Gold Rush 5.10b
American Pie 5.10a
Angel 5.10b
Arctic Rose 5.6
Astral Projection 5.9
Astroglide 5.9
Asymptotic 5.10b
Baseball Nut 5.9
Beckey Route (Frenchman) 5.7
Bicycling to Bellingham 5.10b
Big Tree 2000 5.10a
Blood Blister 5.10a
Boardwalk 5.6
The Bone 5.9
Bucolic Bass 5.9+
Carrot Top 5.9
Catapult 5.8
Chica Rapida 5.10a
The Chossmaster 5.7
Chris and Dave's 5.10a
Clip 'em or Skip 'em 5.8
Cornucopia 5.10a
Crack of Doom 5.9+
Cross-Eyed and Painless 5.9
Crossing the Threshold 5.8
Damnation Crack 5.9
Delightful Cacoffiny Funneled Within 5.8
Desert Shield 5.10a

Diagonal 5.6
Diagonal Direct 5.8
Dirt Circus 5.9+
The Dog Ate My Topo
   5.7
Don's Crack 5.10a
Empire State 5.9
Fakin' It 5.10a
False Impression 5.8
Finishing Touch 5.8
First Blood 5.8
Freedom Fighter 5.10a
Galileo 5.6
Glom Don 5.8
Golden Delicious 5.8+
Green Velvet 5.8+
The Gully 5.0
Gun Rack 5.9
Half-Bassed 5.8
Hallowed Ground 5.8+
Hardening of the
   Arteries 5.10c
Heartbeat 5.9
Hook, Line and Sinker
   5.10a
Hurly-Burly 5.9
Impartial Eclipse 5.8
Insomniac 5.8
Intimidator 5.10a
Jack of Diamonds 5.8
The Jagged Edge 5.7
Jam Exam 5.9
Jesus Saves 5.8
Justified Ancients of
   Mu Mu 5.8
King of Diamonds 5.8+
The Lizard 5.8
Loaves of Fun 5.8
Luke 9:25 5.10a/b
Mandatory Suicide 5.4
Mars Rover 5.4
Medicine Man 5.10a
Mexican Fiesta 5.7
Midway Direct 5.6

Milky Way 5.10b
Mush Maker 5.7+
Nettlesome 5.9
Nightbird 5.10a
99 Grit 5.9
Nocturnal Remission
   5.8
Northwest Corner
   (NEWS) 5.9
November Glaze 5.9
Nutty Buddy 5.9
Old Grey Mare 5.8
On Eagles Wings 5.10a
Orangekist 5.8
Peace, Love and Rope
   5.8+
Peaceful Warrior 5.6
Penny Lane 5.10c
Pete's Possum Palace 5.7
The Pillar 5.10b
Princely Ambitions 5.9
Rappel Grapple II, 5.8
Red Arête 5.9
Reflecting Depths
   Imbibe 5.9
Revolver 5.10a
The Rod of God 5.8
Safe Sex 5.9
Saints 5.8+
Satan's Little Helper 5.9
The Scene Is Clean 5.8
Seven Virgins and a
   Mule 5.7
Silhouettes 5.10a
Some Drugs 5.9
South Arête (SEWS) 5.6
Southwest Couloir
   (SEWS)
Springboard 5.9
Star and Crescent 5.10a
Strokin' the Chicken
   5.6
Tangled Up in Blue 5.9
Taurus 5.9

Terminator 5.10b
Till Broad Daylight 5.9
Tongue in Cheek 5.8
Touching the Sky 5.8
The Tunnel 5.6
Tyndall's Terror 5.7
Unfinished Business
   5.8
Updrafts to Heaven 5.5
Vantage Point 5.8
West Face (NEWS)
   5.10 A1
Wild Thing 5.10a
Windwalker 5.10a
Windward 5.6
Windward Direct 5.8
Zig Zag 5.7

★

Altar of Sacrifice 5.7
Attack of the Butter
   Knives 5.8
Big Tree One 5.8
The Black Caboose
   5.10a
Black Fly 5.8
The Blockhead 5.10a
The Blue Hole 5.6
Bottoms Up 5.7
Butterfly Crack 5.10a
Cactus Love 5.9
Cajun Queen 5.10a
Carnage before
   Bedtime 5.10a
The Cashman 5.10b
Cat Burglar 5.6
Catacombs 5.8
Catatonic 5.6
Cave Route 5.8
Chain Smokin' 5.10c
Charlie Chan's Number
   One Suspect 5.9
Closeness to Forever as
   the Soil Bleeds Black
   5.8

Contraction Action 5.9
Corner Flash 5.7
Cowboys Don't Cry
  5.10a
The Crack 5.7
Cruel Harvest 5.8+
Dance of the Shaman
  5.10b
Deception 5.9+
Desert Shield 5.10a
Diretissima 5.7
Dogleg Crack 5.8+
Dragonfly in Amber 5.8
Easy Street 5.6
Eating Dust 5.6
Edge of Mistakes 5.6
Feather in My Cap 5.6
The 5.5 Route 5.5
Fraggled Pickle 5.10a
Gentry's Face 5.10
Get the Pever Fever 5.5
Gibson's Crack 5.5
Good Timer 5.4
Grey Whale 5.8+
Ground Hog Day 5.7
Half Fast 5.8+
Hanging on A String
  Theory 5.7
Homo Erectus 5.6
Idiot's Delight 5.9
In the Middle Again
  5.7
Jenny's Reef 5.6
Jerry Was a Race Car
  Driver 5.7
Jiffy Pop 5.7
The Joke 5.10c
Left Crack Route 5.6
Level Head 5.6
Light-Headed Again 5.7
Little-Known Wonder
  5.7
Lost Souls 5.9
Lucky Arms 5.6

Magic Bus 5.8+
Me Too 5.9
Meat Grinder 5.9+
Mom, There's Pink in
  my Burger 5.6
The Mounties Big-O
  5.9
My Ex-Wife 5.10a
National Velvet 5.6
Nimrod's Nemesis 5.5
No Holds Barred 5.10a
No Room for Squares
  5.8
Normal Route 5.6
North Face (Concord
  Tower) 5.7+
Northwest Passage 5.9+
Notch Route 5.6
Off Ramp 5.9+
The Open Book 5.6
Overexposure I, 5.8
Patriot Crack 5.8
Pat's Crack 5.9
Perfect Basser 5.11b
Phone Threats 5.10a
Playin' Possum 5.10a
Porpoise 5.4
Potholes (Erie) 5.10a
Preying Mantel 5.10a
Primordial Blues 5.9
Pucker Up 5.10b
Rap Route 5.5
Red Hot 5.8
Redemption 5.9+
The Reflector 5.8
Render Us Weightless
  5.9+
Ring Pin Crack 5.6
Roller Coaster
  Chimney 5.9
Rough Boys 5.5
Ruffled Feathers 5.7
Rug Monkey 5.7
Scarface 5.9+

Scissor Man 5.9
Secret Passage 5.10b
Shake it Don't Break
  It 5.5
Sheena Is a Punk
  Rocker 5.9
Shin Smasher 5.9
Skiing @ 49 North
  5.10b
Slacker 5.4
Snaffle Baffler 5.7
So Funny I Forgot to
  Laugh 5.9
Son of a Pitch 5.10b
South Face (Castle
  Rock) 5.8
Southwest Couloir
  (SEWS)
The Spitz Mark 5.9
Spring Fever 5.8
Stance or Dance 5.10a
Starless in Vantage 5.9
Subliminal 5.10b
Subversive 5.10d
Sumptuous Bits 5.5
Sunset 5.4
Swarm 5.7
Swerve 5.6
Thriller Pillar Direct
  5.9+
Tiers 5.9
Troglodyte in Flight
  5.10a
Twin Cracks 5.8
Under the Boredwalk
  5.7
Underground Economy
  5.9
Upper Notch Route 5.8
Velvasheen 5.6
The Vestibule 5.7
Well Preserved 5.10b
Where the Sidewalk
  Ends 5.1

Wild Child 5.7
Winter Rushing In 5.8
Z-Crack 5.10c

no stars

A Game of Inches 5.9
American Warrior 5.8
Archies 5.6
The Asteroid Crack 5.7
Baptized in the River
    Black 5.7
Big Tree Two 5.7
Black Jack 5.4
Butter Brickle 5.8+
Century 5.8
Crack in the Back 5.6
Eating Rocks 5.6
The Emergence of Man
    5.9
The Fault 5.6
Flammable Pajamas 5.5
Harpoonist 5.10b
Highway Route 5.9
Honky's Lament 5.10a
The Joker 5.6
Kick Start 5.9+

Knife in the Toaster 5.9
Lasting Impression
    5.7–5.10
Leaning Crack 5.5
Lethal Weapon 5.10d
Lust For Dust 5.5
Magnetic Anomaly 5.9
Mickey Mantel 5.7
Mistress Jane's Chains
    5.9
Mountaineers Route
    5.2
Needle Magnet 5.7
New Creation 5.9
The North Face of the
    Eiger 5.4
The Nose 5.8
Old Crack 5.7
Proctology 5.8
Psycho 5.7
Queen of Diamonds
    5.8+
Ray Auld Memorial
    Route 5.8
Right Crack Route 5.2

The Right Stuff 5.4
The Scramble 5.0
Sidewinder 5.4
Sinkerville 5.9
So Easy I Forgot to
    Laugh 5.5
So Funny I Forgot to
    Rope Up 5.7
Sobriety 5.9
Somewhere on Earth
    5.7
Teenage Lobotomy
    5.11a
Thank God for Big Jugs
    5.8
Tree Shadow 5.8
Troglodyte in Flight 5.9
Trouble Maker 5.0
20th Century Clock
    5.10a A2
Your Sister 5.7

ABOUT THE UIAA/TABLE OF DIFFICULTIES

UIAA

INTERNATIONAL GRADE COMPARISON CHART

UIAA	USA	GB	F	D	AUS
V–	5.5	4a	5a	V	13
V	5.6	4b	5b	VI	14
V+	5.7	4c	5c		
VI–	5.8			VIIa	15
VI	5.9	5a	6a	VIIb	
VI+	5.10a		6a+	VIIc	16
VII–	5.10b	5b	6b	VIIIa	17
VII	5.10c		6b+	VIIIb	18
VII+	5.10d	5c	6c	VIIIc	19
VIII–	5.11a	6a	6c+	IXa	20
	5.11b				21
VIII	5.11c		7a	IXb	22
	5.11d	6b			23
VIII+	5.12a		7a+	IXc	24
	5.12b		7b		25
IX–	5.12c	6c	7b+	Xa	26
IX	5.12d	7a	7c	Xb	27
IX+	5.13a		7c+	Xc	28
X–	5.13b		8a	XIa	29
	5.13c	7b	8a+		30
X	5.13d		8b	XIb	31
X+	5.14a		8b+		32
XI–	5.14b		8c		33
	5.14c		8c+		34
XI	5.14d		9a		

The UIAA encourages the inclusion of information in guidebooks that helps visitors from overseas understand the most important information about local access, grades and emergency procedures. The UIAA also encourages climbers and mountaineers to share knowledge and views on issues such as safety, ethics, and good practice in mountain sports. The UIAA is not responsible for, and accepts no liability for, the technical content or accuracy of the information in this guidebook. Climbing, hill walking and mountaineering are activities with a danger of personal injury and death. Participants should be aware of, understand, and accept these risks and be responsible for their own actions and involvement.

Bibliography

Ament, Pat. *History of Free Climbing in America: Wizards of Rock*. Berkeley, CA: Wilderness Press, 2002.

Bates, Malcolm. *Cascade Voices: Conversations with Washington Mountaineers*. Seattle: The Mountaineers Books, 1992.

Beckey, Fred, and Eric Bjornstad. *Guide to Leavenworth Rock-Climbing Areas*. Seattle: The Mountaineers, 1965.

Beckey, Fred. *Cascade Alpine Guide 3: Rainy Pass to Fraser River*. 3d ed. Seattle: The Mountaineers Books, 2008.

Beckey, Fred. *Challenge of the North Cascades*. 1969. 2d ed. Seattle: The Mountaineers Books, 1996.

Beckey, Fred. *Darrington and Index Rock Climbing Guide*. Seattle: The Mountaineers, 1976.

Bland, Marty. *Inland Rock Climbs Northwest*. Self-published.

Brooks, Don, and David Whitelaw. *Washington Rock: A Climbing Guide*. Seattle: The Mountaineers Books, 1982.

Bruce, Garth. *Exit 38 Rock Climbing Guide*. FreeSolo Publishing, 2002.

Carlstad, Rich, and Don Brooks. *Climbing Leavenworth and Index: A Guide*. Lynnwood, WA: Signpost, 1976.

Christensen, Matt, and Holly Christensen. *Tieton River Rock: A Climber's Guide*. Yakima, WA: The Wilderness Athlete, 1989.

Cramar, Darryl, and Dave Gunstone. *Puget Sound Traveler's Guide*. Self-published.

Ford, Marlene, and Jim Yoder. *Frenchman Coulee: A Rock Climber's Guide*. 2d ed. Eatonville, WA: HomePress, 2002.

Harlin, John, III. *The Climber's Guide to North America: West Coast Rock Climbs*. Evergreen, CO: Chockstone Press, 1987

Kloke, Dallas. *Boulders and Cliffs: Climber's Guide to Lowland Rock in Skagit and Whatcom Counties*. Lynnwood, WA: Signpost, 1971.

------. *Climbing Mount Erie*. Self-published.

Kramar, Victor. *Leavenworth Rock*. 2d ed. Leavenworth, WA: Snow Creek Design, 2003.

Martin, Jason D., and Alex Krawarik. *Washington Ice: A Climbing Guide*. Seattle: The Mountaineers Books, 2003.

Nelson, Jim, and Peter Potterfield. *Selected Climbs in the Cascades, Volume 1*. 2d ed. Seattle: The Mountaineers Books, 2003.

Nelson, Jim, and Peter Potterfield. *Selected Climbs in the Cascades, Volume*

2. Seattle: The Mountaineers Books, 2000.

Smoot, Jeff. *Washington Rock Climbs*. Evergreen, CO: Chockstone Press, 1989.

Whitelaw, David. *Private Dancer*. Bethel, AK: Adventure Images, 1985.

Whitelaw, David. *Rattle and Slime*. CD-ROM. Bellevue, WA: Adventure Images, 2003.

Wilkerson, James, M.D., ed. *Medicine for Mountaineering and Other Wilderness Activities*. 6th ed. Seattle: The Mountaineers Books, 2010.

Index

About the Author

DAVID WHITELAW has been an active Northwest climber for more than thirty years, during which time he's written a number of magazine articles and has had some part in the production of ten guidebooks to rock and ice climbs in Washington and Alaska. David has climbed extensively in the Alaska Range, the Alps, the Canadian Rockies, much of the continental United States, a bit of the Caribbean, and several large volcanoes in Mexico and Peru. He estimates that he's been credited with a couple of hundred first ascents along the way, although he staunchly maintains the directions to all of them were given to him in

Photo by Sarah Doherty

1976 by a shadowy one-armed boulderer near Twin Falls, Idaho. David has been an illustrator, painter, and graphic designer for many years, as well as a college-level illustration and stained-glass instructor. Currently he resides in Bellevue, Washington, with his girlfriend Jennifer and two sporty tabular cats.

THE MOUNTAINEERS, founded in 1906, is a nonprofit outdoor activity and conservation organization, whose mission is "to explore, study, preserve, and enjoy the natural beauty of the outdoors.... " Based in Seattle, Washington, it is now one of the largest such organizations in the United States, with seven branches throughout Washington State.

The Mountaineers sponsors both classes and year-round outdoor activities in the Pacific Northwest, which include hiking, mountain climbing, ski-touring, snowshoeing, bicycling, camping, kayaking, nature study, sailing, and adventure travel. The organization's conservation division supports environmental causes through educational activities, sponsoring legislation, and presenting informational programs.

All its activities are led by skilled, experienced instructors, who are dedicated to promoting safe and responsible enjoyment and preservation of the outdoors.

If you would like to participate in these organized outdoor activities or programs, consider a membership in The Mountaineers. For information and an application, write or call The Mountaineers, Program Center, 7700 Sand Point Way NE, Seattle, WA 98115; 206-521-6001. You can also visit *www.mountaineers.org* or contact The Mountaineers at *info@ mountaineers.org*.

The Mountaineers Books, an active, nonprofit publishing program of the organization, produces guidebooks, instructional texts, historical works, natural history guides, and works on environmental conservation. All books produced by The Mountaineers Books fulfill the organization's mission.

 Send or call for our catalog of more than 800 outdoor titles:
The Mountaineers Books
1001 SW Klickitat Way, Suite 201
Seattle, WA 98134
800-553-4453
mbooks@mountaineersbooks.org
www.mountaineersbooks.org

 The Mountaineers Books is proud to be a corporate sponsor of The Leave No Trace Center for Outdoor Ethics, whose mission is to promote and inspire responsible outdoor recreation through education, research, and partnerships. The Leave No Trace program is focused specifically on human-powered (nonmotorized) recreation.

Leave No Trace strives to educate visitors about the nature of their recreational impacts, as well as offer techniques to prevent and minimize such impacts. Leave No Trace is best understood as an educational and ethical program, not as a set of rules and regulations.

For more information, visit *www.LNT.org*, or call 800-332-4100.

OTHER TITLES YOU MIGHT ENJOY FROM THE MOUNTAINEERS BOOKS

Cascade Alpine Guides
Fred Beckey
Columbia River to Stevens Pass (Brown/Vol. 1), 3rd Edition
Stevens Pass to Rainy Pass (Green/Vol. 2), 3rd Edition
Rainy Pass to Fraser River (Red/Vol.3), 3rd Edition

Selected Climbs in the Cascades, Volume 1, 2nd Edition
Jim Nelson and Peter Potterfield

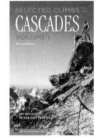

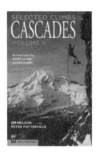

Selected Climbs in the Cascades, Volume 2: Alpine Routes, Sport Climbs & Crag Climbs
Jim Nelson and Peter Potterfield

Rock Climbing: Mastering Basic Skills, 2nd Edition
Topher Donahue and Craig Luebben

Mountaineering: The Freedom of the Hills, 9th Edition
The Mountaineers

THE MOUNTAINEERS BOOKS